A
Farewell to
Heroes

A
Farewell to
Heroes

Frank Graham, Jr.

THE VIKING PRESS/NEW YORK

LIBRARY OF CONGRESS CATALOGING IN PUBLICATION DATA
Graham, Frank, 1925–
A farewell to heroes.
1. Graham, Frank, 1925–   .   2. Sportswriters—
United States—Biography.   3. Sports—United States—
History.   I. Title.
GV742.42.G7A34   070.4'49796'0924   [B]   81-65266
ISBN 0-670-30796-3   AACR2

Portions of this book appeared originally in *Sports Illustrated* in different form.

Selections from the unpublished works of Frank Graham appearing here for the first time are copyright © 1981 by Frank Graham, Jr.

Grateful acknowledgment is made to the following for permission to reprint copyrighted material:

A. S. Barnes & Co., Inc.: Selections from *This Was Racing* by J. H. Palmer.
Bell & Howell: Selections from Frank Graham's *New York Sun* columns.
Curtis Brown Literary Agency: A selection from "Old Men," from *Many Long Years Ago* by Ogden Nash.
Doubleday & Company, Inc.: Excerpt from *Sportswriter* by Stanley Woodward and Frank Graham, Jr. Copyright © 1967 by Esther Rice Woodward as Executrix of the Estate of Stanley Woodward.
Harper & Row, Publishers, Inc.: Selections from *The Boys of Summer* by Roger Kahn. Copyright © 1971 by Roger Kahn.
International Herald Tribune: Selections from William Harrison "Sparrow" Robertson's column in the *Paris Herald,* 1921.
Charles Scribner's Sons: Selection from *The Snows of Kilimanjaro* by Ernest Hemingway.
Simon & Schuster, Inc.: Selection from *A Dual Autobiography* by Will and Ariel Durant.

Printed in the United States of America
Set in CRT Caledonia

To Pop,
our book's senior author

Preface

"**D**o you want to go to the Beach today?"
My father's question did not send me scurrying for trunks and an inner tube. In our household of non-swimmers the word "Beach" was always mentally capitalized, for it meant headier stuff than the surf, sand, and sun of more commonplace vocabularies. My father, who was a sportswriter, was asking me to tag along on one of his professional visits to a stretch of sidewalk on Manhattan's West Side. There, on the north side of Forty-ninth Street, west of Broadway, with Eighth Avenue and the old Madison Square Garden looming at the end of the block, lay that land of boxing gossip and bittersweet dreams called Jacobs Beach.

The boxing mob had named this strip for Mike Jacobs, who used to promote fights from his ticket agency on the block before he took over the programs at the Garden. It wasn't much of a block. Besides several ticket agencies, there was a hotel, a garage, a lunch counter, and St. Malachy's Roman Catholic Church, into which, someone had once told me, French Canadian hockey players used to slip for a brief prayer before a game at the Garden. On nice days fight managers, press agents, and various hangers-on—often jowly men with stomachs sticking out to here—would stand in clusters on the sidewalk and chatter animatedly among themselves.

Jacobs Beach was an enchanted strand, in the years shortly before World War II, for a boy just old enough to be allowed to watch prizefights in the flesh. Walking up the street with my father, I was likely to see broad-shouldered men with dented noses or perhaps a strip of plaster stuck over a gashed eyebrow, emblems of their trade at which I stared with as much wonder as boys on other strands in other times might have regarded mariners home from fabulous voyages with gold rings in their ears. If I had visited one of the small fight clubs around the city the week before, some of those stolid faces would be familiar. The chances were always good of seeing more-celebrated fighters, too—Jack Dempsey, Jim Braddock, even Joe Louis—as they walked along the Beach toward the Garden. Dempsey and Braddock, though their reigns had ended, still shared the "Champ" title with Louis (who was then at the crest of his career) in the greetings called after them by idlers along the street.

Yet a boy's education was advanced not by staring at the fighters but by listening to their managers. Some people seem garrulous to us simply because they don't know how to end a sentence. But for those men, incessant talk was life itself, the tool with which they renewed experience from some distant past or, more likely, created it out of wisps of daydreams. It would be stretching a point to report that either they or their experiences were romantic, but I certainly was, and the world they wove on Jacobs Beach held more significance for me than tales about cowboys and Indians or Arthurian legends. There were stalwart gladiators, treacherous villains, fools and jesters, even a Merlin (Jimmy Grippo, who managed the light-heavyweight champion of the world, Melio Bettina, was a professional magician who performed card tricks on demand).

Two prominent figures on Jacobs Beach were Eddie Mead, a successful manager, and Eddie Walker, who worked for him.

Walker was pointed out along Broadway as the man who wore Damon Runyon's new shoes to break them in for him. Mead dropped dead on the Beach one afternoon, immediately after being told that Liquid Lunch, a horse he had bet on, had won the first race at Belmont Park, paying $16.10. But until that particular curtain was rung down, those two entertained the mob with their banter and their stories.

"Did you see the ring Mead gave me?" Walker asked a gathering one day. On the middle finger of his right hand was a platinum ring set with a diamond.

"Is that the ring you threw at him last month?" a manager asked.

"Yes," Walker said, "and a hat. Remember the hat? He gave me this ring and a forty-dollar hat. One of them hairy hats. But I got sore at him one night and I took the ring off and the hat and threw them at him. He didn't say anything, but he picked them up, and the other night he gave me back the ring. After that he tried to pick a fight with me. I think he wanted the ring back. But I wouldn't fight him, because I might not get it back again."

"What became of the hat?" another manager asked.

"Mead is wearing it," Walker said. "But I don't care about the hat. It don't fit so good."

Many of the beachcombers who stood around gossiping in the afternoon sun on Jacobs Beach could have made comfortable livings in some other profession. But they had turned away from a steady salary and money in the bank to pursue a dream—or rather to wait for it there on the sidewalk. I remember one of those managers, dressed in a threadbare suit that probably had been given to him by a more successful colleague whom it no longer fit, answering the obvious question.

"Why? Because someday a big strong fellow is going to come along and I am going to make him the heavyweight champion of the world and between us we are going to cut up a million dollars."

Harry Lenny was just such a manager. For years he worked with a young giant named Ray Impellittiere. Lenny would talk for hours about his "Imp." There came a time when other members of the mob quietly slipped away when Lenny came in sight; they were not able to stomach any more of the Imp. Yet Lenny believed implicitly in the skill of his fighter and in his eventual success. His faith persisted through repeated disasters. One night Lenny left the Garden after having retrieved the Imp from the center of the ring where he had been flattened by Bob Pastor. His despondency lasted only until he saw my father on the Beach.

"What are you going to do now?" Pop asked him.

"What do you mean?" Lenny asked indignantly. "We're going after the title. Just name one fighter who can lick the Imp!"

My father was about to mention the licking Impellittiere had taken minutes earlier in the Garden. Then he thought better of it, shrugged, and moved off down the Beach.

Horseplay, blighted hopes, some trivial revelation from an otherwise forgotten night in a drab arena; yet this talk had a life of its own, setting off in my father's head certain reverberations that he took with him to his typewriter, and with a journalistic alchemy that I believe was unique to his time, he re-created a naïve, fleeting, and colorful era in sports between the two great wars.

"The most important single change in my business in my lifetime came about in the early 1930s when Joe Vila died and Frank Graham succeeded him as sports columnist on the New York *Sun*," Red Smith wrote in his own column a few years ago. "If anybody had said in Frank's hearing that he invented the 'conversation piece' column, he would have hooted. He only did it incomparably better than it ever was done before, or has been done since."

Before his time, as Smith wrote, "sports columns in America were highly personal essays of opinion and comment expressing the writer's own view of the passing scene." My father, who had been a reporter for almost twenty years, simply went on doing what he did best. As a columnist he wanted to reproduce, as accurately as possible, everyday scenes from the sports that interested him.

This was not an electronic trick. He never carried a notebook or a tape recorder. (He was so incompetent with gadgets that he

couldn't have worked the blessed thing even if he had flourished
in an age of lightweight recording devices.) Instead, he had a gift
for hearing the sporting world's gab, and "the best ear in the
newspaper business" was an appraisal by his colleagues that followed him to the grave. The shadowy bystander, the pipe-puffing
confidant, rather than the manipulator of scenes, he wanted to let
his readers know what it was like in the dugout at the Polo
Grounds on a lazy day in June, on the train taking a losing college
football team back to New York, and on that strip of sidewalk
called Jacobs Beach. Although they may never have glimpsed in
the flesh the great athletes of their day, Frank Graham's readers
probably formed a clearer picture of them than we do of the contemporary heroes who present themselves self-consciously for our
inspection in the restraining glare of the television camera.

My father's enthusiasm for sports was not boundless. As for a
basketball game or a tennis match, he would as soon have been
detected in a Broadway peep show (and he was, when it came to
sexual display, a Puritan). Although he tolerated golfers, he shared
the sentiments of his old pal Francis Albertanti toward the game.
Albertanti, who publicized fights around town, had served briefly
as the sports editor of a New York newspaper early in the century.
When prodded by the paper's editor to print some golf news, he
refused. "But there are many wealthy and influential men interested in golf," his editor persisted. "Then print it on the financial page," Albertanti growled.

Nor was my father a crusading journalist. It wasn't that his allegiance lay with the Devil's party. He was capable of delivering
a stern rebuff to athletes or officials (even old friends) whom he
thought guilty of skulduggery or silliness, but he did not believe in
turning over rocks. Although he seldom betrayed his feelings, he
unquestionably took a dim view of the new breed of sportswriters
who made their reputations by stirring up trouble among athletes,
coaches, and officials. In general, he liked his favorite sports the
way they were. As John Gross, the British editor and critic, has
suggested, "Those whose first aim is to 'appreciate' the world are
the natural enemies of those whose first aim is to change it."

He took a quiet pride in his work, as any true professional does, but he seemed to shrink from advertising his worth to the world. Bob Kelley, his friend for many years, used to speak of his "psychopathic modesty." If this trait restricted his audience (and his income, for his salary never exceeded $24,000 a year), it had much to do with the success of his own minor art.

"There was grandeur in the glorious simplicity of his style, which was quiet and without artifice," his colleague Jimmy Cannon wrote of him. "Those who try to do it Frankie's way don't have his humility or his skill. They get in the way and appear to be bumping into the people they're writing about. He never identified himself as 'I.' It was part of his greatness that he allowed the people he wrote about to create themselves with their conversations."

I grew up thoroughly enchanted by the little universe my father fashioned around me. The reverberations he picked up on the sports beat were passed on and pulsed within me, too, though for a while in a different way. Pop had outgrown the fierce interest in rooting for one side or the other (though he had his favorites to the end) and reveled in the spectacle itself. He told me afterward that during the only hiatus in his newspaper career, a brief period during World War II when he was the sports editor of *Look* magazine, he always came away from an exciting ball game or prize fight with a single thought: "I wish I could write a column about *that one* tonight!" I, on the other hand, had a vested interest in every event, a favorite side for whom I rooted intensely, whose victory uplifted me and whose defeat reduced me, if not to tears, then at least to an evening's sulk.

The partisan interest withered long ago, but the little universe has remained a part of me. It was a-building through the 1920s and early 1930s as my father served his long apprenticeship as a sports reporter for the New York *Sun*, and came into full flower in 1934 when he began writing his column, "Setting the Pace," for that newspaper. This era broke up in World War II, and was succeeded by one that was in some ways brighter but certainly no more fascinating. Although I take over the telling of the story at that point, I have a coauthor in the earlier chapters. While I stand aside, my father conjures up that world as he did nearly fifty years ago in the *Sun*.

His memories of New York's sporting scene stretched back to the early years of our century. He died in 1965 at the age of seventy-one, and my own attachment to that scene waned at about the same time. Here, then, is an attempt to re-create an atmosphere, to set down not a history of sports during that half century or so but a kind of dual autobiography, a very selective overview, gold-tinted perhaps but as honest as the two of us could make it, of an era that now comes dimmering up out of the mists.

A
Farewell to
Heroes

Chapter One
Out of Harlem

My father was born in 1893 in Harlem. He was the youngest of four children, and in giving birth to him his mother died.

Harlem was still an outlying district of the city then, though growing rapidly. Most of the people lived in neat, low brownstone houses, but apartments had already sprung up along Lenox Avenue, Seventh Avenue, and other major streets, and 125th Street was a thriving shopping center that supplied nearly all of the residents' needs. In 1888 Oscar Hammerstein had built the Harlem Opera House, one of the showplaces of the city, where he presented outstanding singers from Europe and often brought uptown, at reduced ticket prices, the leading stars of the Broadway stage.

As the family's "kid" (a nickname by which his older brothers, Harold and Wade, sometimes called him, even in later life), my father bore the brunt of the dislocation caused by his mother's death. I seldom heard him speak about those days, for he had a difficult boyhood, and indeed, almost did not survive it.

He was raised by his grandmother and his sister, Carrie, while his father apparently spent little time around their home, on East 132nd Street. The elder Graham lived on the fringes of politics, associating himself with certain Tammany sachems, his major contribution having been as a bagman between the railroads and those politicians. Later he found employment at Harlem's most renowned edifice, the Polo Grounds, where he was superintendent of the upper deck. On the dresser in his bedroom stood a photograph of one of the era's outstanding prizefighters, Kid McCoy, inscribed "To my friend."

At this time the older residents of Harlem were still trying to live lives of sedate and modest elegance, but the tumult of the great city was crowding in on them. A glimpse of a street scene from that time slipped through, decades afterward, in a column my father wrote about Max Schmeling, the conqueror of Joe Louis, walking with his entourage through Grand Central Station:

They all walked at a brisk pace, heads were turned, and many strays were picked up and tagged along. It reminded you of when you were a kid and somebody was being arrested and marched through the streets to the police station with a mob tagging along at the heels of the cop and his prisoner.

Pop's formal schooling was confined almost entirely to Harlem's Public School 89, whose two most prominent alumni, he always liked to point out, were Jimmy Hines, a powerful Tammany politician, who eventually went to prison, and Sugar Ray Robinson. It was there that he was struck down by a serious disease (meningitis?) which almost killed him and which cost him the sight of his right eye. He missed a couple of years of school and never caught up, though he got through the eighth grade, at last, and immersed himself in higher education for a single term at the High School of Commerce before dropping out.

He was not only "the kid" but also the runt of his family, five feet five and weighing not much more than a hundred pounds as he approached maturity. Despite his handicaps, he was, according to his brothers, a pretty good athlete, a scrappy, sure-handed infielder on the sandlots and a clever flyweight boxer. A visit to one of the neighborhood gymnasiums and the sight of two or three well-known fighters training for future bouts were sufficient to infect him with an enthusiasm for the sport that he never lost. He traveled up to the northern fringes of the city, to the Woodlawn Inn and Cannon's Road House, to watch even better fighters (dressed in their caps and sweaters) walking around their training quarters and later belting their sparring partners in the makeshift rings. After Ad Wolgast won the lightweight championship from Battling Nelson at Port Richmond, California, in 1910, my father traveled all the way down to Miner's Bowery Theater to see the motion pictures of the fight.

"I got a couple of seats in the front row," the man in the box office said, "but I wouldn't take them if I was you because you can't see the pictures so good from up there and, besides, the kids in the gallery like to throw things. Sit back a ways under the balcony."

So you sat under the balcony and saw, in the shadows on the screen, one of the most grueling fights ever held, and one thing you never will forget about it was the scene when the fighters were coming down to the ring. They were silent pictures, of course, but there was a fellow up on the stage who explained everything as the reels were unwound and who warned you to look for certain high spots of every round, and when the fighters were coming down to the ring he said:

"Here he comes—on the shoulders of Youssuf Mahmout—the Michigan Wildcat, Ad Wolgast!"

There was the grinning little Wolgast making a spectacular entrance on the shoulders of a burly Turkish wrestler. . . . Grinning and waving to the crowd on his way to the lightweight championship of the world. Many a time since then you have thought of it and of a story that the great sports writer Bill McGeehan wrote once about Wolgast in a California home for the insane, in which he called Ad the man "who always would be the lightweight champion of the world of topsy-turvy."

My father worked out regularly at a local gym. He fought half a dozen amateur bouts in the small clubs around Harlem, won them all, and allowed himself to dream of turning professional and growing up to win the featherweight championship of the world. But reality soon asserted itself. Even in those days of casual regulations, no one was going to take a chance on a one-eyed fighter.

My father's brother Harold, a tall, slender, very gentle man, became an executive of the telephone company and arranged a job for him as a messenger. But my father was never interested in telephones, or in any other gadgets. (To the day he died he could not screw in a light bulb without causing a short circuit somewhere in the house, and it is a disability I have in large part inherited.) He was interested mainly in boxing, and in the Giants, both of which passions he had an opportunity to indulge freely in Harlem.

"Fight clubs" were just that in New York State during the early years of the twentieth century—arenas where patrons bought memberships to see a boxing program, just as drinks may be bought today in some states only after acquiring membership in a bottle club. The Frawley Law, passed by the state legislature in 1911, removed the club restrictions but limited bouts to ten rounds while making no provisions for a decision one way or the other. A boxer could win in New York State only by scoring a knockout. It was at this time that boxing writers took on added importance, because invariably they rendered decisions in their stories about the fights they covered. Many clever boxers became adept at the whirlwind finish, designed to catch the eye of inexperienced or impressionable writers and thus claim the "newspaper decision." There were also private, or "bootleg," fights promoted illegally.

Many a young New Yorker, ill-fitted for a career of his own in the ring, managed to catch on in some capacity on the fringes of the sport. He took tickets, carried fighters' buckets (and sometimes the fighters themselves) from the ring, or wrote about the action for small publications. Pop's friend Francis Albertanti became a publicity man.

Albertanti's first job as a press agent was to publicize a private fight. He was working as an office boy on the Morning Telegraph and Florrie Barnett, an East Side character and small-time promoter, hired him for ten dollars to build up a brawl between Mickey McDonough and Fred Lucas, neighborhood heavyweights, to be held on an undisclosed date at an undisclosed location. Florrie was aiming at the trade east of the Bowery and knew that if the boys could be interested in the fight they would find out when and where it would take place by inquiring at—well, Jimmy Kelly's Mandarin in Chinatown, for instance. Francis typed his stuff, slugged it "Please Use and Oblige" and delivered it in person to the sports editors. Ever since, press agents have been slugging their pieces "Please Use and Oblige."

That—and the fact that he got his ten dollars—were the only tangible results of the enterprise, for the fight never came off. The fighters were in the ring, pitched on the end of a covered pier at the foot of Catherine Street on a Sunday afternoon, and a couple of hundred customers were banked about it when a cop walked in.

"Hey!" he yelled. "You can't do that! It's against the law!"

A couple of the boys grabbed him and threw him in the river.

"I can see him now," Albertanti once recalled, fondly. "In those days the cops wore those gray helmets and his was bobbing up and down in the water and he was crying for help because he couldn't swim. So one of the boys who had given him the heave-ho jumped in and pulled him out. But Florrie was afraid some other cop might have seen him come on the pier and would come looking for him, so he called the fight off and shooed everybody out."

My father, who made a habit of hanging around the fight clubs and gymnasiums, became acquainted with Ned Brown, who was the editor of a magazine called *Boxing*, and sold his first article to him. (By a curious coincidence, forty years later I earned my first check as a writer for an article in *Boxing*, a publication that had no connection with Brown's long-defunct enterprise.)

"I had given Frankie a quarter to go up to the Bronx and cover Abe Attell's training camp at Woodlawn," Brown recalled years later. "After expenses, I guess he got to keep a nickel. He was enthusiastic, but he didn't know how to begin his first story. I said, 'It's easy. Just pretend you're writing a letter to a friend and tell him everything you saw.' He sat down and wrote a nice piece. For a couple of years he went on picking up small change, and free tickets, writing free-lance pieces about boxing for me and some of the daily papers. At the time, and always after that, I had the feeling he was doing just what he did in the first story—writing a letter to a friend."

Meanwhile, he inevitably became a Giant fan. The Giants had been a part of Harlem since 1883 when New York obtained a franchise in the National League of Professional Baseball Clubs and the new team took over the Polo Grounds, at Eighth Avenue and 110th Street. On this location, James Gordon Bennett, who was the publisher of the New York *Herald* and the man who commissioned H. M. Stanley to go to Africa to find David Livingstone, had introduced the sport of polo to the city. The eighties was a decade of rapid expansion in Harlem, however, and to the struggling team's chagrin, the city soon pushed a street through the middle of their playing field. The Giants found a new location at Eighth Avenue and 155th Street, to which they moved their franchise, keeping the name of their old ball field intact. There they built wooden stands in the form of a huge horseshoe. When the stands burned in 1911, the Giants erected a reproduction in steel and concrete and remained on the site until the franchise was shifted to San Francisco in 1958.

The Giants were a rowdy, roistering crew early in the century. Most of the rowdiness was contributed by Andrew Freedman, who briefly owned the team, a vulgar, vengeful lout who once warned a baseball writer that he was "standing on the brink of an abscess" and threatened to push him in; and John McGraw, who became the team's manager after Freedman's departure in 1903 and led it through its most glorious years. The roistering was attended to by players like "Turkey Mike" Donlin, of whom it might have been said, as Dr. Johnson said of the poet Richard Savage, "At no time of his life was it any part of his character to be the first of the company that desired to separate." Many years later, when baseball was turning enthusiastically to night games, Donlin remarked, "Jesus! Think of taking a ball player's nights away from him!"

Another player for whom training rules were made to be shattered was Bugs Raymond, who pitched for the Giants during their successful rush for the pennant in 1911. My father recalled his abrupt banishment from the team:

During a game with the Pirates on the last home stand, McGraw gave him a new ball and sent him to the bull pen to warm up. It was not until the next inning that he was called in. Hans Wagner was at bat with two out and men on first and third. Bugs' first pitch hit the grandstand and now there was a run in and a man on third. Hans hit the next pitch back to Bugs who, instead of tossing the ball to first base for an easy out, tried to get the runner at the plate and threw it over catcher Meyers' head.

"I took him out," McGraw said, "and as he reached the bench, I saw he was bleary-eyed. He hadn't stopped at the bull pen when I sent him down to warm up but kept going, right out of the park and across the street to a gin mill, where he traded in the ball for three shots of whiskey."

Poor Bugs never appeared in a Giant uniform again. His last appearance in New York, as the world series was coming on, was in a Sunday game with a sandlot semi-pro team.

Aware by now that he could take part in his beloved sports vicariously from the press row, my father was eager to learn all the skills of his new craft. He looked up to the great sportswriters of the day, men like Sam Crane, Joe Vila, Damon Runyon, and Bozeman Bulger. Uncle Boze, as the latter was known, had done much to inject some life into baseball writing. He even wrote a series of articles about an imaginary ball player named Swat Milligan, who was a kind of Paul Bunyan of the diamond, and he later turned the stories into successful vaudeville sketches on Broadway starring Turkey Mike Donlin. The local ball clubs held the likable Boze in such esteem that when he died, in 1932, the flags were flown at half mast at the Polo Grounds, Yankee Stadium, and Ebbets Field.

My father, who was recognized as an eager, persistent young man around the city's newspaper offices, finally found an opportunity to turn his back on the telephone company in 1914 when he was hired by the *Sun*. It is difficult for a younger generation to conceive of the immense prestige of the *Sun* as it existed in the first half of this century. Not only had the paper restored little Virginia's faith in Santa Claus; it also claimed the allegiance of thousands of readers who believed, with Virginia's father, that "if you see it in the *Sun*, it's so." The *Sun* was dependable, its coverage of many fields (including sports) was extensive, and, to a greater extent than was usual at the time, its stories were both lively and gracefully written.

The paper had been founded in 1833 by a printer named Benjamin Day to supplement the earnings from his print shop, which had almost been ruined by a city-wide cholera epidemic. The *Sun* was the first successful penny newspaper, and it revolutionized American journalism. Day was determined that it would not be windy, crammed with interminable editorials and political essays, as its six-penny contemporaries were. Its news items were originally slanted toward the common people it hoped to attract.

A talented and imaginative reporter named Richard Adams Locke played no small part in the *Sun*'s immediate success (illuminating it with the moon's pale fire, as it were). Taking advantage of a well-publicized expedition to South Africa in 1834 led by the British astronomer Sir John Frederick William Herschel, who meant to establish an observatory and complete the study of the "visible heavens," Locke composed a series of articles purportedly based on information furnished him by a scientific publication in Edinburgh. The "revelations" lived up to the *Sun*'s advance announcements of the series. Not only had Herschel's remarkable lenses picked up all sorts of details of the moon's landscape, including lush valleys and large rivers; they had also detected hosts of remarkable birds and quadrupeds, one of which was a bisonlike creature that bore a fleshy retractable appendage across its eyes apparently designed to decrease eyestrain under the great extremes of light and darkness on "our side" of the moon. "We could most distinctly perceive this hairy veil," one of Herschel's colleagues was said to have written, "which was shaped like the upper front outline of the cap known to the ladies as Mary Queen of Scots cap, lifted and lowered by means of the ears."

The series reached its climax with the astounding news that Herschel's party had observed flocks of small, hairy, winged hominids. "In general symmetry of body and limbs they were infinitely superior to the orang-utan; so much so that, but for their long wings, Lieutenant Drummond said they would look as well on a parade-ground as some of the old cockney militia." This revelation made a great sensation all around the world and was picked up and reprinted in much of Europe, where a Paris journal published caricatures of carousing man-bats crooning *"Au clair de lune."* The women of Springfield, Massachusetts, subscribed to a fund to send missionaries to what one chronicler of the event referred to as "the benighted luminary."

The *Sun's* eventual admission that it was all a big joke did nothing to dim its new popularity, and it soon claimed thirty thousand readers, the largest daily circulation in the world. Afterward, Edgar Allan Poe, though scornful of the public's extreme gullibility, applauded the paper's enterprise. "From the epoch of the hoax," Poe wrote, "the *Sun* shone with unmitigated splendor. Its success firmly established the 'penny system' throughout the country, and (through the *Sun*) consequently we are indebted to the genius of Mr. Locke for one of the most important steps ever taken in the pathway of human progress."

The *Sun*, through a succession of able editors, including that giant of journalism Charles A. Dana, and an even greater number of skillful writers and columnists, assumed almost unrivaled eminence. Its price went up to two cents during the Civil War. Although it became a true penny newspaper again for a few years right after my father joined the staff, the contingencies of another war sent the price soaring back to two cents in 1918.

My father wrote local sports for a time. One winter, because of his knowledge of Harlem, he was assigned there to the station house as a police reporter. That Harlem winter stretched on interminably, a monotony of freezing rains and of sordid little burglaries and assaults transcribed from the police blotter. It was relieved only by an occasional three-alarm fire, when my father would chase the engines and excitedly cross the barricades thanks to the magic of his police card. Sometimes the fires seemed the only light in the Harlem sky, and the sun only a rumor up there beyond the murk. Then one day Joe Vila, who was the *Sun's* sports editor, called him over to his desk. He announced that one of the baseball writers was ill and that my father was to pick up a train ticket and leave with the Giants for their spring-training camp in Texas.

Although he was twenty-two years old, my father had never traveled farther from home than southern Connecticut. Now, unexpectedly, unbelievably, he was being sent to see faraway places, and in the company of his heroes. He identified completely with the exuberant remark made a few years earlier by the Giants' gifted second baseman Larry Doyle and reflecting the excitement and naïveté of the time: "It's great to be young and a Giant!" It was a spirited, cocky team, as those managed by John McGraw inevitably were. The Giants had selected the town of Marlin, near the Brazos River in north-central Texas, as the site of their training camp. It lay close to several other towns they could conveniently reach by train in order to play exhibition games with minor-league teams. My father took a sleeper to St. Louis, where he changed for the *Sunshine Special.* Shortly before the train was to reach San Antonio, the ball club's cars were uncoupled at Bremond Junction and then pulled along a short spur to Marlin.

The Giants stopped at the best hotel in town, which was very imposing from the outside. But like the false-front houses you had seen along the line from Bremond Junction, it was a delusion and a snare. There was a broad, balustraded staircase that fanned out in front of the building and the circular lobby had tile floor. The high dome of the lobby was supported by pillars of imitation marble and there were great clusters of lights in the dome. But above the ornate lobby the hotel was a flimsy cavern.

The furnishings in all the rooms were cheap and bare, which was just as well. That was the era when the ball players played rough pranks on each other, such as getting into a rookie's room when he was out, stripping the bed and piling the furniture on it. Among the other lusty diversions were pillow fights, water fights and the heaving of bedroom crockery, such as pitchers and bowls.

There were three staple items on the menu. There were ham, steak and hominy. You couldn't tell, half the time, whether you were eating ham or steak, because both were fried in oil. The hominy was either just boiled, or boiled and then fried.

The members of the Giants' party understandably looked around for more appetizing fare, which they found in Marlin's two Greek restaurants. The players generally ate in one of the Greek restaurants, while the writers made the other their headquarters. Flattered by the attention, one of the Greeks began to advertise his place as the favorite dining spot of the Giants, while the other countered with an advertisement in the local paper: THE NEW YORK NEWSPAPERMEN EAT AT MY RESTAURANT.

A price war began between the two restaurants, one of them reducing chili con carne from twenty-five cents to twenty cents and throwing in an outsize Bermuda onion for nothing.

The ball park was on the outskirts of the town, about a half mile from the main street. The most direct route lay along the single track of the railroad. The players dressed in the bathhouse adjoining the hotel, put their spiked shoes under their arms and walked down the track in bedroom slippers. One day the "jinny," or gasoline-driven car that ran between Waco and Bremond Junction, sneaked up on Jeff Tesreau, the big brown bear of the Giant pitching staff, and nudged him off the track, whereupon everybody rushed to see how much damage had been done to the "jinny."

On St. Patrick's Day every year there was a game between the Irish players and the Germans on the squad. Mrs. McGraw and the wives of the players sold tickets in the town, and even the ball players and the newspaper men had to pay to get in that day. The entire receipts were turned over to the little Catholic church and in

11

the course of the eleven years they trained there the Giants saw it grow from a shack with corrugated iron walls and roof into a charming brick edifice set about with plants and shrubs.

There were various entertainments in Marlin for the players, the writers, and their wives. The townspeople played host to the Giants at a fish fry along the Brazos, and the players and writers in turn invited the townspeople to dance at the hotel, the utterly superfluous dining room having been cleared of its tables and converted to a dance floor. The next day the Giants broke camp and moved southeast from one town to another, playing exhibition games in Waco, Dallas, Fort Worth, and New Orleans. One of the scheduled stops was Baton Rouge, where the Giants played the Louisiana State University team. The chaplain at the state prison invited the players and writers to visit the institution.

The chaplain led the way through the big gate and the warden's office and then through the yards and shops. The prisoners wore black and white stripes, and the Northern boys among the ball players never had seen prisoners in stripes before, except in picture books, and they were quite as much interested in the prisoners as the prisoners were in them. In the shoe shop one of the prisoners greeted Rube Benton, a big lefthanded pitcher with the Giants then, and Rube looked surprised and stopped to shake hands with him. Some of the players wanted to know who the prisoner was, and how Rube knew him, and Rube said he was raised with the fellow and hadn't seen him for years and never knew what had become of him until that minute.

The chaplain led the way through a cell block. At one end of the cell block was the gallows and, at the other end, a big wood stove that heated the whole block. There was a fellow sitting by the wood pile reading a magazine and, as the ball players came along, he looked up, but only for a moment, and then went on reading. After the group had passed, the chaplain said:

"That fellow is going to be hanged. He had an appeal, but it was denied, and they are going to hang him next Thursday."

Naturally, that sort of put a chill on the group. Everybody

stopped talking and looked back over his shoulder at the man who
was waiting to be hanged. Out in the yard you were walking next
to Benny Kauff, the outfielder, and he said:

"And he was sitting there quiet, like that? Boy, if they were
going to hang me next Thursday they would have to start chasing
me around this yard right now."

The team went from Baton Rouge to New Orleans, and then
north by way of Chattanooga and Memphis, playing local teams
and almost everywhere drawing large, excited crowds. In those
days the major leagues were confined to the northeastern section
of the country, bounded by Chicago, St. Louis, Cincinnati, and
Washington, D.C., and for most people in other regions the only
opportunity to see the stars was to catch them as they came by on
the exhibition circuit. None of them could have taken in the
spectacle with as much excitement as my father. He was living
and traveling with his heroes, and he had made friendships among
the players and writers that were to last a lifetime. The only dis-
quieting note was the reaction to his presence by one of the superstars of the newspaper business, Damon Runyon. Runyon, who
was covering the Giants for another paper, seemed to go out of his
way to put him down. He spoke to my father only to contradict
him.

But that was a small cloud in a glorious sky. When he returned
to New York, he reported on the trip to Joe Vila and in passing
mentioned what seemed to be the unfavorable impression he had
made on Damon Runyon.

"That's funny," Vila said. "I saw Runyon yesterday, and he told
me that you wrote the best stuff that came out of the Giants'
camp."

He never numbered Runyon among his close friends, but thirty
years later when my father had become disenchanted with *Look*
and wanted to get back into the newspaper business, it was Runyon who persuaded the Hearst editors to hire him as a columnist
on the New York *Journal-American.*

13

Chapter Two
The Endless Adventure

After my father's death I went through his library, the heart of which he had kept behind glass doors in the top of a tall desk against a wall in the living room. These were the books for which he had a special affection. Aside from the books he had written and one or two that I had written and inscribed for him, they were all from long ago: travel books about faraway places; novels set in London or Paris; several early works by Hemingway, Kipling's *Barrack-Room Ballads*; books on the sea by William McFee and H. M. Tomlinson; books about baseball and boxing, most of which had been written early in this century. I had looked into most of them and read at least several while I was growing up, but now I came across one that I had never opened. It was bound in faded red cloth and entitled *The Story of British Sporting Prints,* by Captain Frank Siltzer. There on the flyleaf (no one had ever mentioned this to me) was an inscription printed in my mother's neat hand:

To Dear Daddy
On my first Christmas 1925
His Boy, Frank

14

The decade in my father's life leading up to that Christmas Day was reflected in the library he had put together. Photographs from that time reveal that he had not changed very much, physically. He still looked like a twenty-two-year-old flyweight, neatly though not flashily dressed, his fedora set squarely on his head. Yet the unschooled kid out of P.S. 89 had become literate and cosmopolitan. He never lost his admiration for rowdies—for gashouse ball players, for old street fighters who flouted the Marquis of Queensberry rules in the professional ring, for tough cops who chastened wise-guy hoodlums by knocking their teeth down their throats. But it was not simply combat and competition that excited him now; it was the prospect of writing about them, and about the men who took part. The isolated literary life, as such, did not appeal to him, because he always wanted to be a part of the action, and later on, when he tried his hand, largely unsuccessfully, at writing "stories," he was stimulated chiefly by a need to supplement the miserable salary of a newspaperman in Depression America.

He was becoming a traveling man at a time when it was still an adventure to go into a new town. Chains of hotels and restaurants, ribbon development, and tangles of expressways had not yet converted a city into a duplicate of another one, two thousand miles away. Each still had its own "feel," its uniqueness. After his first success as a baseball writer, he was assigned to cover the Giants throughout the season, and he traveled with them to all of the National League cities: Boston, Pittsburgh, Chicago, Cincinnati, St. Louis, Philadelphia, and, of course, Brooklyn, where he was drawn by a motive even more romantic than watching the Giants play the Dodgers: Brooklyn became the scene of his courtship of my mother. Meanwhile, once the baseball season was over, Joe Vila discovered that his young reporter was able to handle assignments in other sports, too—boxing, of course, as well as football and hockey. When spring rolled around again, he was on his way to the sun with the Giants. Marlin remained the Giants' spring-training headquarters for several years more, until the base was shifted to San Antonio, and, later still, to Sarasota, Florida.

In 1917, his second year with the team, the Giants and the De-

troit Tigers joined in one of the first spring tours ever made by
two major-league teams. It brought together two of the most colorful and aggressive personalities in the sport, John McGraw and
Ty Cobb, providing the writers with a welcome alternative to
stories about base hits and promising rookies. McGraw and his
players hurled insults at the great outfielder from the first moment
he stepped onto the field against them in an exhibition game in
Dallas. There was nothing in Cobb's background or personality
that permitted him to respond to fellow humans with any tactic
other than confrontation. Accepting the challenge, he stole second base, sliding in with spikes high and ripping a long, jagged
gash in the thigh of Buck Herzog, the Giants' combative second
baseman. The police were required to break up the ensuing brawl
among the players and fans. That night, in the lobby of the hotel
which the two teams had optimistically agreed to share, McGraw
tried to pick a fight with Cobb, but the younger man walked
away.

*In the dining room a short time later, Herzog went to Cobb's
table.*

"What's the number of your room?" he asked.

Cobb told him.

*"I'll be up there at ten o'clock," Herzog said. "I'll bring one
player with me and you can have one of your players there. You
can have Harry Tuttle [the Tigers' trainer] there, too, to act as a
referee."*

*At ten o'clock Herzog and third baseman Heinie Zimmerman
entered Cobb's room. Tuttle was there—and, in addition to Cobb,
eight other Detroit players.*

"Take your coat and shirt off," Herzog said to Cobb.

*They stripped to the waist and started punching. It wasn't
much of a fight. Herzog knocked Cobb to his knees with the first
punch. But Cobb got up and beat him unmercifully until Tuttle
stepped in.*

"They fought like a couple of washerwomen," Tuttle said later.

*Both, however, were satisfied. Herzog considered that he had
avenged himself for the spiking by knocking Cobb down. Cobb fig-*

*ured he had squared accounts by blacking Herzog's eyes, bloody-
ing his nose and pounding him into a state of helplessness.*

Pop's admiration for both gallant rowdyism and a good yarn
resulted in the inside story of the battle, which he had pried from
the fortunate onlookers. Yes, it was great to be young and a Giant,
but there was a self-protective streak in John McGraw that those
around him might run afoul of at any time and that brought on
the first and only serious professional crisis of my father's career.
His competence and integrity were brought into public question.
It is, as I was to find forty-five years later, the most painful experience a journalist can undergo.

When the 1917 season got under way, the Giants moved out
strongly ahead of the field. McGraw, confident, aggressive, raging
at umpires and opposing players alike, led his team on a western
swing and into Cincinnati for a series with the Reds. Tempers on
both sides were heated, and the object of most of the players'
wrath in one of the games was Bill Byron, umpiring behind the
plate. Byron was known as "the Singing Umpire" because he was
a cheerful soul who ordinarily hummed little snatches of song
while waiting for the pitcher to deliver the ball. His tunes must
have soured in his throat that day, however, as McGraw hectored
him unmercifully from the dugout steps. After the game the two
men met on the way to their respective clubhouses and Byron
took the opportunity to deliver a whiff of his own verbal grape-
shot. McGraw, beside himself with fury, rushed at the umpire and
punched him in the mouth, splitting his lip.

Punching an umpire is, and always has been, a mortal sin
within the pale of organized baseball, but McGraw shrugged off
the incident. He insisted that it had nothing to do with the ball
game but was merely a row between two men who had encountered each other off the field. Byron filed a report with John K.
Tener, the president of the National League, and everyone settled
down to see if McGraw would be penalized for his offense.

Nothing happened until the Giants reached Pittsburgh. After
dinner there one evening, my father walked to the telegraph office to write his story and send it to New York. While he was gone,

17

a telegram addressed to him was delivered to his roommate, Sid Mercer, of the New York *Globe,* an older and much respected newspaperman. The two writers had an agreement to open messages delivered in the other's absence in the event his paper wanted to reach him in an emergency. Mercer opened the telegram, which was from Joe Vila, reporting that Tener had suspended McGraw for sixteen days and fined him five hundred dollars and asking my father to file a story on McGraw's response.

When he did not return within a few minutes, Mercer took the telegram to McGraw. The Giant manager's response was sulfurous. He vilified the league's umpires and implied that Tener, a former governor of Pennsylvania, had been given his present position at the urging of the Phillies and that he ran the league to their liking. Much later, my father described the scene in McGraw's room.

"Do you want to be quoted on this?" Mercer asked.

A veteran baseball writer, and noted for the calmness and soundness with which he wrote, he knew that McGraw's outburst, set in print, would be dynamite.

"On every word of it!" McGraw shouted. "Tell all the other newspapermen! I want this printed in every paper in New York!"

Mercer returned to his room, wrote the story, and then, thinking perhaps McGraw had calmed down and might regret publication of his blast, sought him out and offered to let him read what he had written. McGraw, still seething, glanced at it and handed it back.

"That's all right," he said. "Did you tell the other boys?"

"No, I wanted you to see this first. I'll get in touch with them now."

Mercer located my father and two other writers with the team and read them what McGraw had told him. The four men then sent stories about McGraw's charges to their papers. By the next day the country's sports pages were making the most of the brouhaha, reproducing the quotes and wondering what Tener was going to do about it.

They had not long to wait. McGraw was summoned to New

York to appear before the league's board of directors to explain his remarks—and he repudiated them! He had never said any such thing, he told the directors. And there the matter stood.

Pop was astonished. Back at the *Sun,* when Joe Vila questioned him about the circumstances of McGraw's outburst, he admitted that he had not been present during the interview but had heard McGraw say much the same thing on the train a day or two afterward. Vila, like the other writers' editors, stood behind the story. Pop went to the ball park and confronted McGraw, who was in the clubhouse. Under questioning, McGraw candidly admitted that he had been urged to repudiate the stories by the Giants' owner and his lawyers. This was how my father described the encounter.

"They kept at me to sign it and I finally did," McGraw said airily. "I thought that was the best way out for everybody. I made them make one change in it, though. It said that you fellows had written scurrilous stories. I made them strike out 'scurrilous.' "

He seemed to think that had made everything all right for the reporters.

"But you still called us a bunch of liars."

"Don't take it so seriously," he said. "It will all be forgotten in a day or so."

"Not by me, it won't."

"Well," he said, cunningly. "If it comes right down to it, I didn't tell you the things you wrote, did I?"

"You told them to Sid."

"But I didn't tell them to you. If you were put on the stand, you'd have to admit you didn't see me that night."

"I saw you later and you were talking the same way."

He shrugged. "Well, the hell with it."

The interview had gone about as far as he wanted it to. He got down from the rubbing table on which he had been sitting and went out.

Other newspapermen joined in their colleagues' defense. Among the most outspoken was Grantland Rice, who was rapidly becoming the most illustrious man in the profession. Although my father had never met him before, Rice went out of his way to offer him encouragement and, what was unusual for this most mild-mannered of all sportswriters, sarcastically pointed out in his syndicated column the weakness of McGraw's case. The Baseball Writers' Association demanded that the league hold a hearing on the matter. That step proved decisive. Mercer, indignant yet restrained, made a much better witness than the evasive McGraw at the hearing, which was held at the National League's office in New York, and Tener accepted the finding that McGraw had spoken out as he was quoted. He fined McGraw an additional thousand dollars.

Although Mercer refused to speak to McGraw and had himself transferred to cover the Yankees, Pop was sufficiently elated by his vindication to forgive and forget. The Giants were on their way to the pennant, and he basked in their reflected glory, riding with a winner in his second year as a traveling writer. McGraw, undaunted by the turn of events in the legal sphere and supremely confident of his ability to lead the Giants to the world championship, spent much of his energy during the World Series ridiculing the manager of the opposing Chicago White Sox, Clarence "Pants" Rowland, who was a comparative newcomer to the big leagues. To McGraw's chagrin, the White Sox had assembled a powerful team, essentially the same players who, as the infamous "Black Sox," were to throw the World Series to the interior Reds in 1919. But in 1917 the White Sox played in earnest and beat the Giants, four games to two. After the final game, a smiling Rowland walked to the Giants' dugout, hand extended, to offer McGraw the pipe of peace and his congratulations on a well-played Series.

"Get away from me, you goddamned busher!" McGraw snarled, and pushed past him toward the clubhouse. He was not a man to let defeat go to his head.

Constant travel has been the downfall of many newspapermen, their enthusiasm and wits dulled by the endless sitting about in trains, planes, terminals, and strange rooms, with alcoholism the only antidote. But the young Frank Graham was seldom prey to boredom. Although he was not a playboy and, in fact, seldom drank hard liquor before middle age, he enjoyed the parties that were organized by McGraw or the other newspapermen. Singing was his strong suit. He had a thin but pleasant tenor voice, which he liked to raise in concert with his pals, especially if the song was a sentimental one. There were many opportunities to put his voice to use. In parlor cars on long train rides through the South, or in the dining rooms of old hotels after the other guests, and even the musicians, had made their way to bed, the ball players and writers borrowed the piano (and whatever other instruments had been left around) and created impromptu concerts of their own. When the Giants began to dominate baseball after World War I, there were even more opportunities to break into song. After the team won the 1921 World Series against Babe Ruth and the upstart Yankees (until that year perennial losers), the big voices took the buttons off the foils.

That night, in the Giants' suite at the Waldorf, McGraw and Charles A. Stoneham [the team's president] were hosts at a celebration that never will be forgotten by those who attended it—including one Giant player who never had been known to take a drink before, but was carried out, stiff as a board, along about five o'clock of the morning after. There were hams and chickens and turkeys for the guests that night—or steaks for those who wanted them. And rye and Scotch and gin and champagne. Little Jimmy Flynn, a tenor much fancied by the baseball and prize-fight mob, and a great favorite with McGraw, sang. So did Frank Belcher, once a basso with the famed San Francisco Minstrels and a regular companion of McGraw's, who was partial to "Asleep in The Deep" and "I'm Off to Philadelphia in The Morning." So, too, did Lieutenant Gitz-Rice, whose "Dear Old Pal of Mine," composed by him in the trenches during the World War and first sung there to other soldiers, was sung now by him to his own accompaniment on the piano. Someone had clipped the headlines telling of the Giants' victories from the evening newspapers and pasted them across the mirrors in all the rooms of the suite. Endless toasts were drunk to McGraw. The sun was high over Fifth Avenue and

Thirty-fourth Street as the last of the guests emerged and tottered homeward.

But more important to Pop's sense of satisfaction was his capacity for making the best use of his hours of freedom on the road. In the mornings he took long walks through whatever city he happened to find himself in, familiarizing himself with its landmarks and history, so that he came to know many of them with the thoroughness of a resident. When he was out for a walk, he always stopped at the bookstores that he came across, browsing through the shelves and often taking a new novel or a book of travel back to his room to read in the evening. He read a great deal in those days, helping himself to the education he had never received as an adolescent and sharpening his own skills as a writer. His taste was not omnivorous, however. Preciosity in literature did not interest him, and if earthiness spilled over into vulgarity or explicit sex, he was absolutely turned off, which was one of the reasons that he stuck to his old favorites as time went on. (He must have dipped briefly into the *Studs Lonigan* trilogy, for years later, when James T. Farrell wrote a rather sour review of my first book in the *Times*, my father brushed it off with the remark "Forget it. Farrell's only claim to fame is that he wrote a dirty book.")

Hemingway was different, because he came along at a time when my father was taking writing very seriously. He admired Hemingway's exaltation of the manly virtues and his lean, hard prose (which ought not to be underestimated for its salutary effect on the overblown journalistic style of the time). He identified with Hemingway's interest in boxing, and though he did not like bullfighting (or any of the other blood sports, for that matter, if boxing is excepted), he considered "The Undefeated" the best of Hemingway's stories, recognizing in the aging matador many of the washed-up fighters he had known. "The best story about boxing anyone ever wrote," he called it.

Pop made two trips to Europe after the war, the first in 1921. His brothers had fought in France, and the stories they brought back with them made him eager to see Paris and the other continental sights. His first trip was not precisely a "grand tour." He arranged a month's leave from the *Sun* (with an assignment to write a series of articles about European sports to help with the expenses) and sailed for Le Havre soon after the World Series. He carried letters of introduction to people in Paris from his friends in the newspaper business. When he arrived, he made his headquarters at the Paris *Herald*, where he was taken in tow by one of the most flamboyant expatriates of the time, William Harrison "Sparrow" Robertson.

The Sparrow, as he was known by the sporting crowd in Paris, had been born in Scotland but had spent most of his first sixty years in New York, where as a youth he was something of a long-distance runner for local athletic clubs. Later he sold sporting goods, promoted fights, and even contributed sports items to the *Sun*. During the war he had come to Paris with the YMCA (an affiliation he always tried to hide after the fact), found the city congenial, and remained in it for the rest of his life. He was a wispy little guy who spoke out of the side of his mouth in precisely enunciated syllables. Although he was, from a professional standpoint, practically illiterate and knew very little about sports other than boxing and track, he talked his way into the previously nonexistent position as sports editor of the *Herald*. Once the copy editors stopped trying to tidy up his disheveled prose, he gained an enthusiastic readership, who saw in him a kind of latter-day Samuel Pepys. Eugene O'Neill was so mesmerized by the Sparrow's prose that he called him, unblushingly, "the greatest writer in the world." A sample of his prose and subject matter, from his column, "Sporting Gossip," follows:

> The end of a perfect Thanksgiving Day. Early in the forenoon of Thursday, I dropped into Jeff Dickson's office and he prevailed upon me to remain and hear the returns of the royal wedding in London. I did, and during the come-over, some refreshments were offered and not refused. After, it was a case of making a call at Henry's Bar in the Rue Volney, where an excellent free lunch, and drinks included, was served. It was a swell layout and it was deeply appreciated by the mass which attended.
> Then it was a visit to Otto's Bar, where we found the cham-

pion cocktail-shaker in rare form. After an hour or two passed with Otto, it was time to make a visit to Harry's aquarium, and what a bunch we did meet there. While in old Harry's place I met a pal, one well known in the American, English and Canadian colonies of Paris. He said: "Sparrow, come to my home tonight and we will eat cold turkey, drink White Horse and smoke nine inch long Havana cigars." It sounded good to me and I told our pal that I was on.

In the company of such an exuberant guide, my father was treated to a rather special view of war-ravaged Paris, though the reading of a dozen literary memoirs of the time suggests his experience wasn't unique. He also visited the racetrack and the boxing arenas with the Sparrow, then managed to slip away to northeastern France and Belgium to tour the sites of some of the war's great battles and to wander around old cobblestone streets and centuries-old churches. His adventures kindled a brief ambition to become a foreign correspondent, but by Christmas he was back in New York, writing about the actors in a drama he came to believe was much more entertaining than the machinations of European diplomats.

In 1923, when he reached his thirtieth birthday, events crowded in on one another and created one of the most exciting years of his life. New York had no challenger as the center of the sports world. The Giants and the Yankees had won their league pennants in the two previous years, and although the Giants had beaten the Yankees both times in the "Subway Series," Babe Ruth was becoming the city's conquering hero. Yankee Stadium, the House That Ruth Built, financed in large part by the crowds that flocked to see Ruth play wherever the Yankees went, had risen during the off season on River Avenue at 161st Street. On April 18 the Yankees moved into their new stadium, playing the Red Sox on opening day.

This was the greatest, the most magnificent ball park ever seen.
The huge triple-decked grandstands towered, it seemed, almost to
the sky. Wooden bleachers ranged from foul line to foul line. The
exact seating capacity was not divulged, but when all who could

*be admitted had jammed the stands and thousands of latecomers
had been turned back by the police, the attendance was announced as 74,200. Later it developed that the figures had been
padded considerably, but the newspapers were correct when they
said that this was the largest crowd that had ever seen a ball game.
It probably numbered close to 60,000 and before that 40,000 had
been tops.*

With Ruth clouting 41 home runs and batting .393, the highest
average of the long pageant that was his career, the Yankees
turned the pennant race into a runaway and moved toward another confrontation with the Giants. On the way, the Babe's bravado and sense of timing were mingling with his great skills to
create baseball's ultimate hero. At Chicago one day, the Yankees
went into extra innings against the White Sox. Mark Roth, the
team's traveling secretary, had arranged to put the players on a
train for New York late that afternoon, but with time growing
short he began to fidget.

*He called the railroad, explained the situation, and received the
assurance that the train would be held for the team—but not for
very long. On the field, the teams had moved into the thirteenth
inning. Mark Roth watched feverishly from a box next to the dugout. Then the fourteenth inning came, and no score. The Yankees
went to bat in the fifteenth. Joe Dugan singled. Ruth, on his way
to the plate, saw Roth.*

"What's the matter with you?" he boomed. "Sick?"

*"Yes," Mark said. "If you bums don't wind up this ball game in
a hurry, we'll blow the train."*

"Take it easy," Ruth said. "I'll get us out of here."

*Mike Cvengros, a little left-hander with a tantalizing curve ball,
was pitching for the White Sox. Ruth hit the first ball pitched to
him into the right-field stand, jogged around the bases behind
Dugan, and as he returned to the dugout said to Roth:*

"Why the hell didn't you tell me about that before?"

While the Babe was feeding newspapermen the stuff with
which to weave his legend, the Yankees' front office had its eye on

another left-handed slugger. Lou Gehrig had been born in what is now East Harlem and had made more of a mark at the High School of Commerce than my father had, not only earning a diploma but also, in an intercity-championship game, hitting a tremendous home run out of Wrigley Field in Chicago. He went on to excel in baseball and football at Columbia University, where a Yankee scout saw him and informed the front office that Gehrig was "another Babe Ruth." When the Columbia baseball team had ended its season, Gehrig was invited for a tryout at Yankee Stadium.

The Yankees were at batting practice when Manager Miller Huggins brought him out on the field. The players looked at the boy, towering above the manager. Whitey Witt had just finished a turn at the plate, and Dugan was moving up to take a swing when Huggins said:
"Wait a minute, Joe. Let this boy hit."
The boy picked up a bat—one of Ruth's, by some curious chance—and advanced to the plate. He was obviously nervous, missed the first two pitches, then bounced one weakly over second base. Then he hit one that soared into the right-field bleachers, high up, where only Ruth had ever hit the ball. The players were amazed. He hit another ball in there—another—still another. His nervousness had slipped from him now. The balls that flew from his bat crushed into the bleachers or struck the rim.
"That's enough," Huggins cried. He turned to the players. "His name's Gehrig," he said, and walked slowly toward the dugout. The players looked after them in silence. They sensed that they had seen a great hitter in the making.

Also in 1923, Jack Dempsey was at the peak of his career, all fists and killer instinct. With his broad-shouldered, slim-waisted torso, his brakeman's haircut, and his dish nose (later remodeled by a plastic surgeon when he headed toward Hollywood and the vaudeville circuit), he was a perfect fit for those stories about the young savage punching his way out of the West's hobo jungles to win the heavyweight championship of the world. He had already demolished Georges Carpentier, who, if he wasn't quite the Greek god that gushing human-interest writers described when he first came to this country, was at least a canny and suave Parisian. (He was asked, during an interview shortly after he had knocked out the British heavyweight champion, Joe Beckett, in seventy-five seconds, "Will Beckett always be a stupid fighter?" "I don't know," Carpentier said, and shrugged. "I have never met the man.") A succession of other, less glamorous fighters fell before Dempsey's fists, confirming my father in his belief that he was the greatest of all heavyweight champions. And, on September 14, 1923, he fought Luis Angel Firpo, "the Wild Bull of the Pampas," in what my father called the most thrilling fight he ever covered, Dempsey crawling back into the ring from the press row where he had been hurled by one of Firpo's wild rights and flattening the challenger in the second round.

Benny Leonard, whose many skills, my father believed, surpassed even those of Sugar Ray Robinson, then dominated the lighter divisions. Waiting in the wings were the Four Horsemen of Notre Dame, as well as Red Grange, Bill Tilden, Bobby Jones, Earl Sande, and the other superstars who were to make that decade "the Golden Age of Sports" celebrated by the daily newspapers in florid prose that had outlived its Victorian origins. A little education can be a dangerous thing, as many journalists of the time demonstrated. Perhaps Pop's relative lack of education served him well at this time, for he did not have the bright highschool student's breezy vagueness, and he was in the process of working out his own style along sparer lines than those of his contemporaries.

Chapter Three
I Am Born

My father continued his frequent trips across the bridge to Brooklyn, for, at thirty, he had finally acquired the minimal affluence required to propose marriage. It was not a hasty decision. The two lovers had known each other for some years, and both were confident they had found a life's companion.

Gertrude Lillian Whipp was a third cousin to him, and probably several years older. She lied about her age until the day she died, and indeed had knocked off so many years on her driver's license, in apprehension the state might take it away from her because of old age, that it became one of the many sources of anxiety to her during her last years. When she traveled to Maine from New York State on what was recognized within the family as her eightieth birthday, I conspired with Bud Leavitt, the rod-and-gun writer for the Bangor *Daily News,* to have him wish her a "happy eightieth" at the conclusion of his television program. It turned out to be more of a jolt than a surprise for my mother. Aware that Nelson Rockefeller had a summer home in Maine, she shot out of her chair, gasping, "Oh, dear! Now Governor Rockefeller will take my driver's license away from me!"

The doggedness and enterprise that kept her driving New York's suburban parkways well into her eighties were apparent in the young woman courted by my father. George Whipp, her father, was a contractor and bon vivant whose fortunes fluctuated with some regularity between affluence and ruin. In good times he drove his elegant equipage up Flatbush Avenue, my mother, an only child, decked out in her finery on the seat beside him, and treated his little family to regal dinners in one of the restaurants at Sheepshead Bay. Toward his pampered wife and beloved daughter George Whipp was the soul of chivalry, though he turned out to be guilty of the ultimate infidelity: during one of his bankruptcies he contracted pneumonia, abruptly died, and left the two women penniless.

My grandmother, Minnie Whipp, who was used to fine clothes, a maid, and a life of idleness, tried to go on living as if nothing had happened. My mother left high school to support the two of them. She worked as a stenographer ("Going to business," she and Minnie called it) and took courses in the evenings, eventually becoming a librarian. When a small inheritance came their way, as it did once or twice, my grandmother engaged a maid and bought a new wardrobe, living high on the hog until the money ran out and she had to subsist once more on a young librarian's salary. In October, 1923, a few days after the Yankees defeated the Giants in the World Series, my father claimed his bride, taking her out of the library but not away from her mother, who moved in with the newly married couple.

But first there was a honeymoon trip to Europe, where my father prowled London's streets and bookstores and showed my mother the sights of Paris under the guidance of Sparrow Robertson. They lived in a little hotel in the Rue Bréa, met Isadora Duncan and her brother, Jim, in the boulevard cafés, and stored up anecdotes and friendships they treasured all of their lives. John McGraw and his wife, Blanche, also came to Paris that fall, and they made a foursome with them on several evenings.

McGraw knew only one word of French. The word was "tou-jours," meaning "always," and it was remarkable how well he did with it, considering he didn't know what it meant.

Did one of his French friends drop in on him at the Continental? His greeting was a hearty: "Toujours! Toujours!"

Did the friend tell a funny story? His reward was: "Ha! Ha! Ha! Toujours!"

Or was it sad? There would be a shake of the head and a solemn. "Toujours. Toujours."

And when he was departing, McGraw would speed him on his way with: "Well, toujours, old boy! Toujours!"

His expression, his inflection, always were such that no one had the slightest trouble catching his meaning—until one night in the Palais de Glace, on the Champs Elysées. There was a small rink, encircled by a tier of tables. The head waiter, recognizing McGraw, led the party to a table on the first tier, just a few feet above the ice. It was then about eleven o'clock and there were few skaters. One of them was a young man with a small moustache, who obviously was eager to impress the new arrivals with his skill. But, unfortunately, just as he skimmed past their table his feet flew from under him and he sat down very violently. He looked up pathetically. McGraw, in an attempt to put him at ease, said, his voice laden with sympathy: "Toujours, my friend."

The young man's face flushed. Still seated on the ice, he held up two fingers and screamed: "Non, non, Monsieur! Deux!"

Before Christmas, the couple were back in the United States, having rented an apartment for themselves and Minnie on Ocean Avenue in Brooklyn. A year later my mother was pregnant, and in the spring of 1925 my father set off as usual with the Giants, who were then training in Sarasota. The Giants' camp was enlivened by the presence of a movie crew that was shooting a picture somehow designed to depict Florida both as the haven for big-league teams in training and the site of a spectacular but short-lived real-estate boom. Between innings of an exhibition game between the Giants and the Browns, with the Browns in the field, the crew set up cameras around the diamond. The film's hero, dressed in a Giant uniform, stepped into the batter's box to hit the home run that would win the girl or, more likely, an option on a prime lot.

At a word from the director, the pitcher wound up and went through the motion of delivering a ball to the hitter—although, for safety's sake, no ball was used. The hero, who didn't look as though he'd ever worn a baseball uniform or held a bat in his hands before, swung awkwardly. Had there been a ball and had he, by some miracle, hit it, it would have struck the dirt in front of the plate, the way he swung. He started on his round of the bases. Huffing and puffing, he crossed the plate as the crowd cheered.

The director hadn't been satisfied with the performance. "Do it again," he shouted.

The weary actor picked up his bat, and still puffing, took his stance at the plate again.

The press box merely was a continuation of the Giants' bench, a beaver board partition separating the newspapermen from the athletes. McGraw, who sat next to the partition, leaned around it and said to the nearest reporter:

"If he has to run around the bases again, he will either fall down or get sick."

The pitcher went through his motion, the hero chopped at the phantom ball—and was off. He began to stagger as he rounded first base. His legs buckled as he neared second, and he fell across the bag as the crowd howled. Gamely getting to his feet, he went his reeling, lunging way. He fell again as he got to the plate, dragged himself up, and, a look of panic on his face, lurched past the end of the bench. Mercifully hidden from the view of the laughing spectators, he was sick.

The reporter to whom McGraw had spoken leaned around the partition.

"How did you know that would happen?" he asked.

"That was a cinch," McGraw said. "I never saw a well trained player who could run around the bases at top speed twice without a rest in between. So what chance did that poor ham have to do it?"

The movie, entitled *The New Klondike*, had been hastily written by Ring Lardner at a time when he was hard up for ready cash. In his book *The Lardners*, Ring Lardner, Jr., recalls that the finished product was favorably received by the public, though his father dismissed it in his weekly column with the remark "they was a couple of baseball incidence in it that would make a ball player wonder if the author had fell out of a toy balloon in his infancy."

On March 31, 1925, while my father was in Memphis on his way north with the Giants, my mother gave birth to me in a small private hospital on Manhattan's West Side. Pop, characteristically shying away from bestowing anything of himself on another mortal, had hoped to call me Harry, after a close friend of the family, or Bruce, to emphasize my Scottish heritage. But Harry inconveniently committed suicide several months before my arrival, and my mother recalled a pet poodle called Bruce that had belonged to another chum, and so by default I became a Junior. Just Frank; no Francis or middle initial: an elision that prompted the Navy's paper-shufflers to insert the parenthetical "None" between the homely elements of my full name in World War II.

My father, though there were no broad acres or known ancient lineage in his background—he almost never spoke of his own forebears—had a strong sense of continuity. He revered the past; he reveled in tradition. He liked parades, uniforms, martial music, college marching songs. He thrilled to the Brigade of Midshipmen as it marched onto the field before an Army-Navy game, and he loved the hoopla surrounding Ivy League and Big Ten football. (Conversely, he saw professional football as a perversion of the sport, tainted by its removal from hallowed campuses, so that he referred to it contemptuously as "wrestling outdoors" and hoped that it would just go away, like jai alai and the roller derby.) He saw the sports he loved as enriched by a leaf mold composed of brave deeds and rollicking good times. He returned to the Kentucky Derby year after year and, like clockwork, shed a tear when the band broke into "My Old Kentucky Home." His sentimentality served him well in his writing, because it was mixed with an accurate ear and a kind of genius for anecdote.

The book of British sporting prints that, as my mother's proxy, I presented to him on my first Christmas was appropriate, even symbolic. Although the prints in it, I recently noticed, are relatively few, and the text is aimed at the specialist, it represented a sporting life that had disappeared by the time the book was published; it testified to the tradition that expanded the meaning of sport. It also bolstered my father's anglophilia, by which he had been infected on his brief visit to London. He imagined the British Empire as a competitive spectacle on a global scale, where knights or sea dogs or Tommies kept punching, whatever the odds against them. He had once had a glimpse of the Prince of Wales, who seemed a dashing, sporting man himself, and he had put him on a pedestal with Dempsey and Mathewson and Benny Leonard and looked forward to the day when, as Edward VIII, he would shoulder the duties for which he had been bred. The Simpson affair dismayed him, and he took it as hard as the Archbishop of Canterbury.

I spent my earliest years in a Brooklyn apartment hearing not symphonies or birdsong but illustrious names. The most prominent was a person I understood to be called Bay Bruth. I repeated those syllables as if they were a magic incantation. The discovery that I was left-handed was taken to be an omen of sorts, for there was no one else of that persuasion in my immediate family, and it was jokingly suggested that Arthur Nehf, the Giants' ace southpaw, who was my father's closest friend on the team and a frequent visitor to the apartment, had subtly influenced the phenomenon. But when somebody rolled a baseball at me I preferred to kick it.

Perhaps I was saving my arm for a more sinister purpose. In any case, one spring afternoon my grandmother, immensely proud in the expensive pearl-gray hat she had just acquired, took me for a walk. As she led me across a subway overpass, a train came into view and I insisted on being held up to see it thunder beneath us. The train was nearly at the overpass. Under some inexplicable impulse, whether of maliciousness or pure excitement, I tore the treasured hat from Minnie's head and dashed it under the wheels of the speeding cars. She displayed uncharacteristic self-control by refraining from hurling me after the hat, though she burst into tears and there was an awful row when we got home.

I insert this confession not to illustrate childish depravity but to introduce the subject of parental discipline. It was my mother who punished me for the destruction of the hat, though the hiding I got was halfhearted because everybody who witnessed the unfortunate Minnie's hysterics found it hard to insist on the enormity of the offense. In fact, most disciplinary chores in the family fell to my mother. During my first decade Pop was on the road most of the time. By nature he was a gentle man, proud of his children and gifted with endless patience, so that he could go on writing an article even when domestic hubbub boiled around him. The only time he ever struck me was when I had committed the unpardonable sin—impudence toward my mother—and then he merely swatted me on the rump. (Blows to the head and face were ruled out in our household.)

Sometimes, if he had an off day and the Dodgers were playing at Ebbets Field, he would suggest we go to the ball game, and I would always say yes, not because I cared about baseball then but because I wanted to spend a day with him. This was before the Dodgers were widely known as "the Daffiness Boys." Their wretchedness was unrelieved even by comedy. They had one great pitcher, though, Arthur "Dazzy" Vance, who had reached Brooklyn at age thirty-one after years of struggling in the minors and who went on to win 197 games in the National League. We always sat in the press box, a long, shallow enclosure that hung from the grandstand behind home plate. While my father gossiped with the other writers, I willingly surrendered myself to the care of a retired telegraph operator who had sent copy from this press box in past years and now returned there regularly because he knew of no other place to spend a pleasant summer afternoon. When I discovered that he had a wooden leg, I liked to sit on his lap during the game and pound my knuckles on the resonant limb. Even that pastime began to pall after four or five innings, and I would ask to be taken to the zoo (an abandonment of baseball I would repeat thirty years later), whereupon Pop would obligingly walk me over to Prospect Park. My favorite inmate at the menagerie was the llama, whose mobile, rubbery lips screwed its features into mirror images of the funny faces I composed for both our amusement from the other side of the bars.

The necessities of the Depression were to nudge my father into authorhood. By the early 1930s the Graham household was growing in number and still supporting the succession of maids that Minnie had accustomed my parents to. (Obsessed by the vision of the ideal servant, Minnie carped and bullied, driving them away one by one until Emma Akins, the daughter of a former slave, arrived from Florida to stare her down and remain a part of the family for forty years.) I was no longer an only child, and we moved into a small house in Forest Hills. I was followed by Mary, Jim (a beautiful boy with rosy cheeks and golden-red curly hair, born seriously retarded, the great tragedy of my parents' lives), and Judy. The *Sun* had cut the staff's salaries. The letters from my mother that followed my father to various hotels around the country at this time are touching, expressing loneliness amid the expanding family and bewildered gloom in the face of mounting bills. He wrote back, recounting his long walks through urban parks, during which he hoped the idea for a lucrative magazine article would pop into his head.

But it was my mother who came up with the suggestion that he write the story of Andy Blue, the little boy who wanted to be a fireman, and find a children's publisher for it. The Whitman Publishing Company, of Racine, Wisconsin, expressed interest in the manuscript but wanted a companion volume. How about a book on a policeman? And so my father dreamed up Davy Lane, who wanted to be a policeman and one day won a medal for heroism by pulling a drowning man from the icy river. After a successful audition in his own home, my father dispatched the manuscript to Racine; a wonderful check for three hundred dollars, payment for the two volumes, lifted the Grahams temporarily out of debt. In 1932 two little, illustrated volumes appeared that made me as proud as my father was, for I had played a part in their composition, by nagging him into embellishments. To this day I have never seen reds as rich and evocative as those of the fire engines that rushed through the pages of *Andy Blue.*

Meanwhile, the Giants were slowly fading as the center of my father's professional life. McGraw, always volatile and ready for a row, became more difficult as he grew older. He could be utterly charming one moment and vicious, sometimes deceitful, at others. The player on his team most like him in style and temperament was Frank Frisch, "the Fordham Flash," who had come out of college to play second base for the Giants. Tough and aggressive, Frisch became McGraw's team captain, and it was said he eventually would succeed him as manager. But one of McGraw's peculiarities was to blame his captain for all of the team's deficiencies. As the great Giant team of the early 1920s crumbled, McGraw became particularly hard on Frisch after a losing game (as he had on Frisch's predecessor as captain, Larry Doyle). He seemed to blame Frisch for the other players' failures or lack of hustle, endlessly bullying him in the clubhouse. At last, during one of the Giants' swings through the West in 1926, the proud Frisch packed his bag and went off to sulk in New York. Although he was back at second base when the team returned to the Polo Grounds, it was apparent that his defiance of McGraw had numbered his days as a Giant.

In December my father, looking for a story on a dull day, went to McGraw at the Giants' downtown office and asked him if the rumors were true that Frisch would be traded to the Cardinals for Rogers Hornsby. Hornsby, who was the greatest right-handed hitter of his time, had been locked in a bitter contract dispute with Sam Breadon, the owner of the Cardinals. My father, thinly disguised in the third person, recounted the aftermath:

That night the reporter was in Newark, covering a fight between Jack Delaney, then one of the front-rank heavyweights, and Bud Gorman. Just before the principals in the main bout entered the ring, a telegraph operator at his elbow copied a message from his office and handed it to him.

"The Giants have traded Frank Frisch and Jimmy Ring to the Cardinals for Rogers Hornsby," it read.

Unable to reach McGraw on the telephone that night, the reporter confronted him in the office the next day.

"That was a fine steer you gave me yesterday afternoon," he said bitterly.

McGraw was genuinely disturbed.

"I called you at your office last night," he said, "but they told me you were on your way to Newark. I wanted to explain to you what happened. As sure as I am sitting here, when you asked me yesterday if we were going to get Hornsby and I told you no, I was telling the truth, as I knew it then. About eight o'clock Charlie Stoneham and I went to dinner, but got word to come back to the office. Sam Breadon was trying to get us on the phone. We rushed back and called him, and he said:

" 'Do you still want Hornsby?'

" 'Yes,' we said.

"He asked us what we would give for him, and before we could tell him he wanted to know if we would let him have Frisch. We said yes, and he said:

" 'Well, you've got Hornsby.'

"So help me, that's just the way it happened. If you doubt me, ask Breadon."

Upon investigation, McGraw's story stood up. Hornsby and Breadon had had a final bitter dispute on the previous day, and Breadon, who was aware that Frisch was in McGraw's bad graces, determined to unload his star (a trade that brought the wrath of St. Louis fans down on him because the popular Hornsby was also the Cardinals' manager and had just led them to the first world championship in their history). But early the next spring, Pop's love-hate relationship with McGraw took another turn for the worse.

McGraw left the Giants one night to return to New York and bargain with Edd Roush, an outfielder who was holding out for more money. It was twenty-four hours before the team's secretary told the reporters that McGraw was gone. My father was furious, and decided to complain to McGraw when he returned to the training camp. A day or two later, McGraw was back, and he called a press conference.

"Well, Roush has signed," McGraw said. "That's what I went to New York for."

No one said anything for a moment. Then the reporter who had been saving his squawk for McGraw asked:

"Why didn't you tell us you were going to New York?"

"Oh," he said. "I didn't think it made any difference."

"You must have. You told the team's secretary not to let us know until twenty-four hours later."

He flushed at that. "Well, all right then. I didn't want it known. What of it?"

"This much: You put every man covering this ball club in a bad spot and might have cost somebody his job."

"How?"

"By walking out without letting us know. We're supposed to know what's going on around here, and we're responsible for the news. Suppose somebody, seeing you in New York, had tipped off the papers. We'd be a fine-looking lot of stiffs, wouldn't we? Every one of our editors would have been justified in believing we were negligent."

"Oh, come!" he said, forcing a laugh. "I just wanted to get out without any publicity, and if anything had happened I would have squared it with your editors."

"Don't you think," the reporter asked, "that if you had told us you were going, but asked us not to print anything about it, we would have done as you asked? Don't you think you could have trusted us?"

A reporter in the rear of the room got up and, without a word, went out.

McGraw, who had looked after his retreating figure, turned to his inquisitor. "I don't know whether I could have or not," he said sharply.

"You should know," the reporter snapped. "I don't know of a man covering this ball club who has ever betrayed your confidence."

The reporters got up to leave and write their stories. The one who had taken McGraw to task, still angry, was near the door when McGraw took him by the arm.

"Come here a minute; I want to tell you something," he said. As the others left the room he said:

"I just wanted to give you a tip: You were giving me hell a moment ago for not trusting the newspapermen. It might be a good idea for them to find out if they can trust each other. You know what that bird who went out a little while ago is doing, don't you? He's in his room calling his office on the telephone so he can beat the rest of you on the Roush story."

The reporter's temperature rose even higher.

"If I thought you were right—"

McGraw shrugged. "Go to his room and find out," he said. "If he isn't on the telephone talking to his office, I'll buy you the best suit of clothes in New York."

The reporter darted out of the room—then, a little way down the hall, checked his steps. He wouldn't go to his colleague's room. He was afraid he'd discover McGraw was right.

Chapter Four
Star Reporter

Most team sports other than baseball in the 1920s tended to confine themselves to an established season, conforming to solar time, so to speak, rather than sprawling all over one another as they do today when their financial managers puff out the season as long as possible. Football was an autumn sport, getting under way in October and generally finished by Thanksgiving or shortly thereafter, with three or four big bowl games appearing almost as an afterthought on New Year's Day; college teams, and even professional ones, considered seven or eight games a full season. Hockey was a winter sport, though tailored to span the long Canadian winter. By the end of the hockey season, the baseball players were pulling on their rubber suits in sunnier climes to sweat off the fat accumulated since the World Series.

And so, for my father, there was very little conflict in moving from one sport to another—though it raised hell with his domestic life. He spent so much time on the road that once, when he arrived home after a long trip, my sister Mary rushed out the front door to greet him—and kissed the taxi driver who was carrying Pop's bags up the steps. At the end of the World Series he was off to cover college football, mostly in the Midwest and Southeast.

The *Sun* was very big on college football, and on Saturday afternoons much of the front page of later editions was given over to line scores of the major games, followed by play-by-play accounts of three or four of them, telegraphed directly to the office by staff reporters. Thus Pop was on the road for weeks at a time during autumn, doing general surveys of the Big Ten and other leading college conferences during the week and on Saturdays sitting in the press box and giving his telegrapher a play-by-play account of the action on the field. Because the *Sun* did not publish on Sunday, he seldom had to rewrite his running account of a game after it was over but used highlights of the action in a general account of the conference picture for the following Monday. He also kept in touch with all the coaches in his area so that he could send reports back to his paper on prospects for the *Sun's* All-America team, selected at the end of the season.

It must have been a nightmare as the countdown began toward the day when the *Sun* unveiled its own prestigious and highly authoritative All-America team, but it was apparent from the communications that sped to him in his various hotel rooms in the hinterlands that his judgment was eagerly sought.

By then the hockey season was under way, and he joined the New York Americans (now long defunct) on their swing around the National Hockey League. Those were rough-and-tumble days in hockey, with rudimentary protective equipment and few restrictions on mayhem. A favorite anecdote of my father's from those days concerned Punch Broadbent, of the Montreal Maroons, and Cy Dennenny, of the Ottawa Senators.

They were neighbors and friends but they hadn't seen each other for a couple of weeks before this night and as they met going on the ice Punch said:

"Hello, Cy. How are the wife and kids?"

"Fine," Cy said. "And yours?"

"Swell."

Two minutes after the game began Punch almost split Cy's head from crown to chin with a vicious swipe of his stick and Cy lashed

*back at Punch, and they were giving each other a terrific hiding
when they were hauled apart.*

*"The next time you ask me how my wife and kids are," Cy
panted as he was being led away, "I'll hit you over the head first!"*

Boxing, my father's first love, was not a part of his regular beat
during the 1920s, though he covered many of the big fights in
New York when he was not tied up with one of his teams. Whatever the assignment, he took it deadly seriously. He did not bet on
the events he covered, not so much because he doubted his own
objectivity under any circumstances but because he believed a reporter, like Caesar's wife, should be above suspicion. He took
each event he covered as seriously as the athletes did, or were
supposed to. But a rare deviation from rigid professionalism on
one occasion cost him dearly.

Pop had struck up an acquaintanceship with a telegrapher in
one of the Western Union offices where he often filed his copy.
The telegrapher was an enthusiastic boxing fan whose hero was
Dempsey. When Dempsey made a comeback after having lost his
title to Gene Tunney, this man asked Pop to wangle him an assignment as his telegrapher at ringside for the Dempsey–Jack
Sharkey bout in July, 1927. Although the man had never worked
at a major sports event, his enthusiasm was so infectious that caution was set aside in this case.

It was a rousing fight. My father did the best he could to dictate
a blow-by-blow account to his telegrapher, but the fellow's excitement knew no bounds. He was often on his feet at ringside,
cheering his hero on, my father's restraining hand bringing him
back time and again to the business at hand. Finally, in the seventh round, Dempsey delivered the crusher, and Sharkey toppled
to the canvas and was counted out. The telegrapher, by then almost delirious, flashed the message back to the *Sun:* DEMPSEY
KAYOS DEMPSEY. And then he locked his key!

Confusion and dismay took over the sports department at the
Sun. All they had was the cryptic message. Frantic attempts to
rouse a response at the other end of the wire were unsuccessful.
Pop had settled down to write his story of the fight, confident that

the sports desk had the bulletin and was acting on the advice, while his telegrapher at that moment was trying to crawl through the ropes to clap the victorious Dempsey on the back. One of the editors of the *Sun* finally had to call a rival paper to find out who had won the fight. It was the telegrapher's last seat at ringside.

Radios began to proliferate throughout the country and helped to lend boxing an unprecedented immediacy for the public. Before this time, the people who could not get to the arena for a big fight had to keep in touch with the action by hanging around for bulletins outside a telegraph office or a newspaper building. The intrepid radio announcer, of course, did not have a rubber eraser or a heavy lead pencil to expunge his mistakes, and there were some early disasters. Well known in the trade was the account of the abortive broadcasting career of Joe Foley, a prominent boxing writer in Chicago who had been engaged to describe to radio listeners the title bout between Tiger Flowers and Mickey Walker, whose great skills were beginning to desert him. On the night in question, Foley gave an accurate account, round by round, of the pasting that Walker had taken at Flowers' hands.

"There goes the bell," Foley roared. "The fight is over. The announcer is climbing into the ring to get the referee's decision that will mean the retention of the middleweight championship by Tiger Flowers, and—*Jesus Christ! He gave it to Walker!*"

And old Joe Foley was sent hurriedly back to his typewriter.

Behind the scenes, and usually of considerably more interest than the fighters themselves, were the managers and promoters who were artful in the sort of hokum that P. T. Barnum had cultivated decades earlier. One of the boxing men of this stripe was Jimmy Johnston, a friend of Pop's for many years. Johnston, who had been born in Liverpool, was brought to this country by his family when he was still a child. Growing up in a cold-water flat on lower Second Avenue in Manhattan, he learned to use his fists in dozens of street brawls with the Irish kids in the neighborhood who taunted the "limey," and he eventually became a pretty good professional fighter before learning there was a less hazardous role to be filled in the sport. A compact little man with jet-black hair even late in life (friends in his home always visited the bathroom to look for the shoe-blacking they were sure he used as a pomade, but they never found any), Johnston wore a derby at a provocative angle and walked with a strut that seemed to be a challenge to his enemies, who, he boasted, were "numerous." He became a specialist in importing fighters from Europe.

He has been amazingly successful in his exploitation of very ordinary fighters. In 1913, when managers all over the world were seeking a white heavyweight who could beat Jack Johnson, Jimmy bobbed up with a South African Dutchman named George Rodel, who had reached New York from Cape Town via London. He had had many fights and won most of them but was utterly unknown in America. Jimmy promptly tagged him Boer Rodel, had him photographed in an old army uniform he bought in a second hand store and dashed off a graphic description of the young man's hair-raising experiences as a soldier in the Boer War. Some of this got into the newspapers before the unthinking sports writers realized that at the time of the war Rodel was twelve years old. However, Jimmy parlayed that publicity and Rodel's left jab and undoubted gameness into profitable matches with Gunboat Smith, Jim Coffey, Jess Willard and other leading heavyweights of the time.

A few years after Rodel, a grimy Welshman walked into Jimmy's office. He said his name was Daniels, that he had just arrived in this country and that he was a fighter. Jimmy didn't know whether he could fight or not but saw immediate possibilities in the muscular young stranger with black hair, black eyes and a swarthy complexion.

"Also," Jimmy said, "he was very dirty. Dirty enough to be a Gypsy."

Jimmy bought a bandana and two curtain rings in a five-and-ten cent store, knotted the bandana about Daniels' head, stuck the rings in his ears, called in a photographer and then flooded the newspaper offices with pictures of his newest champion: "Gypsy Daniels, Son of the King of the Welsh Gypsies and Born in a Wagon Somewhere in the Rhonda Valley."

Daniels protested that if his father, a respectable coal miner,

*ever learned of this he would give him a hiding the next time he
saw him, but when he saw the crowds drawn by Johnston's bally-
hoo, he stopped protesting.*

*One of Jimmy's greatest feats unquestionably was his promo-
tion of Phil Scott, an English heavyweight and the daffiest pugilistic figure of the daffy late Twenties, when everybody seemed to
spend lavishly and ringside seats brought anywhere from $25 to
$100. Scott was a good boxer and a fair puncher but he couldn't
take it in the belly, and, furthermore, was of no mind to learn how.
He had a much simpler way. Every time he was hit in the belly, he
clutched his groin and sank to the floor, screaming foul. Boxing
writers derided him, calling him "Fainting Phil," among other
things.*

*"Nevertheless," Jimmy said. "My Philip made more money sit-
ting on the canvas than Hoover made sitting in the White House."*

During that period every community that could legitimately
call itself a city, and many that could not, possessed an arena
where boxing bouts were held regularly. Every night the results of
dozens of boxing cards all over the country were sent out on the
wires to newspaper offices, and, under the right conditions, a
fighter could practice his trade once a week, or even oftener.
There was a grim side to this commerce in human flesh. Regulations were even flimsier during the 1920s than they are today,
with communications and record-keeping nearly nonexistent, and
many a state boxing commissioner was the moronic nephew of a
politician who happened to be on the winning side in the most
recent election. A fighter, badly beaten in one place, often was
fighting someplace else a few nights later.

It may be that the most appropriate symbol of that era in boxing was not Dempsey, or his flamboyant manager, Jack Kearns, or
the promoter of the million-dollar gates, Tex Rickard, but a rather
shadowy figure known as Leo P. Flynn. He was not the kind of
man my father found either admirable or entertaining, and consequently he seldom wrote about him, though in later years he occasionally mentioned him without editorial comment. Flynn,
when he died, was said to have assembled not only the largest sta-

ble of fighters (nearly fifty) in boxing history but also a legal estate estimated at half a million dollars and a concealed safe containing two hundred thousand dollars in thousand-dollar bills and a boxful of diamonds.

Flynn was a manager in the true sense of the word. He did not cater to the whims of the young men who placed body and soul in his unsentimental hands. "No purse too small, no opponent too tough" was his motto. Flynn's fighters, many of whom never saw him, were in action somewhere every night in the week. On one Thanksgiving, so the story goes, nineteen of them fought in one town or another throughout the East and the Midwest.

"More than half of them got stiffened, too," Flynn chuckled afterward.

He is said to have coined the terms "palooka" and "hamdonnie" to describe the earnest if inept young men who contributed to his wealth. A Flynn fighter was expected to know his place, and that place implied almost no personal contact with his manager—even at the moment of truth.

"He didn't work in his fighters' corners much in his later years," Ray Arcel, a noted trainer, recalled. "But I remember he was there at a semifinal in Madison Square Garden when a boy got knocked cold. Leo never batted an eyelash. He stared straight ahead and said to me in that deadpan way, 'Go in and get him.'"

The origins of the man, even his name, are draped in obscurity. It is agreed that he came from Providence, Rhode Island, but some old-timers contended that his real name was McManus. In any case, he first appeared in Manhattan hanging out in pool halls on Fourteenth Street and trimming suckers with monotonous regularity. Almost before anyone knew it, he had put together a stable of fighters more remarkable for its number than its quality. Damon Runyon contended he was the first man to call Flynn "the Carpetbagger," a name that stuck and that Flynn relished because of the wily larceny it implied. He became the prototype for Runyon's scheming fight managers.

"I always carried a carpetbag in the early days," Flynn bragged. "When the dough was scarce, you could just drop the bag out the hotel window and pick it up once you skipped past the room clerk."

In more prosperous times Flynn occupied an office in midtown Manhattan where an aide, Arthur Yende, entered on a big board the names of Flynn's fighters and their schedule of bouts. In towns all over the country local promoters knew they could fill half a boxing card on any night by placing a call to Flynn. If Leo was out, his wife, Kate, would take the "order" and drive as hard a bargain as her husband. To supply three fighters for the three ten-round bouts that might have been scheduled on any given program, Flynn would ask for, and usually receive, forty-five to fifty percent of the gate.

At the beginning of each week, Flynn's fighters would visit his office, learn their schedules from the big board, and catch the next train to the provinces. They seldom knew whom they would fight and never how much they would make. After the fight, or fights, they would return to New York to pick up their purses, the size of which had been determined by Flynn. Anyone not satisfied was free to find another manager, but Flynn never suffered a scarcity of fighters. Everywhere in the country the word was out that if a boy wanted fights, Leo P. Flynn could provide them.

In time, the old pool shark, now prematurely gray, began to gather the trappings of affluence. He was the first boxing manager to own a Rolls-Royce, and one of his fighters usually served as a chauffeur. He bought a large house on the Grand Concourse in the Bronx and gradually dissociated himself from the grimy intimacies of the boxing business. It became an event of sorts when Flynn, a covey of Irish politicians in tow, condescended to visit a gym or a local fight club.

In 1926, when Dempsey split with his longtime manager, Jack Kearns, Flynn became Dempsey's adviser. It was during this period that he lost his most tumultuous argument—that of trying to convince boxing officials that Dempsey deserved the victory in his "long-count" battle with Tunney, contending that Tunney had been given too much time by the referee to recover from a knockdown, get back to his feet, and cling to his lead on points.

Dempsey was so impressed by Flynn's acumen that he promised to engage him as his manager if he ever came out of retirement. The former champion also presented Kate Flynn with a nine-thousand-dollar diamond brooch, "for keeping my food from getting contaminated," as she had supervised his training kitchen before the last bout of his career, with Sharkey.

By then Flynn had discovered a bright new horizon in the game of golf. Puzzled visitors to his Broadway office found him chipping trick shots into a straw hat placed upside down on a swivel chair. Flynn moved in moneyed circles now (John McGraw and other celebrated New Yorkers were his frequent companions), and his agile mind made several important deductions. He learned 1) that his skill on a pool table could be carried over to the putting greens and 2) that men with inflated notions of their own skills could be as easily located at the New York Athletic Club as they had been on Fourteenth Street.

On a damp spring day in 1930, Flynn made an appointment to play golf at Van Cortlandt Park with an affluent sportsman whose delusions he had carefully nurtured. Kate Flynn pointed out that he had a bad cold and suggested he cancel the appointment. But Leo P. Flynn was unable to turn his back on a primed gull. He played that damp day, won a sizable bet, and contracted pneumonia. A few days later, the Carpetbagger, age fifty-one, was dead, undone by large purses and easy opponents.

As the 1930s began, my father was the *Sun*'s ranking sportswriter. The paper published two sports columns, one by Joe Vila, the other the syndicated column of Grantland Rice, but Frank Graham's byline was almost always prominent on the first sports page and often on the front page. Saturday, October 10, 1931, was such an occasion, because the final game of the World Series was being played in St. Louis between the Cardinals and the Philadelphia Athletics. The home edition displayed the Graham byline over an article, datelined St. Louis, that covered much of the left-hand side of the front page.

In his advance story Pop set the scene for the game that would take place later in the day, giving the starting pitchers, an idea of the stakes involved, and a summary of what had happened so far in the Series to bring it to a seventh and deciding game. Since there was little new to report about the Series at that point, the rest of the front page was given over to world and national news. The lead story, occupying the right-hand side of the page, reported that Japanese forces, moving into southern Manchuria, had bombed a Chinese railroad junction in the disputed region. In other stories, Thomas Alva Edison had sunk into a "stupor" while reporters kept a "death watch" at his home in West Orange, New Jersey; British prime minister Lloyd George accused the Conservatives of trying to foist a protective tariff on the country; a petty hoodlum was found fatally shot in his car in the Bronx; and Editha Fleischer, of the Metropolitan Opera Company, took an overdose of sleeping powder and slept through a concert engagement in Worcester, Massachusetts.

But by late afternoon, momentous events had taken place elsewhere, and the front page of the *Sun* had been remade into the Sporting Final. The truculent Japanese, the expiring inventor, the indignant prime minister, and the drowsy soprano had been banished to the back pages, while a great, black headline proclaimed CARDINALS WIN 4–2 TO TAKE THE SERIES. The entire right-hand side of the page was devoted to my father's story of the Cardinals' victory and a huge box score of the game. Meanwhile, the left-hand side had been taken over by college football, with line scores of the important games of the day and a story from New Haven (with no byline) recording Yale's defeat at the hands of Georgia. Toward the bottom and center of the page were the horseracing results from Jamaica.

In the spring of 1933, as I turned eight years old, I was introduced to the world that was to occupy so much of my waking hours for the next quarter of a century. My mother had bought an old Ford "flivver" and learned to drive it. (Pop had made one halfhearted attempt to learn, too, but smashed into a garage door and forever after left the driving to my mother.) Although Judy, the youngest of the children, was only six months old, my parents decided to bring the entire family, including my grandmother, to the Yankees' spring-training camp, in St. Petersburg, Florida.

Somehow the seven of us (Judy in a laundry basket) and all our luggage were packed into the little car, and with my mother gamely at the wheel, we set out for Florida. The expense must have been considerable, for the trip took six days and we stayed at hotels, in cities along the route, that my father knew from traveling with the ball clubs. We made it to Philadelphia the first night, where one of us children (no stool pigeon, I) upset an ink bottle over the bed; my father characteristically insisted on paying the hotel for the damage. On to Richmond, someplace in the Carolinas, Savannah, Jacksonville, and finally St. Petersburg, where we moved into a little cottage surrounded by grapefruit trees. The maid assigned to our cottage was short, broad, with arms like a boxer. She used to threaten playfully to discipline us kids with her "Jack Johnson uppercut." Fortunately, she found us congenial, tolerated Minnie's grumpiness, and remained with my mother until her retirement at the age of eighty-eight. This was Emma Akins.

I was surrounded by ball players. In the mornings I went to the ball park with my father and found myself almost literally underfoot in the casualness that presides over a spring-training camp, as the uniformed players mingled with fans and tourists who stood around the field. In the afternoons I romped on the beach with Fred "Dixie" Walker, a young outfielder who became "the People's Cherce" when he played for the Dodgers a few years later. I sat in the wooden stands to watch the Yankees play an exhibition game against the House of David, a team representing a religious organization whose members were densely bearded—an astonishing spectacle to a child in those clean-cut days before beatniks restored the male's right to hirsuteness. I took the ferry across Tampa Bay with the Yankees when they played the Cardinals in Bradenton; as we waited for the return ferry, I stood on the pier with Babe Ruth and Lou Gehrig and watched them pull a small fish from the water on a baited hook.

Ruth was still the great name in baseball, but an era was coming to a close. Ty Cobb had retired, McGraw had died the previous year, and the Babe's days were numbered. It may have been a child's perversity, but I like to think now that I was in tune with changing times when I selected not the Babe but Gehrig as my hero. Handsome, shy, put together along such rugged lines that he was once screen-tested—wrapped in a leopard skin—in Holly-wood for the role of Tarzan, a devastating hitter with men on base, Gehrig served perfectly as the idol of a small boy soon to reach adolescence.

A star-struck Icarus, I was about to soar into empyrean regions on wings that my father's craft had fashioned for me.

Chapter Five
The Greatest Story

In the spring of 1934, Joe Vila, who had been sports editor of the *Sun* for nearly thirty-five years, died and left an enormous vacancy on the paper. A man of considerable energy and forthrightness, he had assembled what probably was the most respected sports department in the country at a time when literacy and integrity were not universally prized in that area. Although Vila had been no great shakes as a writer, his name at the head of the column "Setting the Pace" was a guarantee that its sentiments were fair and had not been bought or influenced. The paper's sports coverage was extensive and expansive, in conformance with Vila's adherence to the *Sun*'s original motto, "It Shines for All," and ranged from a daily feature of baseball gossip and analysis written by various members of the staff under the byline "The Old Scout" to a chess column contributed by a New York master named Herman Helms, who delivered his stuff in the dead of night and, according to one of the few editorial people who had ever laid eyes on him, once accepted the offer of half a sandwich from a copy reader, bolted it down, and, wraithlike, dissolved once more into the dark.

My father had been a favorite of Vila's and was his heir apparent. No false modesty swayed his decision to turn down the vacant position of sports editor. He had seen how hard Vila worked at his job, coming to the office in the early-morning hours to supervise the layout for the first edition of the afternoon paper (due off the presses late in the morning), and how the demands of other business kept him at his desk most of the daylight hours, too. Pop wanted to be "out and around"; he wanted to watch the events of the day and listen to the gossip of the men in the dugouts and dressing rooms. Accordingly, it was decided that Wilbur Wood, the paper's boxing writer, would take over as sports editor, and Vila's old column would henceforward appear under the by-line of Frank Graham.

The column was, and remained, all he ever really wanted out of his professional life. He had almost total freedom to make up his mind about what he wanted to do every day and how he wanted to treat what he saw. If he was covering a contest of some kind, he wrote his column in the press box and gave it to a telegrapher to send off to the paper. If he was simply roaming around town, visiting Jacobs Beach, the gyms, the ball clubs' downtown offices, or an athlete in transit at a midtown hotel, he would always take the subway down to the *Sun*'s offices at 280 Broadway afterward and write his column at one of the temporarily vacant desks in the sports department.

He did not bleed over his prose. The words and phrases he had heard that day were inscribed in his brain (there for instant retrieval at the moment or ten years later), and he composed his column in his head on the way to the typewriter. Puffing on a pipe that he had filled with Blue Boar tobacco just before starting to write, doodling funny faces (never notes) on a sheet of yellow copy paper, he seemed to have shut out the world around him; but at any stage of composition he showed no irritation if he was interrupted by the greeting or the question of a passerby. Once, years later in some stadium's press box, he inserted paper into his typewriter, pecked out the words "by Frank Graham," and settled into a long reverie. His pal Red Smith happened by and looked over his shoulder at what he had written. "It drags," Smith commented, and moved on.

[FRANK GRAHAM, JR.]

In the 1930s there was little interval between the rolling of two sheets of paper into the machine (he never made a carbon of a column but used the double thickness simply to protect the paten) and the onset of composition. He had learned typing by the hunt-and-peck system and jabbed at the keys with three fingers, two on the right hand. His column ran from four to five double-spaced pages, which he would usually finish in a little over an hour, though interruptions might prolong the time. To an admirer who once asked him how he could turn out a readable column six days a week, with such little time, he replied, "There's no mystery to it. You just put down a word, and then another, and then another, and pretty soon you have a column."

He wrote his first piece for the "Setting the Pace" column on May 1, 1934, and continued with the column until August 2, 1943. On that May Day he put one little word after another, indefatigably, writing two thousand words to produce a column that was four inches wide, running the entire length of the page. He seldom wrote one that long again. Most of his later columns ran about fifteen hundred words, but apparently he wanted to prove his endurance to the *Sun's* brass, who were reading his stuff up in the executive offices on the seventh floor at 280 Broadway.

"Quietly, perhaps without ever knowing it," Red Smith wrote later, "he brought about a revolution in the approach to, and technique of, writing a sports column in this country. Gradually editorial opinion gave way to reporting, to conversation pieces and interviews and 'mood' pieces that strove to capture for the reader the color and flavor and texture of the event. No other sportswriter in Frank's lifetime exerted such effect on his own business. None was imitated so widely, or so unsuccessfully."

The subject and style of his maiden effort held, in those eighty square inches of type, the essence of "Setting the Pace" for the rest of the decade. The day before, he had visited Max Baer and his manager, Ancil Hoffman, in their suite in a midtown hotel, and he had a story to tell.

Baer was the Muhammad Ali of his day, or he would have been had he known how to fight. He was a handsome, curly-haired, fun-loving braggart, with shoulders of such astounding width that if he had affected the padded jackets fashionable at the time, he would have looked deformed. In the ring he alternated between strutting, clowning, wisecracking (all prompted not so much by show-business acumen as by the necessity to catch his breath against better-conditioned opponents), and throwing long right-hand punches that sometimes landed on target. To describe his punches as "deadly" would be grimly apt. He had killed Frankie Campbell in a bout in San Francisco in 1930, and in 1932 he had beaten Ernie Schaaf so badly that the unfortunate heavyweight contender never recovered and died a few months later when he was mildly roughed up in a bout with Primo Carnera. Now, in 1934, Baer was the leading contender for Carnera's title and a likely winner in the match that had been arranged for June of that year. The huge, inept Italian, it was said, had been maneuvered into the heavyweight championship of the world by the proto-mafiosi who managed him with the aid of a respectable front man. Baer had come to New York to await the selection of a rural camp where he would begin what passed for him as training.

There was the sudden crash of knuckles against the door and it swung open to admit the challenger for the heavyweight championship. He wore a gray and black plaid suit, a gray shirt, a brown and white plaid tie and gray suede shoes. He was hatless, but a belted top coat hung in the crook of his left arm.

"I was just saying," said Hoffman, "that you are sure you are going to knock out Carnera."

"I will lay him out flatter than a tablecloth," said Max.

"You see?" said Hoffman. "He knows all the answers."

"Sure," said Max. "I can't miss. Everybody who ever fought that big bum has hit him on the chin, but none of them can hit like I can. When I hit him on the chin he will go down and stay there."

He flung the top coat across the chair.

"How do I look?" he demanded. "Pretty good, eh? I look better than that. I look wonderful."

He opened his coat.

"See that?" he asked, patting himself on the stomach. "See how flat it is?"

He pulled his trousers tight across his thighs and calves. "There's no fat on me," he said. "I weigh 220 pounds. I'm in great shape."

He stalked into the next room, bellowing for his trainer, Mike Cantwell.

"Ready in a minute," said Mike. Just wait till I get my pants on."

"Make it snappy," said Max. "I want to get that matter attended to so we can get started tomorrow. I want to get out of the city."

Hoffman grinned and winked. Max came back into the room.

"You know what Tommy Loughran said when he saw me smoking a cigarette this afternoon?" he asked. "He told me I ought to cut out cigarettes, because if I didn't they would hurt my wind. He's right, too. So from now on I'm off cigarettes."

And night clubs?

"Sure. The night clubs will be there when I'm the champion. They'll wait. And no romancing for me, either. I'm serious about this, on the square. From now on I'm going to keep good hours and take care of myself. I'll have my fun when I'm champion."

Cantwell had his pants on now—and his coat and hat, too. They made ready to depart. It was suggested that the pair of them probably would end up in a night club.

"Nix," said Max. "You call up here at half past ten tonight and I'll bet you I'll be here. Do you want to take the bet?"

"If he doesn't," said Cantwell, "I'd like to take that myself."

As the door closed behind them, Hoffman shook his head.

"He's a great fighter," said Ancil, "and a great kid. If you could see the way they chase him you wouldn't wonder that he gets jammed up once in a while. But he is in great shape now. You can tell that by looking at him. Why, he didn't start to train in earnest for the Schmeling fight until ten days before the fight and at that, that's about the longest he ever trained for any fight. But I'll pick out his training quarters in a couple of days and put him to work and I don't think I'll have any trouble with him.

"On this exhibition tour he'd box six rounds every night—two rounds with his kid brother, Buddy Baer, who is as big as Carnera, two with Seal Harris and two with some local yokel who wanted a

shot at him. He'd cut loose, too. It got so after a while that he had Seal Harris crawling through the ropes to get away from him.

"You know what he has Buddy doing? Stepping on his feet, heeling him, roughing him around and hitting him in the face with his elbows. He says that's the way Carnera fights and he wants to get used to it. He boxed some tough local boys, too. But when he got through with them they weren't so tough."

Boxing is a depression sport. It breeds on poverty and tough neighborhoods, both abundantly available in the America of the thirties, when everybody was dreaming of an improbable leap to fortune. Northern cities were especially fertile ground for developing fighters because the mix of nationalities and races—Irish, Italians, Greeks, Jews from Eastern Europe and blacks from Southern farms, even the vanguard of Hispanics from Latin America—generated a friction of its own. Kids from different backgrounds met on the streets and in schoolyards and hurled at each other the taunts and slurs they had learned from their elders. Tempers boiled over, fists flew, and if a boy didn't learn to fight back quickly, he was soon an outcast or an invalid. They battled their neighbors, the cops, and, when there was nobody else around, their uncles and brothers and fathers. If a kid was strong and tough, there was little chance in those days to make a living out of football, or basketball, but there was at least the illusory prospect of earning money in a sport that could be practiced the year round, perhaps in front of thousands of paying customers. There were no scholarships to win, no scouts to impress. All a boy needed was a few dollars to buy a license and a jockstrap and the ability to stand the sight of his own blood; he was in business for himself overnight.

When my father took over the column, boxing was just beginning to revive, following a long period in the doldrums. There may be good fighters in the lighter divisions, but it is the heavyweight division that lights up the sport from within and stirs public interest, and in the six or seven years since Dempsey had left the scene the division had languished. Max Schmeling, though a competent fighter, typified its sorry state. He had won the heavyweight title sitting on the floor, clutching his groin after a foul punch by Jack Sharkey, and lost it standing up, letting a decision slip away to Sharkey in a return bout. Sharkey himself had been displaced by Carnera and his gun-packing manipulators. Game but ill-coordinated and derided as a "circus freak" by the public (he had indeed once worked as a circus strong man), Carnera took some frightful beatings after he lost his behind-the-scenes protectors, and he eventually found his true niche as a professional wrestler.

The beginning of the end for Carnera as a fighter came on that June evening in 1934 when he fought Baer at the Old Madison Square Garden Bowl in Long Island City. Baer had clowned his way through training, defending ineptly against his sparring partners, so much so that one member of the New York State Athletic Commission (the fancy name applied to the boxing commission, which had been created to supervise wrestling, as well) demanded unsuccessfully that the fight be postponed. This notoriety, combined with the rudimentary skills Carnera had somehow absorbed while disposing of the pushovers provided for him on his tours through the tank towns, created the illusion of a contest. But such was not to be.

A battered, weary and bewildered giant, with blood trickling from his nose and mouth, stood in his own corner of the ring at the Garden Bowl shielded by the referee from the raking fists of his opponent. Thus in the eleventh round, the heavyweight championship of the world passed from Primo Carnera to Max Baer. Thus there came into being the maddest of champions in the maddest of championship fights.

That was the finish. In the beginning, Baer picked a right-hand punch up off the floor near the center of the ring and hurled it against Carnera's jaw with less than a minute of the first round to go. Carnera crashed to the canvas and although he got up almost immediately, he never recovered from the effects of that punch. Knocked down twelve times in all, he reeled unsteadily to defeat. Gone was his defensive skill. Gone was his hope of winning. All he had left was courage and that wasn't nearly enough.

The finish came quickly in the eleventh round. Knocked down twice and gone beyond recall, Primo was tottering about on rubber legs when Referee Arthur Donovan put a period to the proceedings. Instantly the ring was filled with Baer's handlers and the champion shouters who always seem to be at the edge of the ropes, poised to leap to the center of the canvas when the last blow has been struck. Out of the swirl came the new champion, straight to the ropes on the side of the ring to the left of his corner where, in solid array, sat the corps of California newspaper men who had come here to cover the fight. He waved and chattered in greeting to them, leaped through the ropes and paraded around the edge of the ring platform, a fantastic figure in victory even as he had been in training.

Events were moving swiftly now, preparing the way for a time when it would be exciting to watch the heavyweights, and to write about them as well. The champion who was crowned that night really had few more skills than Carnera, but he could punch and he knew how to attract attention to himself and the fight game. Yet a preliminary bout had taken place shortly before the main event at the Garden Bowl that, though missed entirely by latecomers to the ringside seats, proved to be the turning point in the story my father always believed was the most satisfying he ever covered. It was the kind of story that one of the big movie studios of the thirties could have turned out, with young Victor McLaglen playing the leading role (how did they ever miss it?). My father would have chuckled at some of the scenes but would have emerged from the theater dabbing at his good eye with a handkerchief.

The traditional graveyard of chronic losers is oblivion, but once in a while a loser earns a measure of fame. He takes a beating from one of his betters, usually a Man of Destiny, and ever afterward his name (always immediately preceded by the word "one") is coupled with his conqueror's. This is the dubious compensation accorded one Corn Griffin for being matched in that preliminary bout on the Carnera-Baer card with James J. Braddock. Dempsey had been one of Pop's great heroes, of course, and he had liked and intensely admired many other fighters—Barney Ross, Benny Leonard, Tony Canzoneri, Henry Armstrong—but he never, before or after, formed so close an attachment to a fighter as he did to Braddock. Indeed, after Braddock retired, Pop made it a point never again to become too sentimentally involved with a fighter's fortunes. It was too painful for him to watch his favorite take a beating in the ring, and he also found that it affected the objectivity he always tried to maintain as a part of his craft. But, if he fell in love with the Braddock story, how could he help himself? Millions of other Americans felt the same way. Here was a man who beat the Depression after starting at the bottom; here was a man who climbed, in the words of the headline writers of the day, "From Relief to Royalty."

In one of his early columns, my father wrote about his visit to Stillman's Gym, on Eighth Avenue north of Madison Square Garden, the most famous of all the training sites in New York, a place where ordinary fighters who could not afford rural training quarters of their own repaired daily to work themselves into shape. He mentioned the usual fresh-faced kids punching arduously at the heavy bag and the punch-drunk wrecks who were once fresh-faced kids themselves. And in a final paragraph he described Braddock, whom he had written about years before in more enthusiastic prose.

Over there, for instance, is a heavyweight whose punch almost took him to the top of his division. Hurled back into the rut, he plods along with neither hope nor inspiration, training doggedly, fighting where he can. He would quit the ring and take a job somewhere at twenty-five dollars a week if he could get it, but jobs are scarce, especially for a fellow approaching thirty who has had no training in any other business. So he goes on fighting because he has a wife and three children who must eat, too.

Braddock apparently had ended up the way so many fighters do—penniless and ignored by the people who once got their kicks from being seen in his presence. In the late 1920s he had been a leading contender for the light-heavyweight championship. A hard puncher, he had scored several exciting knockouts in Madison Square Garden. In 1927 he won five fights by knockout and eight by decision. He defeated Pete Latzo in ten rounds, and fractured his jaw besides. Against all the predictions, he knocked out Tuffy Griffiths in the second round at the Garden. He lost a decision to Leo Lomsky in 1929, but not long after that he knocked out Jimmy Slattery in the ninth round. Then he was outboxed by clever Tommy Loughran in a title fight, and he rapidly plummeted from the ranks of the leading fighters.

It wasn't simply that he lost his ambition. A broken right hand, a fractured rib, a cut eye—these seemed to pile up on him, and before long he was just another second-rater. On a trip to the West Coast he lost to Lou Scozza when the cuts above his eyes opened up; boxing Abe Feldman at Mount Vernon, New York, he injured his hand so badly that the referee decided the fighters weren't trying and ruled the bout "no contest"; when his name was proposed as an opponent for Walter Neusel in Brooklyn, the boxing commission refused to approve Braddock as a "fit" opponent for the big German. By 1934 he was counted among the sport's flotsam, sometimes earning as little as twelve dollars a week.

In a little house in Woodcliff, New Jersey, an alarm clock went off at six o'clock in the morning and James J. Braddock got up. He pulled on a work shirt, dungarees, heavy socks and brogans and went downstairs quietly so that he would not disturb his wife and three small children. He cooked some oatmeal and made a pot of coffee and, having breakfasted, put on a lumber jacket and walked three miles to the Weehawken piers, where he had a job unloading railroad ties from the holds of the ships that had brought them from the South and loading them into gondola cars.

It was hard work. When the sun climbed in the sky he took off his work shirt and, stripped to the waist, toiled until noon. Then he pulled on his shirt and climbed a hill to a lunch room and ate a bowl of stew and some large chunks of bread and drank a pot of tea. By one o'clock, stripped to the waist again, he was hauling away at the ties. At four o'clock he knocked off for the day, put on his shirt, slung his lumber jacket over his arm and trudged three miles back to the little house in Woodcliff.

He played with his children and had his dinner and sat around for a while and then went to bed, not forgetting to wind the alarm clock and put it on a chair near the head of his bed.

Corn Griffin, on the other hand, was not quite so occupied with the struggle for survival. For several years he had been fed and clothed by the United States Army. Now, a civilian again in 1934, he was provided with red meat by an elderly fight manager named Charley Harvey, who labored under the delusion that Griffin was going to be the next heavyweight champion.

Griffin had the face of a loser, with a dented nose and scar tissue around his eyes, but his other credentials were good. He was squarely built, with a solid punch and an aggressive style. Harvey arranged for him to be a sparring partner at Carnera's training camp in Pompton Lakes, New Jersey, while the big man was preparing for his unfortunate meeting with Baer. It was reasoned that Griffin would pick up valuable experience and Harvey would be relieved of his meat bill. The sportswriters who traveled into the New Jersey hills to inspect Carnera in training came away babbling about Griffin. Earlier in the workout, Carnera had speared his other partners with his long jab and bulled them about the ring.

Now comes Corn Griffin. He looks small beside Carnera, but he is a full measure heavyweight for all that, being about five feet eleven inches tall and weighing upward of 185 pounds. You never have heard of him doing any fighting, but he must have done some because the mark of the trade is on his rugged features. It is on his work, too, as you see when he goes into action.

As a sparring partner, he is no mere catcher. He is a pitcher— and he pitches with both hands. He drives straight into Primo and his fists thud against the champion's jaw and into his stomach. Carnera fights back hard, but he cannot keep Corn away. The soldier piles him up in a corner, belts him savagely with both hands and then drives him out. Carnera, stung and slightly bewildered

*by the force of the attack, flounders. Griffin nails him with a long
left to the jaw, drives his right under Primo's left and nails him in
the stomach.*

*The crowd applauds and Carnera's manager calls for silence.
Carnera gets straightened out and his huge fists bounce off Grif-
fin's jaw, but the soldier keeps plunging in and hammering away.
The round ends and the men climb out of the ring. It seems that
only one round had been allotted to Corn, which is just as well.
The champion's dignity already has been ruffled.*

"How long has this been going on?" a visitor asks.

"Every day," a regular at the camp replies.

Jimmy Johnston, who was promoting the Baer-Carnera fight,
had booked Griffin in one of the preliminary bouts on the card,
but he could not find an opponent for him. Managers of the
second-rate heavyweights are seldom squeamish about having
their charges butchered, but they are reluctant to have the job
done by a fighter nobody has ever heard of. In the end there was
one interested party—Joe Gould, who managed Jim Braddock.

Gould was a bright-faced little man with a quick mind and a
nature that harbored no illusions. He and Braddock had been together from the start, and his fortunes had risen and fallen with
his fighter's. Now that the promoters no longer were interested in
Braddock, Gould had been forced into the final indignity of going
to work for a living. He sold appliances from door to door. Occasionally he sent Braddock a few dollars to help him over a particularly rough period. "This is a strange business," an old-time
manager has said. "You can't run it like a grocery store." Gould
spent every moment he could in promoters' offices, talking about
Jim Braddock. Even his best friends got tired of listening to him.
He had become a bore.

One afternoon he was in Jimmy Johnston's office, sitting on the
edge of the promoter's desk and swinging his legs while he gabbed
with the other boxing men who sat on chairs along the wall. Corn
Griffin's name had been mentioned by someone.

"Do you have an opponent for him yet?" Gould asked Johnston.
Johnston shook his head.

"What about Braddock?" Gould asked hopefully.

The other managers in the room shot each other "here-we-go-again" looks. Johnston screwed up his face. "This is no match for Braddock to take, Joe," he said. "I'd like to help you, but Griffin's been fighting regularly and he's been up there with Carnera getting in shape. Do you want to see Braddock get killed?"

"Give me that match, Jimmy," Gould pleaded. "Braddock can take care of himself."

Johnston shrugged. "It's your funeral," he growled. "Nobody else wants it, so I guess it's yours. I hope he's ready."

Gould rushed out of the room and called Braddock. "I got you on the Carnera-Baer card," he told him. "It's only two days away, but it was the best I could do."

"Two days, two hours—what's the difference?" Braddock said. "Hauling railroad ties keeps a guy in shape."

The early arrivals among the fifty-six thousand people who came to the Garden Bowl that night saw a brawl that made up for the one-sidedness ("a pig-sticking," the fight mob would call it) of the main event. Griffin, well tanned, his hair close-cropped, walked confidently out to meet Braddock at the opening bell. Braddock advanced in his usual heavy-footed, stiff-legged way. Before the round was many seconds old, Griffin landed solidly against Braddock's chin and the older man went down. The crowd, indifferent to the preliminary bouts until then, came alive in the vast Bowl and urged Griffin on as Braddock got to his feet.

Suddenly there was a war going on in the ring. Braddock staved off Griffin's rushes, dodging his punches on wobbly legs. In a few moments his head cleared and he began to fight back. A short right-hand punch stopped Griffin and sent him reeling into the ropes. Braddock followed him now, punching at him savagely, raking him with the accurate and deadly flurries that had made him a local hero five years before. At the bell Griffin clung to Braddock to keep from falling.

The rest was anticlimax. Braddock continued to hammer Griffin toward defeat in the second round, and in the third he punched him along the ropes and caught up with him and knocked him out. In the dressing room a few minutes later, Braddock turned to his excited manager and said, "I did that on hash, Joe. Wait till you see what I can do on steak."

Corn Griffin thereafter was remembered only by Braddock's friends and biographers. Contrarily, Braddock's ambition and confidence, which had faded after his defeat at Loughran's hands in 1929, returned with the destruction of the ex-soldier. But his luck hadn't completely turned. He had broken his right hand in battering Griffin, and there were further months of inactivity while he waited for his injury to heal. It was during this time that Braddock went on relief. He had no choice. Jobs were scarce, and his small check for the Griffin fight did not equal the grocery and electricity bills that had mounted for almost a year. But Braddock, when he earned his first big purse, repaid the $350 he had accepted in local relief funds. Gould, of course, fashioned a gripping human-interest story from this episode as Braddock climbed toward the title.

His hand mended, Braddock was eager to return to the ring. He beat John Henry Lewis (who was later to become the light-heavyweight champion) and Art Lasky (a leading heavyweight contender) in main bouts at Madison Square Garden. The fight mob began to take his comeback seriously.

With characteristic modesty James J. Braddock was sitting on a bench in the outer office of Jimmy Johnston's suite in the Garden. It had not occurred to him, apparently, that as the hero of the ring's most astonishing comeback in many years he was entitled to move inside and drape himself over one of the many easy chairs in Johnston's private office. Joe Gould found him sitting out there and brought him in to join a group consisting of three reporters, a couple of fight managers and a detective. The flesh about his left eye was puffed and discolored, but the friendly grin was as wide as ever.

"Been in a fight?" one of the reporters asked.

"No," he said, still grinning. "I ran into a door in the dark."

"I never knew you were such a good boxer," the detective said.

"You didn't think I knew what to do with my left hand, eh? I was always a pretty good boxer, but when I got in there I usually didn't do much boxing."

"You mean," the detective said, "that fighters don't begin to get smart until they get old."

"You don't get smart in this business," Braddock said. "You just get cute."

"We haven't had a fight around here in a long time that stirred people up like that one," said a reporter. "I met some hard-boiled guys after the fight that told me they were praying for you. Did you know that?"

Braddock grinned again. "The priest over in my parish told me that after Mass on Saturday morning he met a lady coming out of the church and she said to him:

" 'I was listening to Jimmy Braddock's fight on the radio last night and all the time I was listening to it I was praying.'

"And the priest said: 'What do you think I was doing?' "

Meanwhile, the other contenders were systematically eliminating themselves. When the time came for Baer to defend his championship in 1935, the New York State Athletic Commission decreed that the twenty-nine-year-old Braddock was the outstanding challenger, and Gould agreed to terms with Baer's manager, Ancil Hoffman. Boxing managers are, as a breed, intensely jealous of their rivals, but now all of them stood in awe of Gould. Billy McCarney, one of the oldest and most respected managers of his time (and called "the Professor" because of his reputed erudition), said aloud what many others were thinking:

"The greatest job any manager ever did was done by Gould. Lots of managers have taken vigorous young fellows and brought them along, but for a manager to stick to a guy everybody thought was washed up, even after he must have begun to think so himself, and then to build him up and make him over and work him into spots where he could keep going until he won the championship of the world—well, that's tops with me."

Gould thought this estimate a fair one. "I take my hat off to no manager," he said when things were going especially well. He was overheard by Dumb Dan Morgan (so-called because of his excessive volubility), who admired Gould but did not like to see him give himself airs. "Your hat means nothing," Morgan interrupted. "You don't even take off your hat when you eat."

Braddock became a national hero. Gould talked and talked, and soon there wasn't a soul in America who didn't know that Braddock had a devoted wife and three lovely kids and a background of hard knocks and poverty. A country just beginning to hope again after six years of unrelieved Depression loved every word of Gould's "From Relief to Royalty" spiel. Jim Braddock seemed to typify and exalt the national soul in the mid-thirties. As the date set for the fight in the Garden Bowl drew nearer, excitement began to peak all over the country. Baer demanded that an ambulance be kept ready outside the arena in case he broke Braddock's neck or fractured his skull, and most professional boxing men and the gamblers gave odds of as high as ten to one against the challenger. But the public sentiment was obviously with Braddock, and a few of the experts were also beginning to think his chances were good.

The sentiment was there on June 13 when the fight began before thirty-five thousand people. "Bang him one for the wife and kids," a fan would shout, and his neighbors, linked by the pious conviction that they were doing their bit for a worthy cause, added lusty cheers of their own. Anyone unfortunate enough to find himself on Baer's side was made to feel ashamed of himself. Those who bet on Braddock at splendid odds felt doubly pleased with themselves as the fight took what might have seemed to them its preordained course.

The incredible has happened and James J. Braddock is the heavyweight champion of the world. The march that began when he got up off the floor in the Garden Bowl a year ago to knock Corn Griffin out ended last night when he took a fifteen round decision over Max Baer. Nothing like this ever happened before in the long history of the prize ring. It just goes to show you how far a stout heart will take a fellow, provided he has a good left hand to go with it.

The Braddock who belted his way into a chance for the light-heavyweight title six years ago and then blew it relied almost solely on his right hand to bring his foemen down. The right hand won for him over Griffin a year ago and spun John Henry Lewis on the canvas a couple of times last fall. But Braddock beat Art Lasky with his left hand and did the same to Baer. Probably nothing like that ever happened before, either, because usually when a fighter is right-hand crazy he remains that way until they carry him out for the last time.

Baer, losing the title, made a showing that shocked those of his admirers who, a year ago, were calling him another Dempsey and, as recently as yesterday, were saying that he could call the round, the minute and the punch where Braddock was concerned. Broken hands, Max said, prevented the slaughter of Braddock, but the bubble of his invincibility had burst long before the round he named as that in which the first fracture occurred. He had grimaced and postured and thrown the sucker punch to the winds through the first couple of rounds and bore no more resemblance to a champion than he did in the closing rounds, when, with the wildness of desperation upon him, he sought to recapture that which he had lost.

It wasn't a very good fight, but that was Baer's fault, not Braddock's. By stabbing his left hand in Baer's face and moving around, Braddock held Baer's right hand so closely in check that only two or three times in fifteen rounds did the fading champion land it. When he did, the crushing, blinding, paralyzing force that had been claimed for it was missing. It was just a sucker punch— only this time there was no sucker waiting for it.

It was known that Max's plan was to tear into Braddock in the first round and bowl him over or hurt him so badly as to soften him up for a sickening beating in the later rounds. Actually, Braddock carried the fight to Baer from the opening bell, landed the first punches, threw Max off his stride, tied up his right hand and started him skidding toward defeat. That's all he had to do, for Baer, strictly a one-handed fighter, was completely at a loss. Whether he broke his hands doesn't matter. They weren't any good to him anyway.

Thus began the most placid reign in heavyweight history, a sort of *Pax Braddockiana,* in which the champion retreated above the fray to pursue the less arduous chores of showing up at banquets and boxing occasional exhibitions, while violence was confined to the lower orders in his division.

For the next two years, in fact, the focus was to be almost entirely on a remarkable young fighter named Joe Louis. In the young black man from the cottonfields of Alabama and the Ford assembly plant in Detroit there was mixed the excitement and ruthless efficiency that had not been seen in a fighter since Dempsey. Crowds flocked to see a succession of terrified victims—including Carnera, Baer, and Sharkey—served up to him. While boxing fans had their lust for blood satisfied by watching "the Brown Bomber" (who was, nevertheless, as fight-club announcers assured the patrons, "a credit to his race"), they felt a certain satisfaction in knowing that "the world of fistiana" was still ruled by Jim Braddock, as comfortable and respected a figurehead for the public as Queen Victoria had been less than half a century before.

Meanwhile, on that memorable evening in the Garden Bowl, somebody asked Braddock what his first act as champion would be.

"Well, I guess I gotta go out and buy some pet turtles," he said, and grinned. "When I was leaving the house, I told the kids I was going to bring home the title. They thought I said 'turtle,' so naturally I can't let them down."

One afternoon during Braddock's two-year reign, he and Gould sat idly on the porch of his rural training camp at Loch Sheldrake, New York. With them was Francis Albertanti, the champion's publicity man. Albertanti hated the country. The birds and the flowers made him nervous, he spent his time wondering "what the boys in the Tombs are doing," and he often expressed the wish that he could be sitting at the moment in Mickey Walker's saloon with a fan blowing on him.

"If it wasn't for Corn Griffin, I wouldn't be here," Albertanti growled through the cigar that was stuck perpetually in the middle of his face. "The next time I see him I'm going to punch him in the nose."

"If it weren't for Corn Griffin, you know where we'd all be, don't you?" Gould said.

"Sure. On relief."

"That's right," Gould said. "The next time I see Corn Griffin I'm going to kiss him."

Chapter Six
In the Dugout

O ne of the contradictions of progress is that the developments in media technology, while offering millions of people a clearer image of what "the game" is all about, make absolute mush of the athletes themselves. When a player walks before the camera, or the camera probes the dugout and the dressing room, naturalness atrophies. The proscenium— or the arena—has expanded to include even those two retreats, and the sterling southpaw, whether he is plugging a six-pack, sitting for his portrait by Howard Cosell, or even celebrating a World Series triumph by drenching the commissioner in bubbly, falls into the TV role he has chosen for himself. Just as the real Nixon, as revealed in the tapes, metamorphosed before the cameras into the weepy poseur saying farewell to his troops, the off-duty athlete on the tube is clearly not going through his accustomed paces. Snotty ham, maybe, charming ham, perhaps, but pure Smithfield all the same.

Readers of "Setting the Pace" during the middle thirties were given the first accurate picture of life in the dugouts and clubhouses of big-league baseball. Although my father had experimented with these portraits in dialogue earlier when writing "The Old Scout" feature, or in other articles in the *Sun*, he used the roominess of his new column to bring the technique to a kind of perfection, exploiting the form in a way that has seldom since been equaled in simplicity and accuracy. He carried no electronic gear to nudge the athletes into either silence or histrionics. He was just a little, bland-faced man, sitting in a corner, or next to the manager, puffing on his pipe, storing neatly in his brain for future use the fragments of conversation and horseplay that were going on around him.

When he had sifted the elements of the scene afterward, he reconstructed it, usually without editorial comment. He made no attempt to flesh out the characters or milk their interplay for the human-interest angle. The banter was the message. The unrelieved dialogue may have been patterned on pages of Hemingway's short stories ("Fifty Grand," perhaps, or "The Killers"), but he never pretended that it was anything beyond the kind of reporting that most interested him. Like a Currier and Ives print, here was simply a reproduction of a moment in a certain time and place.

By 1936 great changes had taken place among baseball's *dramatis personae* in New York. Bill Terry, a great first baseman and the last National League player to hit .400, had succeeded McGraw as the manager of the Giants. Most of McGraw's other "boys" were gone, but the Giants were building once more, piecing together a winning team around Carl Hubbell and his dazzling screwball pitch, and Mel Ott, the little right fielder who, when about to swing at a pitch, lifted his right leg so high that he looked, as somebody said, like a dog peeing against a fire hydrant. The roster included other good players: a scrappy shortstop named Dick Bartell; left fielder and leadoff man Jo-Jo Moore; pitchers Hal Schumacher, Fred Fitzsimmons, and Frank Gabler (the latter recently brought up from the minor leagues); and catchers Gus Mancuso and Hank Danning.

Babe Ruth had retired from baseball the year before, permitting Lou Gehrig to emerge from his shadow and to shine briefly as the game's finest player before he went back into eclipse with the rise of his young teammate Joe DiMaggio. Under manager Joe McCarthy, the Yankees had once more assembled a crew of devastating long-ball hitters, with DiMag and Gehrig followed in the batting order by catcher Bill Dickey, right fielder George "Twinkletoes" Selkirk, and second baseman "Poosh-'Em-Up" Tony Lazzeri. "Just a bunch of window-breakers," scoffed traveling secretary Eddie Brannick of the defense-minded Giants. But the window-breakers were at the onset of a reign in which they would capture seven pennants and six World Series under McCarthy's leadership in the next eight years.

Prediction—"especially about the future," as someone once said—is a risky business, and no one would have hazarded the guess that the man doing the heavy thinking for the ragtag team across the river in Brooklyn would someday surpass even McCarthy's string of triumphs at the Yankees' helm. "Is Brooklyn still in the league?" Bill Terry had asked facetiously one afternoon before a gathering of reporters, thus bringing the wrath of a proud borough upon him. The Dodgers' management had retrieved an old clown and journeyman ball player named Casey Stengel from the minors and made him the manager at a salary below that with which they were paying off his recently terminated predecessor. Stengel labored at Ebbets Field in an atmosphere that can only be described as perpetual frustration against a background of farce. The Dodgers, to put it bluntly, were hopeless. After one particularly messy game, Stengel settled into a barber chair and said to the proprietor, "A haircut and a shave, but don't cut my throat. I might want to do that myself later."

There were a few promising players under Stengel's command, including an eccentric, hard-throwing right hander named Van Lingle Mungo, who matched the humorist Bugs Baer's description of a similar pitcher: "He could throw a lamb chop past a wolf." But otherwise Stengel was bedeviled by such chronic failures as Ox Eckhardt, a brawny terror in the minors who showed up at the Dodgers' spring-training camp trailing an enormous St. Bernard on a leash. "He always came to camp with me in the minors," Eckhardt explained, "and I thought he'd enjoy seeing a big-league layout." A leader among the "Daffiness Boys" was

Stanley "Frenchy" Bordagaray, who astounded the baseball world by appearing on the field wearing the first mustache and goatee seen in the majors since the turn of the century. "Shave it off," Stengel urged the young man, whom he had acquired to give the team a little speed on the bases. "That hair's going to slow you down." But, as a Brooklyn writer pointed out, "Frenchy's speed would have helped the Dodgers had he run in the right direction."

On opening day, 1936, Stengel led his Dodgers into the Polo Grounds to play the Giants. It must be remembered that in that era, before night baseball came to the majors, weekday baseball was patronized chiefly by the leisure class, the unemployed, and people who worked nights, and thus games usually began at three-fifteen to allow the Wall Street crowd to make it uptown on the subway in time to swell the attendance. Certain figures of baseball speech were keyed to this traditional starting time; for example, "a one-o'clock hitter" was a dud whose best efforts were restricted to batting practice, whereas "five-o'clock lightning" was the phrase in which the press then alluded to the power-hitting Yankees' predilection for erupting in a barrage of late-inning home runs.

They opened the gates at eleven o'clock in the morning, and by two o'clock only some of the reserved seats were empty. The sun was shining, and everybody was glad to be there, and you could tell, even then, that it was going to be the biggest opening day in many years.

In the dugout the Giants watched the Dodgers closely as they began their batting practice.

"That must be Eckert," Gabler said, as the first Dodger went to bat.

"That is Eckert, or Eckhardt, or whatever the hell his name is," Terry said. "He can't bunt a ball to right field."

"But he can hit," Moore said.

"I'll say he can hit," Terry said. "Take the bat and ball away from him and he could still hit."

"Who's that pitching?" Jackson asked.

"That's Baker," Terry said. "He's fattened up."

"He hasn't fattened up," a reporter said.

"He looks fatter to me," Terry said. "He's got a great motion, hasn't he? Look how he pitches. Nice and easy."

"He sure has," Gabler said. "Who's this hitting?"

"That's Cooney," Danning said.

"He used to be a pitcher, didn't he?" Gabler asked.

"Yes," Moore said. "But he got smart."

"Who's this?" Gabler said.

"That's Frey," Danning said. "You ought to recognize him."

"I do now," Gabler said. "But he looks bigger to me than he did last year."

"He looks smaller to me," Terry said. "They all look smaller to me."

"Wait till the game starts," Jackson said. "They'll look big enough then."

Lindstrom hit the first ball pitched to him into left field with a perfect stroke. He hit another ball to left field, then one to right.

"Three for three," Gabler said. "Gee, he gave an exhibition, didn't he. Who's this?"

"Booker, or Boocher, or whatever his name is," Danning said.

"He pronounces it Bew-ker," a reporter said.

Hassett stepped to the plate.

"This is their first baseman, isn't it?" Gabler asked.

"Yes," Danning said.

"I been reading a lot about him lately," Gabler said. "I never heard of him before."

"Well," Danning said, "the chances are he hasn't heard of you yet."

Jack White, the comic, handed a scorecard and pencil to Gabler.

"Sign that for me, Gabe," he said.

Gabler signed it and handed it back.

"Now, get Hubbell to sign it and you'll have fifty-one thousand dollars worth of pitching talent on it," he said. "Fifty thousand for Hubbell and one thousand for me."

All around were familiar faces. Governor Hoffman of New Jersey posing for the photographers . . . Detective Lieutenant Johnny

*Broderick standing in the aisle back of the front row of boxes . . .
Former Governor John K. Tener of Pennsylvania, who used to be
president of the National League . . . Boxing Commissioner Bill
Brown . . . Groundskeeper Henry Fabian making a final inspection
of the infield turf.*

*In the underslung press box they were standing up, too. There
wasn't even room for a cop to sit down. Brass hats of the Police
Department stood up with the late arriving reporters.*

*Just before the parade to the flag pole, there was a great stir and
craning of necks in the grand stand. Babe Ruth was coming in.*

*"Who is it, the Mayor?" a police inspector in the press box
asked.*

"No. It's the Babe."

The inspector craned his neck, too.

*The teams marched out to the flag pole, and the band played
"The Star Spangled Banner," and everybody stood up. When the
last strains of the anthem died away, everybody sat down except a
hockey writer, who remained standing with his hat in his hand.*

*"What!" he exclaimed. "No Maple Leaf Forever? These must be
two American teams."*

*The teams marched back. Mayor LaGuardia was with them,
bowing and waving his black soft hat to the crowd. Half way to
the home plate, the Giants appeared to lose interest in the parade,
and the Dodgers finished in front by six lengths. LaGuardia
reached his box and stood posing for the photographers.*

*A few minutes later former mayor Jimmy Walker came in and
sat near LaGuardia. Again there was a great stir and craning of
necks.*

*"They can't tell me old heroes are forgotten quickly," a reporter
said, as he unlimbered his typewriter. "The guys that got the most
attention around here today were Babe Ruth and Jimmy Walker."*

*Then the ball game began, with the teams attacking each other
with more spirit than skill . . . Schumacher pitching against Earn-
shaw . . . Terry and Geraghty out of the line-up . . . the Giants
taking the lead in the third inning, and the Dodgers taking it back
in the fourth, largely because of two errors by Bartell . . . Terry*

batting for Schumacher in the sixth inning . . . and Coffman com-
ing in to pitch for the Giants.

In the seventh inning Bordagaray went to right field for the
Dodgers in place of Eckhardt. He called for time and ran around
in circles in right field.

"Look at Frenchy warming up," one reporter said. "It would be
funny if he ran out of breath and then somebody hit one out
there."

"He isn't warming up," another reporter said. "He just wants to
give the crowd a chance to see his mustache and goatee."

In the eighth inning Bartell made a home run that won the game
for the Giants. Two runs followed Bartell's homer, but it was the
homer that won the game. The Giants' winning made it a perfect
day . . . or ruined it . . . depending on the viewpoint.

Every sportswriter has his favorite athletes, and in most cases
they are not the ones whose names dominate the headlines and
whose pictures stimulate sprawling feature stories in the big national magazines. Skill is a part of the attraction, of course, but
other qualities strengthen the bond. My father had his favorite
ball players—Ross Young, Arthur Nehf, Pepper Martin, and Tony
Lazzeri. In writing about Lazzeri, he could never put down the
urge to explain what the Yankees' second baseman meant to him
as a player. The Yankees had a tremendous year in 1936, winning
the pennant by nineteen and a half games, then going on to
beat the Giants (who were no patsies) in the World Series. That
winter, the New York baseball writers decided to honor Lazzeri as
Player of the Year at their annual dinner. Lazzeri was one of the
three Italians from San Francisco who played in the Yankees'
starting lineup, DiMaggio and shortstop Frank Crosetti being the
others. At times they carried the "strong, silent" image to incredible lengths. A reporter once told of eavesdropping (if that expression may be used in this context) in the lobby of the Chase Hotel
in St. Louis.

"I came down in the elevator," the reporter said, "and the
three of them were sitting there, watching the guests coming and

going. I bought a paper and sat down near them, and after a while I became aware that not one of them had a word to say to the others. Just for fun, I timed them to see how long they would maintain their silence. Believe it or not, they didn't speak for an hour and twenty minutes. At the end of that time, DiMaggio cleared his throat. Crosetti looked at him and said:

" 'What did you say?'

"And Lazzeri said: 'Shut up. He didn't say nothing.' "

Now, at the beginning of February, 1937, Lazzeri arrived by train in New York to attend the writers' dinner.

Seeing him there made you think of the many times you had been around with him since he came up with the Yankees eleven years ago. Watching him on the ball field . . . Sitting with him in the dugout before a game . . . Seeing him playing cards or reading a magazine or eating on a train . . . Walking through the lobby of a hotel . . . Or sitting by the window of his darkened room in a Cleveland hotel one night when it was so hot nobody could sleep and everybody was sitting around in the dark trying to catch a breath of air coming in the windows overlooking the lake.

And you thought that of all of the ball players who have come up and stuck around for ten years or so Tony has changed less than almost any you could call to mind. Maybe this is because the mark of the busher never was on Lazzeri. He wasn't like some of these kids who come up out of the tank towns with their brakeman's hair cuts and their mail order clothes. Tony is a big-town guy. Born in San Francisco, which is a big town in all its aspects. Ball players who come out of San Francisco always are big-town guys. Fellows like Lazzeri and Crosetti and DiMaggio and Frank O'Doul and Joe Cronin.

The readers of "Setting the Pace" were invited behind the scenes. For a complete description of what took place on the field they usually had to look elsewhere on the sports page, because, though my father liked to watch baseball and invariably stayed for the game, his professional interest lay in the encounters (and what they stirred in his memory) before play began. But once in a while events took a dramatic turn. There was a day at Yankee Stadium during the 1937 season (long before players wore batting helmets) when a frightening accident stunned fans all over the country.

Mickey Cochrane was the manager of the Detroit Tigers. One of the finest catchers in baseball history and an inspiring leader who had won pennants for Detroit in 1934 and 1935, he led his team into New York to begin a series with the Yankees. The Tigers, who had been knocked out of the pennant race the year before when their huge slugger, Hank Greenberg, was kept from the lineup by a broken wrist, appeared strong once more. They possessed artful pitchers like Schoolboy Rowe and Tommy Bridges, and Cochrane was still unsurpassed by any other catcher in the game with the exception of Bill Dickey of the Yankees and Gabby Hartnett of the Chicago Cubs. The day began quietly.

The player dressing nearest the door in the Tigers' clubhouse was Gilbert English. English is a fair-haired young man who tried to play third base for the Giants five or six years ago without much success, but he is a better ballplayer now than he was then. Every time you see him you think of the time he was seated next to Smoky Joe Martin, also a busher with the Giants, in a bus that was taking the second team to Newark for an exhibition game the day before the season opened. Martin was fresh from Oxnard, California, and some of the regulars had been kidding him about the wonders of New York, and when he asked English, about midway through the Holland Tunnel, where they were, and English told him they were under the Hudson River, Martin snarled at him:

"I've taken enough of that nonsense from the regulars," he said. "Don't you start it."

Mickey Cochrane and Cy Perkins, who is one of his coaches, had just come in and were drinking milk as they got into their uniforms. You asked Mickey if he didn't think that when the clubs were all straightened out it would be a two-club race.

"That's the way I see it," he said. "The Yankees are the club to beat, and it looks as though we have the best chance to beat them. We've been going pretty good, considering the breaks we have had. Anyway, we've been hitting."

In a little while the ball game started and in the fourth inning Mickey Cochrane was hit in the head with a ball pitched by Bump Hadley. From the press box it looked as though Mickey had tried to pull away from the ball and it struck him full in the right temple. He dropped unconscious, and the players gathered about him. Dr. Robert Emmet Walsh, the Yankees' physician, examined him and sent to the clubhouse for a stretcher.

They carried Mickey into the clubhouse and laid him on a rubbing table. Eldon Auker and Babe Herman had helped to carry him and stood there looking at him with drawn faces. Police Lieutenant Joe Murray was there, and Doc Painter, the Yankees' trainer, and Dukie, who trains the Tigers, and newspapermen came down from the press box. Cy Perkins, badly shaken by the accident, stripped off his uniform and began to get into his street clothes.

"Is he conscious?"

You told him Mickey had just regained consciousness.

"He almost got hit yesterday," Cy said, fumbling with the collar of his shirt. "The ball didn't miss him this much yesterday."

Lou Gehrig came in and stood over Cochrane, looking down at him. He stood there silently for a moment and then said:

"Get well in a hurry, Mike. There aren't enough like you."

He went out, and in a moment Lazzeri came in. He looked at Mickey but didn't say anything and then went out.

Painter brought some ice from the Yankees' clubhouse, and Dukie put it in a bag and placed it under Cochrane's head. A boy brought a blanket from the Yankees' clubhouse, and Auker and Herman spread it over Cochrane and tucked it around him.

"He has a definite concussion," Dr. Walsh said. "I don't think there has been any fracture. But I want to see the plates first."

Lieutenant Murray came over to the newspapermen, standing at one side of the room.

"Please go out now," he said. "They want him to have absolute

quiet. We have sent for an ambulance, and after he has rested for
a bit they are going to take him to St. Elizabeth's Hospital."
    The newspapermen filed out. In the stands the crowd was roar-
ing. The Yankees had just made two runs.

Although Cochrane recovered from his grave injury, his career
was shattered. The Yankees went right on winning, but the faces
were beginning to change there, too. Lazzeri, aging, was near the
end of his career. Gehrig, "the Iron Horse," unaccountably began
to lose his awesome power at bat and even his mobility in the
field, a victim of "lumbago," or so they said. Meanwhile, the
Giants faded as perennial contenders, Terry departing and being
replaced as manager by Mel Ott. But across the river the Dodgers
were stirring from their long sleep in the league's nether regions.
Derisive jokes about the team ("Overconfidence cost the Dodgers
sixth place this year") were replaced by an enthusiasm for their
scrappy, colorful play that spread far beyond the boundaries of
Brooklyn.
    As the decade waned, even more astonishing changes came to
baseball. Arc lights appeared over the staid old Polo Grounds. It
was just in time to give the fans an appetite for night baseball before the glow was snuffed out with the advent of the blackouts
that brought a side of World War II to dwellers in coastal cities.
Cincinnati had been staging night games occasionally since 1935,
when President Roosevelt pushed a button in the White House
that turned on the lights in the Reds' Crosley Field. On May 24,
1940, night baseball came to Manhattan.
    If a reader wants to shine in a trivia quiz, he might store in his
memory the fact that the Giants' opponents that evening were the
Boston Bees (a twist in the long nomenclatural history of the
Braves), who were managed by Casey Stengel.

The gray afternoon had waned and dusk was settling over the
Polo Grounds, and the Giants, who ordinarily would have been on
their way home by that time, were coming into the dugout. They
looked a trifle bewildered. All of them had played night baseball at
some time or other, the older players in exhibition games at such

widely scattered points as San Antonio, Houston, San Diego, San Francisco, Dexter Park, Staten Island and Bridgeport, the younger players in regular games in the minor leagues. Frank Demaree and Bill Jurges, when they were with the Cubs, had played in Cincinnati. Now night baseball had caught up with them as a team.

"What time do we hit?" Mel Ott asked.

"Twenty minutes to seven," Travis Jackson said.

Ott shook his head.

"It sounds funny, don't it?" he asked.

The dusk deepened as the batting practice wore on and then the Giants were through and the Bees began to hit.

"You ought to do pretty good in this league," Jurges yelled at Al Lopez, the Braves' catcher. "You like to stay up late."

Lopez grinned and swung on the ball.

"Do they hang a lantern on you in night games?" Jurges asked. "I can't see you very well, even now."

"Why don't they turn on the lights?" a player down the line on the bench asked.

"Wait until it gets dark," Jackson said.

"It's dark enough to suit me now. I'm glad we're through hitting. I wouldn't want to be standing up there."

Over in the Bees' dugout a few minutes later they, too, were asking why the lights weren't on. The Bees are no stranger to night baseball. But they wanted batting practice under the lights.

"They'll turn 'em on for fielding practice," Stengel said.

Somebody asked Stengel how he liked night baseball.

"I like it all right," he said. "But I guess the best place to be in a night game is right here on the bench. Those fast ball pitchers can't hit you in here."

It was quite dark when the Bees' batting practice ended. The lights in the stands went on and gleamed down on 22,260 fans who had come out in spite of the threatening weather. The players dawdled about for a few minutes. Then the lights were turned on and the crowd cheered.

The throwing of the switches that set the eight light towers blazing put New York in the list of towns that play night baseball and marked a new era in the colorful history of the Polo Grounds. For

*those—and there may have been some in the crowd—who remem-
ber the old wooden stands and the horses and carriages in front of
the old clubhouse where helmeted policemen stood guard, it must
have been a strange sight. The light towers blazing and the field
flooded with light on a misty night and the Giants and the Bees
moving to their positions.*

*Make no mistake about it, it is a scene that will be repeated with
increasing frequency. Night baseball, once scorned and derided by
the major leagues, is in keeping with the tempo of American life.
There may be a difference between baseball in the daytime and
baseball under the lights—although no difference was perceptible
on this superbly lighted field last night—but the demand for the
night game is here and the ball clubs are meeting it and, as they go
along, the demand is going to become heavier.*

Chapter Seven
The Blood Sport (I)

L ord Macauley pointed out that the Puritans disapproved of bear-baiting not because it gave pain to the bear but because it gave pleasure to the spectators. The hold of the blood sports on intelligent and otherwise sensitive people is a mystery and, often, an abomination to some of their peers. To derive pleasure from converting a beautiful and graceful animal into a blood-soaked lump of fur or feathers, or from watching one man beat another to the point of death, is a phenomenon that most of us don't care to examine very closely. We cast off a remark about atavistic impulses, or the manly virtues, and turn back to the carnage.

Pop was the gentlest of men. Yet he could come away from a brutal fight, in which he and his typewriter at ringside literally had been spattered with the gore of the combatants, seething with excitement, replete with admiration for the ferocity of the conqueror and the courage of the poor wretch deposited, twitching and half-blinded, on the canvas. *Biff! Bam! Pow!* Nor did he ever want boxing's elemental violence disguised. Boxing, he believed, was no place for the rule-makers; the Marquis of Queensberry simply confused the matter. Pop had no patience, for instance, with the concoction of such niceties as scoring systems, where the winner of a fight was decided by the number of rounds a man won or the total of points he had piled up. Boxing was an elemental sport.

"If two men were fighting on a streetcorner," he said, "every bystander could tell you who won the fight. The winner was the guy who was punching the other fellow around when the cops arrived to break it up."

It was an obvious absurdity, he believed, that a man could win the first six rounds of a fight, take a shellacking in the last four, and be given the decision. Of a fifteen-round fight he used to say, "You can throw out the first ten rounds. The fighter who is in charge during the last five rounds wins it." Nor was he tolerant of the attempts of boxing commissioners and referees to turn an alley fighter into a gentleman boxer, an exercise he compared to sticking a bear into pumps and a frilled skirt. Insisting that the Dempsey-Firpo fight was the most exciting anybody ever saw, he wrote, "The champion and the Wild Bull not only tossed the rule book away, they went back through the ages and fought like a couple of cave men." To keep warning fighters about illegal tactics, to keep calling fouls was—well, to reduce boxing to the level of basketball, and he could say no worse. He admired Joe Louis, he loved Jim Braddock, but he positively reveled in Two-Ton Tony Galento.

There have been very few prize fighters like Tony Galento, which is too bad, because if there were a few more prize fighting would be a gayer business from the spectators' point of view. Until yesterday you merely had seen Tony climb into the ring while the fans around the ringside giggled and wanted to know how a little fat man like that could fight and you had seen him belt out some big ham and everybody had said something like:

"My goodness, but that little fat man is a terrific puncher."

Then you sat with him in a dressing room at Stillman's Gymnasium after he had finished his day's training for the fight with Eddie Mader at the Garden next Friday night and suddenly he didn't look as funny to you. In spite of his rotund body, thickly matted with hair, he has a fighter's face—deep set black eyes, a short, thick nose, lips that have been thickened by the punches of his opponents, close set ears. It is a rugged face in which courage and a love of combat are written plainly. He isn't really a very good fighter. He isn't as good a fighter as he thinks he is. But in spite of his limitations, he was made for fighting. Street fighting, barroom fighting, ring fighting. War. He never has had enough of fighting, not even when—as not infrequently has been the case— he has been beaten.

"When I was 15 years old I was working on an ice wagon," he said. "That was over in Orange, New Jersey. Well, I always wanted to be a fighter. When I was 15 years old I wanted to fight Paulino Uzcudun. I saw him in some newsreels and I knew I could lick him. I could lick all those fellows around then. I used to see their pictures in lunch rooms and places like that. I was interested in them because—well, I guess I wanted to be a fighter ever since I was old enough to want to be anything.

"I used to fight in the streets, like most kids do. I'd start at one end of my street and fight a guy right down to the other end, and my old lady—I mean my mother—would come out with a broom and start swinging at me and I'd go on fighting and—

"Say—I'm not talking too much, am I? I'll bend your ear talking to you if you sit there long enough. Well, all right. There were a lot of kids in our school that wanted to be fighters, too, and they were always coming around looking for me, which was all right with me, because I always wanted to fight.

"When I was about 17 I wanted to fight some of the pros around there, but they wouldn't fight me. They heard all about me and they were afraid to fight me. So I went into the amateurs because I knew I would get plenty of fights there. I weighed only about 130 pounds then, and I fought lightweights, middleweights and heavyweights. They would throw me in with the heavyweights because they wanted to see me get knocked off, but I would hook those big bums with my left and curl them right over, head first, like this. I can't do it like they did because I'm not double-jointed, but any-

way they would wind up with their heads right down at their feet. You know those guys were hit.

"Is it all right to talk so much? Because you know what I told you. I'll bend your ear . . . Well, I finally got a fight with Babe Farmer in the pros. I was supposed to be a setup for him. I was fighting in one of the preliminaries, and Farmer was in the semifinal, but the fellow he was supposed to fight didn't show up so they said I could get a hundred dollars if I fought him. The manager I had then said he didn't know about that, but I said I would fight ten guys like Farmer for a hundred bucks. So I knocked him out in three rounds—I could have knocked him out in one—and by the time they got through cutting up my hundred bucks there was only thirty left for me."

There followed an outline of a robust and rollicking career.

"I knocked out DeKuh in four rounds. I broke his nose in the first round. . . . I beat Johnny Risko in ten rounds . . . I could have knocked him out, only I had sore hands, and I was afraid to let one go too hard for fear I might break my hand, but I could feel him go weak a couple of times when I hit him. Any good fighter—I don't mean I'm such a good fighter—well, maybe not the best fighter in the world . . . although I think I am and I am not afraid of any of these fellows . . . but what I was going to say is that any good fighter knows when he has the other guy going. You can feel him go weak when you hit him.

"I knocked out K. O. Christner . . . I knocked him out in eight rounds, but I could have knocked him out in a round, but my hands were still sore. . . . But in the eighth round I hit him a left hook under the heart and as he was falling I hit him with my right on the chin. . . . I knocked out Natie Brown in one round and Joe Louis couldn't knock him out in ten. . . . Ernie Schaaf beat me in ten rounds, but I could have . . . but Lord have mercy on him, he's dead and I won't want to say I could have licked him if I had fought him again. Although I could have. . . . I wanted to fight Braddock but . . . well, I don't want to put in a knock on him, because he is a great fellow and a good fighter. . . . If he wasn't he wouldn't be up there where he is.

[FRANK GRAHAM, JR.]

*"I knocked out George Panka in four seconds.... Of course, he
wasn't much of a fighter, but I am telling you about it because it
was one of the quickest knockouts on record. It was in Motor
Square Garden in Pittsburgh, and the ring was only thirteen feet
long. I just had to take a couple of steps out of my corner, and as
he came across I let one go like this and knocked him dead. My
trainer was going down the steps and had his back turned to the
ring, and when he looked up and saw me standing in the corner he
says to me:*

" *'What are you waiting for? Why don't you go out and fight?'*
"So I points to Panka lying on the floor and says:
" *'It don't look like he's going to get up, so get your things to-*
gether. We're moving.'

*"I made some bad fights, too.... I got swell-headed, and I ran
around and did some drinking and didn't train, because I could
knock out a lot of those fellows without training, and I thought I
could lick anybody without training.... So I lost some fights and
made some very lousy ones, and I missed a lot of chances. But my
manager, Joe Jacobs, has put me in a good spot now and I won't
miss any more chances. All I want him to do is to get that Louis for
me and I will attend to him. I am training now like I never did before.... Can I tell you about some of the lousy fights I made?"*

*You told him it wouldn't be necessary, because you saw him in
one of them not so long ago. And he said:*

*"Well, I guess your ear is bent pretty good now, anyway. I told
you it would be, if you sat there long enough."*

Day after day, the places to write about boxing in New York
were the gymnasiums. Lou Stillman ran the busiest gym, charging
admission to fight fans who wanted to watch a couple of neo-
phytes slug it out in one of the rings, or just stand and gawk at the
well-known fighters and the mass of humanity that swirled around
them. The newspapermen were free to visit the fighters in their
tiny dressing rooms off the main hall, asking them questions (or, in
Galento's dressing room, simply standing back to listen) as they
got a rubdown from a trainer, or had their hands bandaged with

88

protective tape. Sometimes the spectacle of the gym itself was quite enough.

Freddy Steele was going to work out, and James J. Braddock was there, and so was Lou Ambers, and the opportunity to see three world champions all at once had drawn a crowd. All the seats were taken, and there were spectators standing up behind the seats and hanging out over the rail of the balcony at one end of the gymnasium. Steele, the middleweight champion, has been working out at Stillman's ever since he has been in New York, but this was his first formal workout, and there were a number of reporters and photographers there. Steele, who fights Babe Risko in the Garden next week, never has fought in New York, and everybody wanted to see what he looked like in the ring. Up to now he had been just a nice looking young man who dropped into Jimmy Johnston's office once in a while. He looked like a college hero, somebody said.

The crowd was milling around on the floor, and fighters were belting each other around in the two training rings. Frankie Carbo, who is a fight manager, said:

"Steele is back in his dressing room, if you want to see him."

Steele was sitting on a rubbing table, and he didn't look like a college hero. He looked like a fighter. Like a fighter who could be hard and vicious and merciless when he got in there and started punching. He wasn't on parade now. He was at work, and you could tell by looking at him sitting there that there wouldn't be clowning done when he climbed into the ring.

He had on a sleeveless white shirt and black trunks, and his trainer, Al Lang, was standing behind him and handing him strips of tape with which he was binding the gauze bandages on his hands. Nick Masters and Freddie Lenhart, who were going to act as his sparring partners, were sitting around waiting for him. Masters has done a lot of fighting around here, and Lenhart is Steele's stablemate. They are heavyweights, and Steele said:

"They give me a good workout. It's a great thing to have fellows like that to box with."

Masters didn't say anything, but Lenhart said:

"That's a lot of baloney."

Steele laughed and went on bandaging his hands. The door of his room was open, and Art Winch, who manages Barney Ross, came in. Winch is here with Davey Day, the Chicago lightweight who fights Lou Ambers in an over-the-weight bout at the Hippodromo tomorrow night.

"Where's Davey?" Steele said.

Day was dressing in the cubicle across the narrow hall from Steele, and Winch called him in. He is a slim, white-faced Jewish boy with big dark eyes. He came in and shook hands with Steele, and they wished each other luck.

Now Lang was picking up Steele's stuff and Freddy got down off the rubbing table and started for the ring, and Masters and Lenhart and Lang followed him.

Steele looks big for a middleweight, but as Sammy Goldman, who manages Tony Canzoneri, pointed out, his weight is well distributed.

"Some middleweights are heavyweights from the waist up," Sammy said. "But this fellow is built like a middleweight all over. That's why, although he is taller than most middleweights, he doesn't have any trouble making the weight."

Ambers was boxing in one of the rings, and Steele was going to use that ring, so Lang took his time getting him ready. He put his headguard on and laced his gloves on and smeared his cheek bones and eyebrows with vaseline. Ambers bobbed up and down in front of a Negro sparring partner and hurled punches at him from all angles, which is the way Ambers always fights, seldom setting himself for a punch. Then the bell rang and the lightweight champion climbed out of the ring and Steele and Masters climbed in.

They went a couple of rounds and, as you had suspected, there was no clowning. Steele has a good left hand. He stabbed Masters with it and hooked him with it, hooking it short so that there was no waste of motion or force. Now and then, as Masters bore in on him, he snapped his head back with a right uppercut. And when Masters tried to bull him around the ring he roughed him and hauled him and tied him up.

Between the first and second rounds Braddock, wearing a green one-piece suit, climbed up in the other ring. The two rings are on one platform, separated only by ropes, and Steele was walking up and down along the ropes when Braddock climbed in.

"Hello, Jim," he said.

"Hello, Freddy," Braddock said.

After the second round with Masters, Steele took on Lenhart, who fights John Henry Lewis shortly.

Braddock finished his workout and pulled a dressing gown over his shoulders and started for the showers and the crowd on the floor opened up for him. Doc Robb, his trainer, and Tex Sullivan, his secretary, almost had to run to keep up with him, and the crowd closed in behind him and they had to elbow their way through.

Ambers having left the floor, Day came out to the ring.

"He'll give Ambers a lot of trouble," Jimmy Johnston said. "I just said that to Al Weill, Ambers' manager, and he laughed because he thought I was kidding him, but you wait and see."

"What do you think, Sammy?" somebody asked Goldman.

Goldman shrugged. "I don't know," he said. "He's little more than a preliminary fighter. He shouldn't make any trouble for the lightweight champion of the world."

Steele finished his two rounds with Lenhart and punched the bag and skipped the rope. Then Lang put his dressing gown around him, and they started back to his dressing room. The three champions had left the floor and the crowd began to break up. In one of the rings Day was boxing with a sparring partner.

The payoff, of course, arrived when the fighters completed their training and squared off before thousands of fans in one of the big arenas. Galento, after regaling my father with his saga of triumph, returned to real life to reenact a few more "lousy fights," then righted himself and eventually advanced to a memorable evening in the ring at Yankee Stadium in 1939, when, for one second, he stood over the fallen Joe Louis; he finally succumbed to the champion, bloodily, gloriously, in the fourth round. Freddy Steele went on from training at Stillman's to defend his title against Babe Risko, while Davey Day acquitted himself well in a losing battle against Ambers. (Later, Day was recognized for a time as the lightweight champion by the National Boxing Association.) Lenhart, the sparring partner, proved to have a not very substantial chin after all. He lasted only into the third round when he fought John Henry Lewis, and disappeared from history.

Chapter Eight
The Blood Sport (II)

Boxing fans, looking back to the thirties and the succession of fights that will always stick in their memories, are apt to recall the big outdoor shows at the ball parks and the Garden Bowl, or the almost weekly indoor fight cards (except when the circus, the rodeo, or the ice show was in town) at Madison Square Garden. Wild nights! The Garden produced its share of them, with Joe Louis, or Henry Armstrong, or Fred Apostoli hammering a victim across the ring, pinning him on the ropes, and battering his face and skull until the referee (always a little tardily, complained onlookers in whom the milk of human kindness flowed more readily than in their neighbors) leaped in to pull the better man away and stop the fight. There was the night the crowd booed Louis because he could not catch up with the hastily retreating Bob Pastor. Or the night when the crowd booed Braddock because he had passed over Louis' conqueror, Max Schmeling, to defend his title in a far more lucrative match with Louis in Chicago. And the night Schmeling fought Harry Thomas in the Garden in 1937, when swarms of pickets, under the watch-

ful eyes of mounted policemen, filed up and down in front of the
Garden to protest the German's appearance.

"Don't send money to the mad dog of Europe!" a woman
screamed at the ticket holders as they hurried toward the entrance. "Schmeling is an agent of Hitler!"

But for a short time one of the hottest boxing arenas in the city
was the old Hippodrome, striving for elegance, with its red plush
seats, on Sixth Avenue between Forty-third and Forty-fourth
streets. The Sixth Avenue elevated trains rattled overhead in
those days, before the wrecking crew came to dismantle the
structure; it was sold as scrap to the Japanese (who allegedly
turned it into bombs and dropped it on American ships at Pearl
Harbor). Jimmy Johnston still controlled boxing in the Garden,
while Mike Jacobs bided his time and kept a foothold in the business by promoting at the Hippodrome and at some of the ball
parks. That was the time when the sands of Jacobs Beach shifted
from Forty-ninth Street down to the strip of pavement in front of
the smaller arena, and the fight mob stood around there in small
groups making their shadowy deals, cutting up old touches and
seldom avoiding opportunities for malice in discussing their ab-
sent colleagues. And on fight nights they moved inside to carry on
their conversations.

*The Hippodrome was almost filled and the fight mob was stand-
ing in the foyer. Fighters, managers, match makers, newspaper
men and gamblers. Cops and cloak and suiters. And Mike Jacobs,
the man who never sits down, prowling through the crowd.*

*In the long dead days when they were putting on "A Yankee
Circus on Mars" and similar spectacles at the Hippodrome, it
seemed like an enormous place. But it has been dwarfed by the
Garden and the motion picture cathedrals, and now it is a very
snug place. It is the almost perfect fight club, with the ring pitched
where once there were orchestra seats. In a manner of speaking, it
is a middleweight club. It is too large for the little fellows, and too
small for the big ones. It seems almost as though it was built especially for a Solly Krieger and a Fred Apostoli, a Babe Risko or a
Harry Balsamo.*

Boxing Commissioner Bill Brown was in the foyer. And Al Weill, who manages lightweight champion Lou Ambers. Just outside the door was Detective Lieutenant Johnny Broderick, who never misses a fight.

In the semi-final, fighting Caspar La Rosa, was Attilo Sabatino, a Negro middleweight from Puerto Rico. Sabatino is a stablemate of Pedro Montanez. He and Montanez roamed the highways of the world together and finally reached Paris, and there they found Lew Burston, the manager they had sought from the time they entered Europe by way of Madrid. Burston brought them to this country, and Montanez moved into the big money, and Sabatino is at his heels. Not in the big money yet, but getting into the better clubs, fighting in the preliminaries or the semi-finals.

Burston and Jimmy Bronson were in his corner last night. It is interesting to hear the seconds map out their plan of operations before a fight, so there will be no confusion when the bell rings at the end of a round, and they go up through the ropes into their fighter's corner. It is arranged who will go first, and who will take the stool, and who will handle the bottle. And they know who, if the fighter is cut, will patch the wound. Every one of the sixty seconds between rounds is precious, especially if the fighter is hurt or tired, and precaution is taken that none of them will be wasted.

In Sabatino's corner it was agreed that Bronson should go up first and take the stool, and that Burston should follow him, prepared to staunch a blood flow, patch a cut or treat a swollen eye. And do the necessary talking, since Sabatino speaks only Spanish and French, and Burston is a linguist. Behind Bronson and Burston, crowding up through the ropes, was a second who handled the bucket.

The semi-final was a hard but not spectacular fight. Because it followed some rowdy preliminaries, the crowd hooted and stamped a good deal. But the fighters were doing their earnest best. Sabatino was lean and hard. La Rosa, an old stager, and carrying what is known in the trade as a spare tire around his waist, depended on his experience to win for him. But Sabatino pounded La Rosa's soft-looking middle and took the decision. Everybody cheered when it was over. It was a hard fight that interested no-body.

Then the main bout, introducing Apostoli and Krieger. And the lucky sweater of Hymie Caplin, who manages Krieger. The sweater is brown and green, and the pattern is such that at first glance it seemed Hymie was wearing a brown vest over a green shirt. It is rumored that Hymie bought the sweater in Hollywood. It sounds plausible. Surely no sweater like it ever was seen around here before.

Krieger and Apostoli fought savagely, as they figured to, re-membering their first meeting. In the fourth round Krieger suf-fered a bad gash on his lower lip, and when the round was over Dr. William Walker, the Boxing Commission physician, climbed up in the ring and looked at it. Hymie asked the doctor to let the fight go one round more, promising that if the lip didn't stop bleeding he would stop the fight himself.

The fifth was a rousing round, in which Krieger fought gamely and opened an old cut over Apostoli's right eye. At the end of the round Referee Jack O'Donovan and Dr. Walker went to Solly's corner and looked at his lip and shook their heads, and Hymie readily agreed to having the fight stopped.

"He was winning, too," Hymie said, leaning over the ropes to the newspapermen. "He had the guy licked in the last round."

Hymie was wrong about that. But he was right about one thing. He had said before the fight that his tiger has a tough potato, and he does have a tough potato, even if they did have to stop the fight to keep him from bleeding all over the place.

The fight mob—meaning the managers, trainers, press agents, and various hangers-on—had their favorite after-hours hangouts, which were scattered through midtown. Notable among them was Mickey Walker's, on Eighth Avenue at Forty-ninth Street, across the street from the Garden. Walker, "the Toy Bulldog," had been a great fighter for many years and, like Dempsey, lin-gered on as something of an attraction on his own premises. One had to remain alert to stay out of trouble there. The mildest sort of fellow could come in for a couple of quiet drinks, but an hour or so of sitting at the bar could work wondrous changes in him. Hanging on the wall behind the bar were dozens of photographs of illustrious fighters, all striking pugnacious poses and staring balefully down at the solitary drinker. After the liquor took its effect on the patron, he began staring back with equal aggressiveness at the photographs and occasionally might be seen even to square his shoulders and clench his fists in the approved manner. If, at that moment, another patron happened to brush the solitary drinker accidentally as he passed, the fellow might leap from the stool, his fists raised in emulation of the dozens of immortals behind the bar, and the first thing anyone knew there would be a serious altercation in progress.

Francis Albertanti, the press agent, was a familiar figure at the bar and a close friend of the proprietor, whom he was not above needling if the mood was upon him. A classic "drunk" story emerged from the relationship.

One night, when Albertanti and Walker were sitting at a table in Mickey's place, a stew at the bar spied them and came over.

"Mickey," he said, "I've seen all the fighters for forty years and there were two of them who were tops in my book; Dempsey among the big fellows and you among the little fellows."

"Thank you," Mickey said.

"Yes, sir, Mickey, you're the greatest middleweight that ever lived. There was nobody even close to you. Let me shake your hand."

Mickey shook hands with him and thanked him again. This went on for a while. Unable to stand it any longer, Albertanti said to the stew:

"You say you've seen all the fighters for forty years?"

"Yes, sir! For forty years!"

"Ever see Stanley Ketchel?"

"Ketchel? Fifty times I seen him! Fifty times!"

"He was a pretty good middleweight, wasn't he?"

"Pretty good? He was terrific! Terrific!"

Now for the jab. Francis knocked the ashes from his cigar.

"Well," he asked, diabolically, "how do you think he would have done with Walker?"

"With Walker!" the stew roared. He whirled on Mickey. "Why, you bum!" he sneered. "You couldn't lick one side of Ketchel!"

By the fall of 1937 Jacobs Beach had been restored to Forty-ninth Street, east of Madison Square Garden. Mike Jacobs, the most powerful and skillful boxing promoter of his time, had played his trump card, and he and his Twentieth Century Sporting Club had supplanted Jimmy Johnston at the Garden, promoting the fight in which Henry Armstrong knocked out featherweight champion Petey Sarron to win the first of his three world titles. Armstrong was to be the Garden's most consistent drawing card. But Jacobs' chief weapon in forging the monopoly he soon gained in the sport was the exclusive contract he had the foresight to sign with Joe Louis. Louis could fight only for Jacobs, and the Garden couldn't have him unless Uncle Mike was in charge there. So the Garden's administrators bid Johnston a reluctant farewell, and when Jacobs moved into his office, Jimmy went back to managing fighters on a full-time basis (though it was said that he had a share of the promotions with his brother, Charley, at the little St. Nicholas Arena uptown, in the neighborhood that is now dominated by Lincoln Center)

Jacobs was a slender, gray-haired man with a funny, curled-over walk and ill-fitting dentures that were said to clack uncontrollably when he grew excited. He signed every young fighter of promise to a contract, binding him to fight only under Jacobs' promotion. If a promoter in another city wanted the fighter's services, he was obliged to make a financial arrangement with Jacobs. Boxing picked up considerably under Jacobs' domination, despite the cries of "monopoly," and there was work for everybody—managers, trainers, and other promoters, as well as the fighters themselves.

Much of my father's passion for sports was sustained by this world of petty larceny, derring-do, vanished arenas, gallant banditti, high courage, well-nursed vendettas, and other trappings of romance retrieved through the golden filters of memory and handed down by the eyewitnesses themselves. The contest swelled in interest as it reflected and amplified a rich past. The anecdotes of old-timers, even the bland dressing-room chatter of the athletes, were freighted with references to other times, other places. Like the sound of the wind in the rigging for an ancient mariner, the thud of a gloved fist against bone and muscle had the ability to summon up instantly for my father this pageant of heroes and rascals.

Yet, in his enchantment for the theatricals of his beat, he never completely ignored the effect of those thudding punches on the men who took them. The story of that savage, long-ago brawl between Ad Wolgast and Battling Nelson at Port Richmond, California, might be milked for drama or comedy by the ringsiders who carried their tales down to the present, but the romance was always clouded by the consequences of dozens of similar battles on poor little Wolgast, who was to live out his days in a state asylum. The fighters, of course, looked on pain and disfigurement as a part of their bruising trade. Here is Babe Risko, born Harry Pylkowski in Syracuse, New York, who had a swift rise to the middleweight championship in the thirties and an even swifter fall, talking matter-of-factly in the gym about the bulging scar tissue on the ridges above his eyes.

"I got so when I turned this way I couldn't see you if you stood over there," Risko said. "I went to Dr. Dudley in Seattle after the old scars opened up in my fight with Freddy Steele, and he fixed me up. He took a mold of my face, and then when he was ready he put me on the table and gave me a local anaesthetic. I was on the table for three hours and a half. It didn't hurt when he cut out the tissue, but I could feel it like he was cutting out pieces of rubber or something. I laid off about eight weeks after that."

Scar tissue can be cut away, broken noses can be mended or even remodeled, but some injuries are beyond the doctors' skills.

[FRANK GRAHAM, JR.]

There was a paragraph in the newspaper the other day that may have escaped your notice. It came from Oakland, California, and it set forth that Sammy Mandell, former lightweight champion of the world, had been stopped in the sixth round of a scheduled fight with Joe Bernal.

"Mandell showed a flush of his old fire in the fourth and fifth," it read in part, *"but Bernal came out strong again in the sixth and staggered Mandell with lefts and rights to the jaw. About fifteen seconds before the end of the round Mandell walked into a neutral corner and dropped his hands to his sides. Referee Jimmy Duffy then awarded the bout to Bernal."*

You have just read the latest chapter in the tragic story of a little man who once was a first rate fighter. Sammy Mandell—or Mandello, to give him his proper name—came out of Rockford, Illinois, some eight years ago to win the lightweight title from Rocky Kansas. Sammy was a bright-eyed, rather handsome little fellow in those days, a superb boxer and a fair puncher. At the Polo Grounds one night after he had won the championship he made Jimmy McLarnin look so bad that the boys in the ringside seats laughed fit to die. He was on top of the world that night—but the world rolled over on him very shortly thereafter.

His managers, to whom he must have seemed a lesser fighter than he actually was, refused to take any more chances than were necessary, once he had got by McLarnin. They kept him campaigning through the sticks, meeting obscure opponents for small purses and wasting his energy and his effectiveness. The next time McLarnin caught up with him, which was in an over-the-weight match in Chicago, Jimmy gave him a terrific beating in ten rounds and from that time on Sammy's decline was rapid. He lost the championship here on a one-round knockout by Al Singer, but he continued to fight.

As his skill left him his weight increased. He moved up into the welterweight division. Lucrative matches were denied him and he fought where and when he could. Boys who could not have carried his bag for him that night at the Polo Grounds, when he toyed with McLarnin, began to punch him soggy. But he kept on fighting be-

100

cause, for one thing, he did not know anything else, and for another, he needed the money.

In the succession of lightweight champions he is only three removed from Barney Ross, the present title holder, and he is but thirty years of age, yet he is an old man of the ring, a gray figure wandering through the tank towns.

"I saw Sammy Mandell in Chicago a little while ago," Ross said the other day, "and I never felt so sorry for anybody in my life."

Barney did not say any more. He did not have to. The picture his words had drawn was complete.

But despite the tragedy and the sordidness that was always just beneath the surface, and sometimes right out in the open, my father never lost his conviction that there was a profound nobility in the spectacle of two strong, brave young men squaring off against each other in the ring. It was primal stuff, and it had the power to stir him. One of his favorite fighters was Tony Canzoneri. Years later, after he had retired from boxing, Canzoneri became part of a comic act that often appeared in night clubs and on early television. For some reason, an occasion for exquisite hilarity was when one of the comics cuffed Canzoneri around, but Pop could never watch this part of the act. The sight of a sleazy vaudevillian slapping a once-great fighter across the mouth with his open hand was, to him, heartbreaking. Earlier, he had described in a column his discovery of an old photograph of Canzoneri being pinned against the ropes by Jimmy McLarnin's flailing fists, and the sources of his admiration for a game little man shine through.

That must have been taken in the first round of their first fight, and it made you think of the story Sammy Goldman told you of that moment, near the end of the round, when Tony had been nailed on the chin with a right hand, and it looked as though he might not last out the round.

Sammy said that when Tony came back to his corner at the end of the round he berated him for having gotten in the way of McLarnin's right hand.

101

"I told you to box him carefully and to keep away from his right hand and look what happened!" he said.

Tony didn't say anything, and Sammy said:

"Well, what are you going to do now?"

Tony looked up at him.

"What am I going to do now?" he demanded. "What is he going to do when I walk out in this round and hit him right in the kisser?"

You always will believe that was as game a thought as a fellow ever had in a spot like that because many another fighter, having been tagged by McLarnin in the first round, would have been looking for a gate in the ropes. But all Tony wanted to do was to get a shot at him. When the next round opened Tony walked right out and hit him on the kisser, and from then on the fight was in his hands.

Chapter Nine
A Vanished World

Only the antediluvians among us remember that college football once was able to excite large numbers of people in New York City. There were some pretty good local teams during the thirties. Columbia beat Stanford in the Rose Bowl in 1934, and a couple of years later, Fordham rooters devised a slogan, "From Rose Hill to the Rose Bowl," which was their optimistic scenario for the team's prospective march from the campus to a national championship. Although the invitation to the Rose Bowl went elsewhere, the Rams put together perhaps the best defensive team in the country for a time, and New Yorkers still recall the three successive scoreless ties they played against the University of Pittsburgh's juggernaut in the years 1935–37.

Nevertheless, the visiting teams provided most of the excitement and interest in the city.

One Saturday during the fall was taken over by the Army–Notre Dame game at Yankee Stadium. The stands for the game would be jammed with Notre Dame's "subway alumni," the thousands of New Yorkers who had never attended any college at all but, Roman Catholics or not, were attracted by the Notre Dame spirit and tradition and came out in force on this day every year to display their allegiance. The spirit and tradition, of course, were a legacy from Knute Rockne, who had built fine teams in South Bend and then taken them on the road, harrying the countryside, as it were, playing big-name colleges all over the country and accumulating fans and gate receipts in quantities that would not have been possible in what was then the comparative insularity of South Bend, Indiana. (His teams, indeed, were sometimes called "the Ramblers" before the press settled on "the Fighting Irish.")

But there was another wandering football team that made its mark in the big city during the thirties. While the drums were beginning to beat for the Army–Notre Dame game, a continent away an observer might have noticed a string of eighteen Pullman and baggage cars slowly making its way out of California. A peek inside the cars might have convinced the observer that he had stumbled onto the set of one of Busby Berkeley's Hollywood musicals, though Dick Powell and Jack Oakie were nowhere in sight. But the impression would have been misleading. It was simply the football team of little St. Mary's College, accompanied by more than two hundred singing, swinging industrialists, shopkeepers, secretaries, and other camp followers who were fans of the team and friends of the coach, Edward Patrick "Slip" Madigan. Their destination: New York.

Most college football press agents lack imagination. All they tell you about the young men on their squads is how big they are and where they come from and how well they play their positions. But not the press agents at St. Mary's, which is in the Moraga Valley back of Oakland, California, and which sends its football team East nearly every year to play Fordham. Like the press agents at St. Mary's before him, Tom Foudy really holds his football players up for you and turns them inside out—in type, of course.

For instance, to lift bodily from Foudy's description of Anthony August Falkenstein, one of the halfbacks:

"Came to St. Mary's from Pueblo, Colorado. Tousled haired,

shaggy browed, mighty muscled. Looks like story-book footballer.
Works summers in steel mill. Can lick any man in the college.
Only pronounced weakness, blondes, brunettes, redheads."

The regular quarterback is Louis Francis Ferry. Want to know
about him?

"Gloomy Lou. Austere Prussian-type quarter. Rarely speaks
and no one at St. Mary's ever has seen him smile. Rooms alone.
Has lived nearly all his life on a small vegetable farm near Rich-
mond, California. He has one brother and six sisters and his hobby
is traveling, which is why St. Mary's appealed to him. He prefers
neither blondes nor brunettes and says he has never got a thrill out
of football."

James Lawrence Austin, a right end, works in the movies in the
summer and is a friend of Jean Harlow.

"But he denies she means more to him than a half dozen other
girls. Jean made a mysterious visit to San Francisco just before the
Gonzaga game, and Jim was late for practice. Roared Slip Madi-
gan: 'You can play with Jean Harlow or you can play with St.
Mary's. I won't have any glamour boy on my ball club.' As a soph-
omore Jim was voted America's handsomest football player by the
co-eds at Mills College. No brothers and two sisters.

My father always wrote about the Galloping Gaels, as St.
Mary's team was called, when they came to New York. He also
spoke about Madigan and St. Mary's so often around the house
that I became interested and insisted on attending my first football game when they came to play Fordham in the Polo Grounds.
I rooted for the Gaels, but though they lost to Fordham by a
point, their dim place of origin, their colorful uniforms, and the
outlandish Coach Madigan brought me under their spell. I would
have gone to see a movie about them, provided Busby Berkeley
had found a role for my favorite actress, Ruby Keeler. (She might
have roused Gloomy Lou Ferry from his misogynic seclusion.)

Even the trip to New York by the Gaels had something heroic
about it. Before the introduction of regular commercial planes
between California and New York (covering that vast midland
Hollywood moguls later came to call the "fly-over"), the journey

consumed four days on a train. In addition to its sleeping, dining, and reveling facilities, therefore, the St. Mary's special contained a "gym car" equipped with rubdown tables, exercise mats, bucking machines for the linemen's use, and a battery of showers. For the latter purpose, the gym car carried its own supply of water, a commodity one was not likely to find anywhere else on the train; Madigan, the perfect host, had provided his Pullman alumni with all the trappings of an American Legion convention to beguile the tedium of an arduous journey.

Although St. Mary's College antedated Madigan, its existence had been a well-kept secret until Slip arrived there. Fewer than a hundred students were enrolled in 1920 when its football team earned a small measure of notice by losing to the University of California, 127–0. The following autumn the Christian Brothers who ran the school hired Madigan to help spare it that sort of publicity. Madigan, who had played under Rockne at Notre Dame, was a large, cocky Irishman with a booming voice and a louder wardrobe. He set to work assembling husky young men to preserve the school's honor and a sufficient number of uniforms to clothe them. Since football players came cheaper than uniforms in those days, Madigan spent much of his time buying up second-hand jerseys and repairing damaged cleats.

Soon St. Mary's began to acquire a reputation as a "giant killer." Madigan, however, dubbed his team the Galloping Gaels, though his failure to secure many genuine Gaels prompted the following verse from a lyrical New York sportswriter named George Phair:

> The Harp that hangs in Tara's Halls
> Sings out in accents rich,
> As Herman Meister throws the ball
> To Luben Popovich.

Undaunted, Madigan did the best he could with his young men, bolstering their reputations with nicknames that promised to titillate the fans and writers in distant cities. Angel Brovelli became "the Dark Angel of the Moragas," George Wilson appeared as

"Icehouse" Wilson, and John Podesto rode east under the rollicking cognomen of "Presto Podesto from Modesto." As increasing
gate receipts enriched St. Mary's treasury, the school moved out
of its dingy building in Oakland and found a bright new campus in
the Moraga Valley. At the same time, Madigan began to shun the
dark plumage worn by conventional teams of that era in favor of
the wildest colors of the rainbow. He experimented with tear-
away jerseys as well as with the T formation. Rival coaches also
accused him of concocting the "forward fumble" to pick up
needed yardage.

In 1930 Madigan arranged to play Fordham annually in New
York. St. Mary's president at first objected to the plan, fearing
that the players would lose too much time from their classes, but
Madigan argued persuasively that the educational opportunities
such a trip presented outweighed the loss of class time. By 1936
the St. Mary's–Fordham game had become a football attraction in
New York second only to the Army–Notre Dame game. When the
special train arrived there, its passengers whooping and hollering,
Madigan dispatched his players to their rooms at the Westchester
Country Club. Then he took himself and his followers to a massive
"press party" at the Waldorf. Although many of the team's ardent
rooters missed seeing a football game because of what went on at
the party, Madigan made dozens of friends among both the press
and those strangers who happened to wander in off the street.

There were fifty thousand (including the Grahams, father and
son) in the Polo Grounds on that Saturday in 1936 when the St.
Mary's players, glittering in their red silk jerseys with white
epaulets and their shiny green pants, rushed onto the field. Strolling proudly after them, no less resplendent, was Coach Madigan
in a natty light suit, pink shirt, and orange cravat. By the end of
the first period, Slip looked as rumpled as his players. Storming up
and down the sidelines in his usual manner, ranting at the officials, pulling his hat down over his ears, he worked himself into a
lather. At halftime the Fordham band formed a giant tolling bell
on the field and played "The Bells of St. Mary's." The hung-over
camp followers, sitting together in the upper stands, cheered
wildly and rained confetti down on the sidelines.

Shortly after St. Mary's lost the game, 7–6, the special train pulled out of New York. In addition to memories of another lively visit to the Big Town, Madigan carried with him a check for $36,-824.15. This sum, St. Mary's total share of the gate receipts, was collected by Madigan because the college had fallen behind in paying him his agreed-upon share of the receipts.

"I paid Mr. Madigan," Brother Albert, the president of St. Mary's, was to say during the college's subsequent financial difficulties, "because it was a just debt and I recognized that he had brought certain assets to St. Mary's."

A year later Madigan's bright creation began to flicker. St. Mary's was unable to meet the payments on its new campus and nearly fell into the hands of its bondholders (partly, it was said, because Madigan's salary and bonuses, as well as the team's travel expenses, considerably exceeded the gate receipts). The college was bailed out finally by the archdiocese. Meanwhile, unable to carry out his educational ideas under the new directors, Madigan departed for good in 1940, leaving New York's sportswriters almost as bereft as the Pullman alumni.

During those years New York was invaded annually, from the opposite direction, by an even more unlikely cast of characters. The six-day bike riders had a special hold on New Yorkers. They were Europeans, and this great city of immigrants, many of whom still felt closer to the amusements of their youth than to the incomprehensible, foreign sports of baseball and basketball, crowded into the Garden with their arrival. Yes, the race went on for six days, without letup. The spectators came and went, day and night, watching the riders grind round and round on the wooden oval track.

The contestants in the race were broken down into two-man teams, so that while one of the riders kept to the grind, the other ate his dinner or lounged in one of the bunks set up along the track. The race had gained a unique popularity among the sporting crowd, and it became a meeting place during that wacky week, usually in late February, when fight managers, newspapermen, horse trainers, wrestling promoters, and, of course, gamblers came together to reminisce away the hours wholly undistracted by the action taking place on the wooden saucer below them. Live musicians or mechanical contraptions supplied appropriate music, garish lights shone down, and the bright-jerseyed riders cruised in tight little packs. At intervals, especially during the evening when the crowds were likely to be largest, a sprint would be announced, the riders would begin pedaling furiously, gamblers would give their odds and place their bets, and the music would submerge beneath a throaty roar. Abruptly the sprint would end. The gamblers paid off, the riders slowed their pace, and the spectators returned to their interrupted confabulations.

Like most other native-born Americans who showed up at the Garden for the race, Pop hadn't the faintest idea what was going on. It was just something one did in the dead of winter in New York, as rustics gathered around the cracker barrel in the general store.

Four young men were playing "The Way You Look Tonight" on four pianos in the infield, and the riders were circling the track at an almost leisurely pace. Smoke hung heavy over the arena. Pop and hot dog vendors hawked their wares. The crowd cheered, shrilled, whistled.

The brazen voice of Baldy was lifted in song. Baldy is almost as much a part of the six-day race as the riders themselves. During the race he spends his days and nights in the Garden, yelling at the riders and the fans. Singing . . . whistling . . . playing the clown. The riders marvel at his stamina. They say he sleeps less than they do and works twice as hard.

Somebody offered $10 for the winner of a sprint. Somebody else offered $25. Both got action for their money. The riders feel that $25 here and $25 there . . . or even $10 . . . runs into money. Detectives prowled through the crowd or stood about the portals looking for pickpockets. Or alert to stop fights. But the modern six-day bike crowd is an orderly one. In the old days . . . and the old Garden . . . thugs and crooks were numerous. They once called it the Gunmen's Derby. But that doesn't go any more.

It is an unusual crowd, made up of segments of the crowds that go to ball games, the prize fights, the race tracks and the hockey games. The press box offers a cross section of the crowd. There are few sports writers who write about bike racing exclusively. The six-day race is covered by baseball writers, fight writers and turf writers. Most of them have been doing it for years and know this curious sport as well as they know those about which they write regularly.

But press box conversation rarely touches on the bike race. The writers sit around in dull moments and talk about fights, football games, races, dames, crimes and the newspaper business.

It wasn't quite as it once had been, when memories of the old country still glowed in the minds of many of the spectators and gunshots resounded in the bowels of the Garden and the whole arena pulsed with excitement. That was when the most colorful of all the six-day riders, Maurice Brocco, fired the crowd with his lung-bursting sprints. He had been born in France, but New York's Italian community claimed him as its own, and he came pedaling down the stretch under the urging of the deafening chant *"Brocco! Brocco! Brocco!"*

Torchy Peden was the biggest contemporary name among the riders, but he was aging fast; the younger riders jammed him up in the turns now and pushed him unmercifully in the straightaways and he was, as my father wrote, "riding uphill." The newcomers were faceless athletes to all but the most enthusiastic fans—members of teams from Germany, Italy, France, Belgium, and the Netherlands. Yet their courage and endurance won my father's admiration. They pushed themselves day and night, surviving sickening falls on the harsh boards only to climb back on their bikes and go on riding with broken collarbones, wrenched backs, and various gashes and bruises. To withdraw from the race would be to betray the teammate, who could not stave off the pack alone. Only the more serious injuries took a rider out of the race.

The score board showed that the Red Devils team, composed of Emile Ignat and Emile Diot, both Frenchmen, were leading. Last year they almost won the race here. They were leading in the last forty minutes, when Diot crashed to the boards and broke his right shoulder. Ignat tried desperately to keep the combination in front, but against the frenzied riding of the other teams no man could compete alone.

Now they are trying again, and the bike bugs who hang over the rail peering down at the whirl of colored jerseys think they can win. They are young, strong and ambitious. They won the race in Chicago last November.

Diot was waiting to relieve Ignat. Diot had just had his lunch, and he had come up refreshed and ready to get on his bicycle again. Ignat pedaled slowly around, and Diot rode into the pack and relieved him, and Ignat stopped by his trackside bunk and climbed off.

"Come downstairs, if you'd like to talk to him," Big Speak said.

Big Speak is a tall, slim, nice-looking young Frenchman who trains Ignat and Diot. He has come to this country so often that he speaks very good English and acts as interpreter for the riders and trainers. Thus he is known as Big Speak.

"Just call me Big Speak, and then everybody will know who it is. If I told you my name, nobody here would know."

He led the way down the stairs to the quarters where the riders eat, take their showers, change their clothes and do their serious sleeping—those trackside bunks are for catnaps only. At the foot of the stairs was a wide space in which the riders' trunks are kept for the week, so that they are easily accessible. The trunks are plastered with labels. Paris . . . London . . . Berlin . . . Rome.

The dining room is large enough to hold a half dozen long tables, three on each side, at which the riders are served. The walls are white-washed, and it is a noisy room, at least at that time of the day, because the riders are coming in and going out, and their trainers are hustling up their meals for them. Just beyond there are the clatter and smells of the kitchen. A white-jacketed bus boy took away the empty dishes and put butter pats and pitchers of water and knives and forks on the table, but the trainers did all the waiting.

Ignat sat down at one of the tables, and Big Speak disappeared into the kitchen and came back with a bowl of vegetable soup and set it before him. Ignat looks like a middleweight fighter. His dark hair is brushed back straight from his forehead. His blue-gray eyes are set deep behind his high and rounded cheek bones. His nose has been broken and his mouth is a straight, harsh line. He looks a little as Paulino Uzcudon must have looked before he got mussed up.

As he ate his soup Frans Slaats and Alvaro Georgetti sat down across the table from him. Slaats is a Dutchman, and Georgetti an Italian, but they managed a conversation. Now and then, when Georgetti did not understand what Ignat said, Slaats or Big Speak would interpret for him.

Ignat finished his soup, and Big Speak hustled out and brought back a plate of lamb chops and French fried potatoes; side dishes of peas and spinach; a bottle of beer; and a fruit cup for his dessert. He talked, sometimes with his mouth full, across the table, because he was hungry and was of no mind to stop eating, even for a moment, just to carry on a conversation. Now and then he gesticulated with a fork or a piece of toast.

Big Speak pulled up a couple of chairs at the end of the table where Ignat sat and explained to him that you wanted to talk to him. Or, at least, to ask him some questions about himself. He acknowledged an introduction by smiling and sticking out his left hand. Maybe he is a left-hander, but the chances are he put out his left hand only because, at the moment, he was reaching for a lamb chop with his right.

He said he was born in Paris and was twenty-seven years old. He was born in the Vaugirard quarter. This is close to the Grenelle quarter, which means that it is close to the Velodrome d'Hiver. Almost everybody in Paris rides a bike, but near the Velodrome d'Hiver everybody rides one. It was natural that he should become a bike rider when he grew up. He rode in many road races and won most of those in which he rode. That was when he was an amateur. He decided to turn professional and soon became a six-day rider.

You asked Big Speak to tell him he looks like a fighter.

"He was a fighter," Big Speak said. "When he was in the army, he was the lightheavyweight champion."

112

You said he looked more like a middleweight.

*"He does," Big Speak said, "but he weighs 179 pounds. He has
to be careful about what he eats, or he will be a heavyweight."*

*You looked at the plate from where the lamb chops and potatoes
had vanished and at the empty beer bottle and the empty side
dishes.*

*"Between races, I mean," Big Speak said. "It takes a lot of food
to keep him going during a race. This was his lunch. Come down
some night and see him when he is eating his dinner."*

The six-day bike race was fading and would not survive the
war, but another sport was beginning to attract my father. Now,
Pop was not a betting man. He clung to his belief that a journalist
ought to have no financial interest in the events he covered. But
the racetrack was to catch and hold him: by the end of his life, it
was the only sport that really interested him. He found a good
race exciting, though the track meant more to him than a race. It
was the mingling of the old and the new, sitting around the horse
barns with the old-timers, who spoke about the way racing was
long ago. It was the sounds and smells and the bright sunlight of a
today that was always interesting to him. He found there the history, the continuity, that gave him his keenest satisfaction in
sport.

*The shade of Father Bill Daly walked under the trees in the
paddock at Belmont Park between the fourth and fifth races yesterday. It was invoked when somebody asked Willie Brennan, who
trains for Mrs. Charles Payson, how long it took to mold a raw stable boy into a jockey.*

*"It depends," Brennan said. "It depends on the boy and the
trainer. I guess it depends on the times, too. Silvio Coucci was riding in races after only six months around a stable."*

He pointed across the paddock to the jockey's room.

*"Some of those boys have been around only a couple of years,"
he said. "But Father Bill Daly used to keep us for five and six years
before he was satisfied we were riders. When he thought we were
ready he would sell us. He'd sell a boy for as little as a hundred*

dollars, if that was all he could get."

"How much did you bring?" somebody asked.

"I don't know exactly," he said. "Four or five thousand, I think."

"How much of that did you get?"

"How much did I get?" Brennan asked. "You wouldn't ask me that if you'd ever known Bill Daly. I got nothing. As a matter of fact, the way he had it figured, we all owed him something when we left him."

The fourth race was over and the crowd was coming back to the paddock.

"Who won it?" Brennan asked a man who was hurrying by.

"Teacher," the man said.

Brennan looked at his program and then flipped the page over to the fifth race.

"Daly was a hard man," he said. "But he could get horses ready to run, and he made jockeys to ride them. He made some great jockeys. Mickey Miles, here, and Danny Maher and Winnie O'Connor and the Lamley boys, Johnny and Jimmy, and Snapper Garrison and Jack O'Brien."

"And Monk Moran," a man sitting next to him said. "Him that was killed at the beach."

"That's right," Brennan said. "Monk Moran. Daly was harsh with us. He treated us like slaves. The first year you worked for him you didn't count. You were on trial then. If he thought he could do anything with you, he would sign you up for five years more. He gave us nothing but board and clothes. We slept in the stalls with the horses or in a loft over the stalls. And when we didn't do what he told us to, he batted us around. He'd give us our instructions before a race and, if we didn't follow them—and it didn't make any difference to him whether we were in a position to follow them or not—he'd belt us.

"His place was at Gravesend. Not right on the race track, but only a stone's throw from it. It was down a lane they called Daly's Lane. He was a big man and hard and not afraid of anybody. He kept us in line, I'll tell you. We had to be in bed every night, and he'd check us to make sure we were there, and we had to go

114

to church every Sunday morning, whether we wanted to or not.

"He used to have us exercising horses on the Boulevard—a lot of trainers did that—and sometimes he would have us ride right down to Coney Island and swim the horses in the ocean. It didn't make any difference to him whether a boy could swim or not. Out he had to go, even if he would have been drowned if he slipped off the horse.

"Every day after the races we would go back to the barn and wait for him. He'd come down there, and he'd take a stick and draw a race track in the dirt, and he'd show you exactly where you'd made your mistakes that afternoon, and then he'd take you by the neck and clout you. He had a terrible grip and a heavy hand . . . he hit me so hard once I had a headache for a week. I ran home and told my father, who was in the Fire Department, and he was going to go down to the barn and beat Daly, but I talked him out of it. And I went back, of course. Why? Well, I wanted to become a good jockey, and everybody that wanted to be a jockey went to Daly."

Mickey Miles is Brennan's friend. They were boys together in Daly's stable and became great jockeys and won big races and rode in Europe, and they have come down the years together.

"He was a hard man," Mickey said. "That's right. But give him credit. He knew a lot about the race track. He knew a good horse when he saw one, and he knew a good boy. There were times when we hated him, as Willie says. But when I look back on it I can see some of the things he did for us. Of course there were things that he did that he shouldn't have done. He shouldn't have beaten us the way he did. No trainer today could do that—or would want to. But he was a hard man and that was his way.

"He was born in Ireland, and he drove trotting horses and trained them before he came to flat racing. As Willie says, he knew how to get horses ready and how they should be ridden.

" 'Get off in front,' he'd say. 'Get off in front and stay there. When you're out in front you can't get into trouble. That's a good thing to remember as you go through life, too,' he'd say.

"You hear them say around a race track still that when a jockey gets off in front he's 'On the Bill Daly.' That's where the expression came from. He wanted you to get off in front and stay there, but if you couldn't stay there he wanted you to ride your horse out. The worst thing a boy could do was to pull up when he saw he was beaten. Daly used to want that show money, if he could get nothing else, even if it was only fifty dollars, which it frequently was. And if you didn't get that fifty when he thought you could, he'd thrash you. Well, I suppose—looking back, as I say—you couldn't blame him. It isn't every man who could see a boy throw away fifty dollars and like it.

"Naturally we used to hold grudges against him and try to get even with him," Mickey said. "Once in a while we did. Like the time we brought a boy in to fight one of Daly's boys that he had brought down from Hartford with him. In those days, when all the jockeys lived around the stables, we used to put on fights in the barns, and Daly thought this stable boy, who weighed about 130 pounds, could beat anybody around the barns.

"Terry McGovern—he was the great 'Terrible Terry' later on—was the best amateur fighter around Brooklyn at the time, and he used to come around the barns a good deal. He loved the horses, and he could ride them, too. You know his brothers, Hughie and Philly, were jockeys. Daly knew him by sight, but he didn't know anything about him being a fighter, and one time when he was telling us how good this boy from Hartford was, we said we would arrange a fight for him with McGovern. Daly didn't think Terry was big enough to fight the boy—Terry weighed only about 115 pounds—but we said that was all right. So the match was made.

" 'Do you want to bet?' Daly asked me.

" 'Sure,' we said. We didn't have much to bet with, of course. But Willie had fifty cents and I had a quarter, and Daly said:

" 'All right. I'll bet you a dollar against seventy-five cents.'

"Well, Terry tore into this boy and belted him on the chin and drove him up against the wall of the barn, and his head hit the wall and down he went—out cold. Naturally we wanted our money, but Daly said: 'No. That's a foul. His head hit the wall.' We said: 'Sure, but who drove his head against the wall?' But he said it didn't make any difference. He said his boy won on a foul, *and he kept our money. But we had the satisfaction of seeing his boy knocked out, anyway."*

"How much did he sell you for?" somebody asked.

"He didn't get anything for me," Mickey said. "My time was up, but he hadn't noticed it, and one day I said to him:

" 'I'm leaving you, Mr. Daly.'

"He still didn't understand. 'All right,' he said. 'Take a good vacation and come back.'

"I laughed and walked out—and never went back."

Chapter Ten
Security Blanket

My father's baseball glove, though not an antique, offered his left hand little more cushion against a ball's impact than one of those fingerless gloves that weekend tennis players wear to prevent blisters. It was an ill-made, bright orange affair. He had probably picked it up in a five and-ten-cent store somewhere, and it made me think of pictures I had seen of old timers with handlebar mustaches who fielded their positions with flimsy strips of leather covering their horny hands. (Until quite recently, box scores of ball games contained columns for a player's putouts [o] and assists [a], as well as for his at-bats [ab], runs scored [r] and hits [h], a holdover from the period when it was something of a triumph if a player was able to snag a hard-hit ball with his primitive glove.) The glove was fished out of a bushel basket of roller skates, marbles, and other boyhood things whenever we played ball together. We usually did this on his days off after we had moved into a roomy old house owned by my grand-aunt Nellie in Lewisboro, New York, near the Connecticut line.

On the wide, lumpy front lawn of this house he taught me how to hold a bat and hit a ball. I would fetch my own glove, a cheap first baseman's mitt with a rudimentary webbing linking the thumb to the rest of it. This spared my tender hand when I was fortunate enough to have a pitch find its way there. Pop volleyed bursts of professional lingo at me as he kept me moving after the ball. When I dropped a throw, he called, with mock gruffness, "Take the rubber heel out of your glove!" When the ball he rolled at me bounced up and thudded painfully into my forearm, he barked a peppery "Rub it off! Rub it off!" And when I lifted a leg high to let a grounder skip past, he wagged his head in disapproval: "The old Arlie Latham, eh?" (Latham having been a big-league third baseman of his own boyhood, notorious for his agility at dodging sharply hit grounders). Although my father harbored no illusions about making a big leaguer of me, he hoped I would learn to play the game well enough to get some fun out of it.

At this stage of my supposed athletic development, baseball was not a popular pastime among my classmates at grammar school in Ridgefield, across the state line. There were no Little League programs in those days where I might have been taken in hand and my enthusiasm for playing the game either nourished or quickly smothered. Nor were there many accessible neighborhood children. We lived in a rural area—exurbia had not yet engulfed it—and my grandaunt's house had the aspect of an ancient country inn in decay, which in fact it was. Her husband had died a long time ago, and she and her bachelor brother operated the place as an inn. After he died in turn, our large family, including the four children, my grandmother Minnie, and Emma Akins, solved our domestic financial crisis by moving in with Nellie.

Pop rather enjoyed the idea of being a country gentleman at this period of his life, though neither my mother nor my grandmother was quite so enthusiastic. Since he refused to learn to operate any vehicle, including a bicycle, it was my mother's duty to drive him to the commuter train in New Canaan every day and, if he was kept late in the city by a fight or a hockey game, to manage the thirty-six miles, round trip, to Stamford where the train stranded him after midnight. Minnie lamented being cut off from her fashionable Flatbush friends and often confided to visitors that Emma Akins was slowly poisoning her. I accepted this enforced isolation, and went about building a world of my own out of books and newspapers. There was an old set of the *Encyclopaedia Britannica* with cracked spines in a glass-enclosed bookcase in the main hallway, and I took to reading in it about foreign countries. I read dozens of history books—about the Revolutionary War, the opening of the West, the wars and revolutions in India, South America, and China. Livingstone, Clive, Kit Carson, Simón Bolívar and other heroes swarmed through my inner life. The bales of newspapers that my father brought home, tabloids as well as those of more respectable size, presented added grist for my romantic mill. There were gangland slayings, sharpshooting G-men, wars in Manchuria, Ethiopia, and finally Spain. King Arthur's knights had to work overtime to cleave as many torsos and shatter as many brainpans as were piled up in the contemporary press.

This concern with romance had its practical aspect. Enough of the geography, chronology, and other facts adhered to the gossamer with which my mind was stuffed to win me something of a reputation as a scholar. I excelled in subjects such as current affairs. I could point without hesitation to Bengal or Tasmania on the world map that hung from the sixth-grade blackboard, and I could name the capital of the rebel forces in Spain. I knew what my classmates did not: that an A-plus was more likely to spring from *Barrack-Room Ballads* than from what passed in those days for a social-studies textbook. In the next year or two this reputation was eroded by the distractions of sports and social affairs, and it would be a couple of decades before I regained this peak of erudition.

But no heroes were so ready at hand as those my father wrote and talked about. None of my other mental landscapes was so precisely delineated as the arenas in which those larger-than-life figures struggled to victory or defeat. The morning papers gave me the details of the game itself, which I read hungrily. A casual fan tends to dismiss this part of sportswriting, finding the minutiae of scoring tedious and preferring only summaries and "angles." The true fan wants to know how the home team put together its sixth-inning rally—the chronological account of the walks, hits, force-

outs, and sacrifice flies that produced the runs, just as a chess fan
wants to see the masters' games reproduced in print move by
move. A special pleasure of the football season was the *Sun*'s
practice of printing in its late Saturday editions the play-by-play
of several important games, so that I was able to relive their
events almost as if I had witnessed them. Even though my father
was a columnist, he continued to cover games for the paper several Saturdays a year, dictating the play-by-play to a telegrapher
as the action progressed. Here, from three columns of small type,
I could extract the essence of the second-quarter drive that gave
Army its 6–0 victory over Navy at Philadelphia's Municipal Stadium in 1937:

Army—*Rain continued to fall and between each play the referee dried the ball with a towel. Army took possession on Navy's
43. Wilson gained a bare yard on a line plunge, and was tackled
by Wallace. Ryan, on a straight plunge, got 2 and was stopped by
Antrim. Wilson hurled a forward pass to Schwenk for a gain of 20,
Schwenk being brought down by Wood on Navy's 19. Navy took
time out here. Wilson, swinging wide around Navy's left end, was
thrown for a loss of a yard by Wallace. Long threw a forward pass
to Ryan, who was brought down on Navy's 2 by Wallace. Wilson
smashed at the line, but was stopped by Antrim before he could
gain. Antrim was hurt on the play and Navy took him out. Craig
replaced Wilson in Army's backfield and Samuel replaced Sullivan. Case went in for Franks of the Navy. Craig smashed over
right tackle for a touchdown. Ryan failed to add a point with a
placement kick. It carried wide of the post.*
    Score—*Army 6, Navy 0.*

Those columns of small type sang like a ballad through my
consciousness, evoking the thud of padded bodies against each
other, the orchestrated roar of the smartly uniformed young men
in the stands, and the incessant drizzle over all. On the following
Monday that scene would be annotated for me, as it were, in my
father's column. He would have enriched the action on the field,
perhaps, with an account of the dialogue among the coaches and

West Point heroes of other years in the club car on the train returning to New York.

Radio played a large part in stimulating America's craze for spectator sports, but, curiously, the New York teams did not broadcast their games during most of the thirties. Living on the fringes of New England, however, I was able to pick up Boston games on my set. Thus, eleven times a year I heard Yankee games when they visited Fenway Park, and on other days I kept in touch with their fortunes as the Boston announcers relayed the inning-by-inning scores of the other big-league games. The Yankees were unyielding in their preservation of tradition. They held out against most innovations, disdaining night games and broadcasting as "bush league" until long after most other teams had introduced them.

In one sense this attitude widened my experience, because the Yankees at least thought that both night games and broadcasting were appropriate for their farm team in Newark. The Newark Bears had outstanding teams in those days, players like Charlie "King Kong" Keller, Joe Gordon, and Spud Chandler giving promise that pennants would be flying over Yankee Stadium for years to come. I remember my satisfaction in feeling a part of this process one day in 1937 when Pop took me into Joe McCarthy's office adjacent to the Yankee clubhouse. McCarthy sat at his desk, filling out his lineup card for the day. (I noticed that the famous Yankee pinstripes on his uniform, which looked black from the stands, were really a dark purple.) Oscar Vitt, who managed the Newark team, dropped by for a visit while we were there, and McCarthy asked him about Gordon.

"The kid has it all, Joe," Vitt told him. "He's going to be the best second baseman you ever saw."

Joe Gordon and his prowess were already familiar to me from the radio broadcasts, and I was able to nod as knowingly as Vitt in assuring McCarthy of the kid's worth.

Although I was too young to be admitted to a prizefight (sixteen being the minimum age for spectators), I could get in on the bloodletting via the radio that stood, gawky and top-heavy on its

spindly legs, just off our dining room. We were allowed to stay up
late for a big fight, and in those years a big fight almost always involved the shadowy, rather frightening figure of Joe Louis. When
my sister Mary disputed Pop's prediction that Louis would defeat
Max Schmeling in their return bout, he relaxed his standards for
the nonce to wager a nickel with her on the outcome. She looked
mildly shell-shocked after listening to the two minutes and four
seconds of mayhem Louis visited on her gladiator, but the next
morning she was pettish as she handed over the coin.

"Schmeling would have won," she asserted, with the losing
gambler's unfailing logic, "if Louis hadn't hit him so hard."

Mary's interest in sports spurred my own. Judy wasn't much
past the toddler stage then, and poor Jim, though sweet in both
looks and temperament, was just being recognized by our parents
as irremediably retarded, so Mary was often my only companion.
One summer we played a game called "jockeys." This boisterous
diversion consisted of galloping imaginary horses (in the style
later adopted by Monty Python's knights in pursuit of the Holy
Grail) up and down the driveway while shouting vulgarisms at
the country air. No one would have confused us with the devil's
children at play. Because our parents never let an unchaste expression escape their lips, and the rural school was pretty tame, our
repertory was so meager that we soon cast about for other amusements.

I turned to the sedentary pastime of collecting baseball cards, a
more suitable hobby, considering my inclinations, than philately.
Each card cost a penny and came wrapped in colored paper with
a pinkish, usually stale and brittle square of chewing gum. On one
side of the card was an illustration, purporting to be the likeness
of a big-league player, and on the other a brief account of his
career. My aim was to possess cards depicting all the Yankees.
Each purchase was a gamble, however, the identity of the player
concealed until the purchaser had put down his penny and unwrapped the package: my Yankee collection remained incom-
plete while my card box (and my consciousness) teemed with
names like Milt Gaston, Fabian Kawalik, Fabian Gaffke, Billie

Urbanski, and Jim Walkup. I even acquired an Eddie "Doc" Farrell, the ball-playing dentist, who was a good friend of Dave Sloman, our own dentist in Stamford.

Pickings at the local store, I soon realized, were slim. But one evening my father came home from New York with the ultimate birthday present—a box of one hundred baseball cards. I unwrapped them with high expectations, only to find that twenty-eight of them were Horace Fords. Ford had departed from the majors in 1933 after a long and undistinguished career as an infielder in the National League, and the gum company apparently was trying urgently to reduce its inventory.

Fortunately, Mary took an interest in the cards, and I was able to swing some deals with her. She preferred good-lookers, especially those in whom she thought she detected a resemblance to Nelson Eddy. Mary wasn't simpleton enough to have any Horace Fords palmed off on her, but I was able to unburden myself of a number of smiling, wavy-haired journeymen and pick up a Yankee here and there in return. Her craving for a Mel Ott became so intense that I profited handsomely from the transaction, and when she had salted him away somewhere, he immediately became her real-life hero and the Giants her favorite team. This development yielded me a further dividend. I was able now to conform to the highest standards of fandom, having found not only a team to root for but also one to loathe.

The baseball cards likewise confirmed in me a fan's devotion to statistics. I don't mean adulation for some superb performance ("He hit .393 that year! Wow!") but figures for figures' sake. Turning over cards and reading the capsule biographies, I grew just as interested in, let's say, Milt Gaston's record of two victories and thirteen defeats with the also-ran Red Sox in 1931 as in Lefty Grove's 31–4 record with the pennant-winning Athletics in the same year. Two and thirteen—it summoned up a picture of long, hopeless days in Fenway Park, with base hits rattling off the wall, which was a part of baseball, too. Each of those thirteen defeats (and the two victories as well) meant something to me: one game among the thousands that had already been played in baseball's history, with its hits, runs, and errors, each in turn going into the record books and enriching that history.

Here was baseball's ecology. The two-base hit that a batter wallops at Fenway Park this year is related to all of the other two-base hits made there in past years. Perhaps someday a broadcaster will announce to his audience, "Well, fans, that breaks the record for extra-base hits against a right-handed pitcher in Fenway Park for a single game. The original record was set against Milt Gaston way back in 1931." Then, again, maybe he won't. But, in any event, the hits and runs, the wins and losses, were in the record books for keeps, as deathless as Elizabethan sonnets. This is how one boy measured permanence. Every play of every game took on relevance within the 154-game season. When, in the early 1960s, the game's Procrustean leaders tampered with that structure to fit it to their expansion plans, stretching the season onto its new, 162-game frame, they wrenched sixty years of baseball out of focus. Roger Maris' sixty-first home run was hit outside the framework of the Babe's sixty, and the asterisk that accompanied it into the record books was as abasing as the scarlet letter.

Another reflection on the psychology of the fan: Grantland Rice and the One Great Scorer represent the sportsman's point of view, not that of the rabid rooter. It isn't how you play the game, at all. There is no such thing as a boring game, or even dirty tricks, when the rooter's side is winning. Action, controversy, colorful antics, are of no moment, the suspense of what will happen is the only thing that matters. Even an outrageously lopsided game is no bore to the true devotee on the winning side; one either enjoys the rout immensely or bites one's fingernails at the dreadful possibility of blowing such an enormous lead. I saw a number of games as an adolescent, listened to a great many more on the radio, and savored every Yankee victory. Some were tight pitching duels; others were won with thrilling, last-minute rallies. But after all those years, the game that sticks in my mind as the most pleasurable of all was the second game of the 1936 World Series. I sat in the upper right-field stands at the Polo Grounds and watched the Yankees demolish the hated Giants by the incredible—the delicious—score of 18–4. All of my heroes weighed in with damaging blows, so the satisfaction was complete.

Parents, educators, and child psychologists are constantly in a dither about the effects of all this sterile passion on young minds, and if it persists into adulthood, even the neighbors begin to wonder, Is it good or bad? What does it all mean? Although reams of prose have been written in attempts to shed light on the subject, I think that Joe H. Palmer, the *Herald Tribune*'s incomparable racing writer, made as much sense in as few words as anybody.

"The theory here," Palmer wrote, "is that an intense interest in any sport, and perhaps in any hobby, is a form of escapism, an attitude of mind of which this department is heartily in favor. Persons who find the world a little big and disheveled and are either unable or unwilling to cope with it can retreat to a microcosm, a smaller world inhabited by a few hundred ball players or a few hundred stables, a world in which the paths are pretty well charted and the patterns fairly stable. These small, comfortable worlds are not threatened with the H-bomb, or with subversive groups or water shortages, and life within them is cleaner and more sanely ordered than life outside."

What impact did my own excessive interest in sports have on my life? It certainly narrowed my outlook, closing me off from many experiences, a pattern that I reacted against later on. But in one sense my febrile interest in the Yankees proved a security blanket all through my adolescence. I was seldom tortured by the pangs of inferiority. No matter what else went wrong in my life— imagined slights at home or in school, inadequacies in studies or athletics—my team was invariably a winner, and I wrapped myself spiritually in the security of that pinstriped pelt. I fed on the accounts of my heroes' victories, as the hunter on the flesh of a tiger, and absorbed some of their strength. What would have happened had my team been the Browns or the Braves? ("I'm a Yankee fan, but you're an Athletic supporter," I used to wisecrack to a young friend from Philadelphia.) I might have ended up besieged by insecurities, in the hands of a shrink. As it was, I have never harbored much sympathy for underdogs. God, I became convinced early in life, is on the side of the big battalions, and so was I. (Someone with a bent for grantsmanship ought to make a study of American men—their insecurity or aggressiveness, their humility or insufferable pride, etc.—based on the teams they rooted for as adolescents.)

In college football, I settled for tradition. We were practically Connecticut residents then, and on several Saturday afternoons every fall we drove over to New Haven to watch Yale play its ivied rivals. The Merritt Parkway had not yet been opened, so we picked up friends in Stamford and drove up the Post Road, then cut across backcountry to the Yale Bowl. We always packed a picnic lunch in a large basket and ate in the parking lot before the game, standing around the car. I believe it was at the Yale Bowl that "tailgate" picnic lunches first became popular among football fans.

Yale was by no means a football powerhouse, but few schools in the country could claim such a long history of outstanding football. That history went back to the last century and the heroics of Pudge Heffelfinger, almost the prototype of the All-America player, and the "inch men"—stalwarts of the line who were said to have given ground against the enemy only inch by inch. In the period when I began to take an interest in its fortunes, Yale was graced by two of the most extraordinary college players of the decade, Larry Kelley and Clint Frank. Kelley won the Heisman Trophy as the outstanding player in the country in 1936, and Frank succeeded him as the trophy's winner in 1937. Kelley played end, where he was a fine defensive lineman and a superior pass receiver, but he built his reputation as an "opportunist." An extremely alert athlete, he seemed always to be at the right place in a moment of crisis, whether that meant settling under a long forward pass in the end zone or falling on somebody else's fumble. (This was an era of limited substitution, when football players were just that—football players—and not specialists restricted to either offensive or defensive duties.) But the play that brought Coach Ducky Pond's 1936 Yale team a dramatic victory in Baltimore over Navy, and Kelley national attention, was, Kelley stoutly maintained, purely accidental.

Coming back from Baltimore on the Yale special they were talking, naturally, of the Navy game and somebody asked if anyone in the group had the statistics.

"I have," somebody else said. "We outpunted them and ran punts back further. But they outfumbled us—and we outkicked them on fumbles."

Droll—but true. It was the story, in its essence, of a game that reached its outlandish climax in a play that brought victory to Yale and heartbreak to Navy. For Navy had counted very heavily on winning the Yale game and was winning it when Larry Kelley kicked it out of the Middies' reach.

"Give us credit," Ducky Pond said, with a grin. "We are the first team in the East to use that play."

The play at Baltimore came in the third period with Navy leading, 7 to 6. Tony Mott of Yale punted and Sneed Schmidt of Navy fumbled the ball at his own 20 yard line. Kelley, who had been covering punts skillfully all afternoon, was down the field under this one and joined in the frantic pursuit of the bounding ball. Accidentally—or so it seemed to you and so Kelley later said—he kicked it toward Navy's goal line and then chased it and kicked it up on the 2 yard line and rushed across the goal line. Of course, the ball was brought back to the 2 yard line, but in two plunges Clint Frank put it over and that was the ball game.

There were some who thought the Yale captain kicked the ball deliberately. This is because Kelley has a hair-trigger mind and can think of a lot of things in a split second. But the mental picture you carried away from that thrilling moment was of Kelley running and the ball bobbing right into the middle of his stride so that he couldn't have avoided kicking it. And for all the drama of the play and the sudden, downward sweep of Navy's fortunes, there popped into your mind a memory of the forgotten clown, Marcelline, who used to convulse Hippodrome audiences with his trick of stooping over to pick up a rolling ball and, in feigned awkwardness, kicking it out of his own reach.

But it was Clint Frank, not Larry Kelley, who became my football hero. Frank was a pile-driving running back who took on the characteristics of a jackrabbit once he shook off tacklers at the line of scrimmage. He called the team's plays in the huddle, had a strong, accurate passing arm, blocked acceptably, and tackled as ferociously as an All-Pro middle linebacker. (I have checked this estimate—admittedly the effusions of an aging man ranting about his boyhood hero—with newspaper accounts of the time, and it seems to hold up.) I had read a feature story about Frank somewhere, and he turned out to be a player I could identify with: quiet, an earnest student, and afflicted with weak eyes, so that he had to wear glasses off the field. I hadn't started wearing glasses then, but I suspected that before long somebody would notice my squint and I would be fitted for ignominy. Soon Frank's picture, autographed to me, went up on my wall beside Lou Gehrig's. It was one of those traditional photographs they take of Yale captains—Frank backed against a fence in front of a painted background with a football tucked under his arm. It was even larger than my sister's autographed picture of Nelson Eddy.

I spent some memorable afternoons in the Yale Bowl during the 1937 season. Larry Kelley was gone, but Yale had a strong backfield built around Frank and a passable front line. They beat Cornell, 9–0, in a steady drizzle as Frank ran 68 yards for the game's only touchdown, but he must share that day in my memory with Brud Holland, who was the first Negro athlete I ever saw. There were no black athletes in my local school circles, certainly (unbelievably, it must seem to anyone today) none in major-league baseball, and none that had ever come within my ken in football. Holland was impressive in his team's defeat, smashing through several times from his position at end to dump Yale's ballcarriers in the backfield. Apparently his appearance at the Bowl was a novelty to others besides myself, for the subhead over my father's story of the game in that evening's *Sun* read:

HOLLAND, NEGRO END, WAGES
STRONG BATTLE FOR ITHACANS
BEFORE 40,000 CROWD

A week later, Yale played a good Dartmouth team and was leading at the end of three placid quarters, 2–0, having trapped a back in the end zone early in the game. Then, high excitement welled up. One of Frank's passes was intercepted by Dartmouth's Bob MacLeod, who ran it back 77 yards for a touchdown. Dartmouth was soon hammering at the Yale goal again, gaining a first down with less than a yard to go for a touchdown, but the line held and Dartmouth settled for a field goal. As the minutes ran out, Frank led a Yale charge down the field. He completed a pass for a first down at the Dartmouth 35-yard line. His next three passes were batted away from potential receivers. On fourth down, with only seconds to play, he passed to a speedy back named Al Hessberg for a touchdown. A player named Gil Humphrey, whom even I had never heard of, was rushed into the game to tie the score with a placekick. That the spectacle ruffled even Pop's declared neutrality can be seen in the account he wrote for his column on the following Monday.

"How could he miss—with 72,000 people kicking that ball for him?" asked Gregory LaCava, the movie director, who was sitting behind you in the press box.

That was the way you felt about it, too. That even the Dartmouth rooters wanted to see him kick it. A lone kid, standing out there on the field, looking at the ball and at the goal posts, and 72,-000 persons standing, breathless, and looking at him. What a spot for a kid to be in! The fellows in the press box are hard-boiled. But the fellows in the press box stopped banging their typewriters or chattering to their telegraph operators and sat there looking down on the field at that kid getting ready to kick. And the kid walked up and kicked the ball over the bar ... and everybody in the Bowl went crazy for a moment ... including the hard-boiled fellows in the press box.

Just a moment in a college football game. But a moment like that never will come again into the life of Gil Humphrey ... and maybe never again into the lives of those who looked on. It was a moment in which the world beyond the rim of the Bowl stood still. And all that mattered was that Humphrey should kick the goal.

Silly? Maybe. But you hope not. Because you believe that the moment in which a seemingly hopelessly beaten fighter gets off the floor to flatten his opponent with a punch . . . or a horse coming out of nowhere roars through the stretch and sticks his nose under the wire first . . . or a hitter with two strikes on him and two out and a couple of runs needed to tie the game or win hits a home run . . . or a kid from Cleveland steps out and kicks a goal after touchdown in the Yale Bowl on a glorious fall afternoon . . . is a moment never to be forgotten and that the very memory of it enriches your life.

And if you still haven't made out a case for yourself, all you can say is that if the time comes when you don't get a bang out of things like that you will give up and go home.

Two weeks later I saw Frank play for the last time. Under a cold, bleak sky he put on one of those exhibitions that old Yalies still babble about, running for four touchdowns to lead his team to a 26–0 rout of Brown. Yale's final game, of course, was against Harvard, and it was played in Cambridge. I tuned in the old radio in Lewisboro on that Saturday afternoon, and settled in serenely for the season's climactic victory, which by now, as a veteran Yankee fan, I had come to expect. But Yale, I learned that day, was not the Yankees, or even Notre Dame. Although Frank played brilliantly, scoring Yale's only touchdown and making half the tackles for his side, Harvard's better-balanced team walked off with the victory. I don't think I have ever again experienced the defeat of a favorite team so keenly. When I worked for the Dodgers later on, we suffered a few defeats that can only be described as dillies, for no one could lose quite so heartrendingly as the Dodgers, but by then I was an adult somewhat inured to slings and arrows, and I was surrounded by equally stricken comrades from whom I could take comfort. But on that fall day in 1937, I was a twelve-year-old boy sitting alone by the radio in a big country house, and the full weight of that defeat seemed to fall heavily on my ill-prepared shoulders. I might have reflected that my hero, Clint Frank, probably felt lousy about it, too, though on second thought he at least had had the satisfaction of playing a whale of a game. I didn't even win my letter.

I never sat by that radio again. My grandaunt Nellie had died, my mother had wearied of the midnight drives to the Stamford railroad station, and the Grahams' financial picture had brightened. That fall we moved to New Rochelle, New York, a suburban city where we rented a white frame house on a quiet residential street. Although I still planned to attend Yale when the time came, I thought I had left the rest of that vicarious adventure behind me. Then, one Saturday morning, when Pop had taken my brother to the barber, the front doorbell rang. I answered the door and was confronted by a dark-haired, broad-shouldered young man wearing spectacles.

"Are you Frank Graham, Jr.?" he asked.

"Yes."

"Hello," he said, sticking out his hand. "My name is Clint Frank."

Well, you could have knocked me— In any case, I pulled myself together, shook hands, and at last summoned the presence of mind to ask him in. Frank explained that Joe Stevens, Jr., whose father was a member of the family of caterers who serviced the New York ball parks, was a friend and classmate of his at Yale. He had been visiting young Joe and his parents, who also lived in New Rochelle. Somehow talk had come around to my father, and Joe, knowing of my enthusiasm for Yale and for Clint Frank, had suggested he stop at our house on his way out of town. I haven't the faintest recollection of what we talked about, if anything. I remember only that I kept hoping my father would come home, not only to share this moment with me but to keep the conversation going. I guess my hero and I soon ran out of things to say to each other, because he left before my father returned.

Pop's absence, however, did allow me a moment of true satisfaction. When he and Jimmy came in, he asked if everything had been quiet. I shrugged and, in what I hoped was a matter-of-fact voice, replied, "Clint Frank stopped by to say hello."

Chapter Eleven
Father and Son

Some time after the *Sun*'s demise in 1950, Charles Addams drew a cartoon for *The New Yorker* in which a lone pedestrian stands, mouth agape, on a deserted nighttime street in Manhattan as a *Sun* delivery truck dashes past. Rolling along in its ghostly aura, the truck is a kind of Flying Dutchman. I think Addams caught something there, the restless spook forever roaming those streets, which are, in a sense, pathways through the minds of thousands of old newspapermen. Like the Dodgers and the original Metropolitan Opera House, the *Sun* haunted its surviving admirers long after it had ceased to exist.

Even before World War II, the *Sun* was an anachronism. It was a clean, airy paper—no jumble, like the proliferating tabloids and yellow journals—and for all its managerial conservatism, it presented to its readers a more inviting page than the stodgy type and layouts then favored by the *Times*. Yet, while the other afternoon papers in the city were pawns in extensive newspaper chains, like those owned by Hearst and Scripps-Howard, the *Sun* was still run as a family-owned business with managers and methods pegged to the past.

Although most of its rivals were produced by members of the Newspaper Guild, the *Sun* had created its own innocuous in-house labor union, and the wages it paid were consequently among the lowest in the business. Philosophically, this suited my father. He had no serious quarrel with big labor, believing that big business was getting only what its rapacity deserved, but he was not a joiner. Newspapermen should not tie themselves up with unions, he argued. Part of his stand was based on a belief that the unions would eventually help to kill the newspaper business as he knew and loved it. He agreed with one of his journalistic heroes, H. L. Mencken, that "it is one thing to sass a cruel city editor with, so to speak, the naked hands, and another thing to confront him from behind a phalanx of government agents and labor bravos." But Pop also had a gut fear that someone might stick him on a picket line. I occasionally saw him express disapproval, even anger, at the behavior of other people, but the only open contempt I ever saw come over him was at the sight of men and women parading the sidewalk with signs on their chests. That sort of action, he believed, was beneath a professional's dignity.

In accordance with these principles, he resolutely went out and worked a little harder to support his family. Some of his colleagues had turned to magazine writing to supplement their incomes and had done very well at it, even forsaking their newspaper jobs in the end to enter more lucrative careers writing for the big national periodicals. More often, the shift from writing news stories and columns to longer articles for magazines confounded veteran newspapermen. Pop belonged to the latter category. Although magazines were to figure in his future, he was neither happy nor very successful writing within their impersonal framework. He had tuned his skills to the length—a thousand to fifteen hundred words—of the daily newspaper column. This was his lyric art. Like the sonneteer who fails in the attempt to write an epic poem, my father found himself, in most cases, uncomfortable within the roomier province of the magazine article. He tended, then, to write inflated columns, attaining the desired wordage by tacking on anecdotes and comment as if they were afterthoughts.

Grantland Rice provided him with the ideal alternative. Rice was more than a sportswriter; he was an institution in sports, a courtly, literate, and beloved father figure to both newspapermen and athletes. Yet he was curiously unaware of the prerogatives of such eminence. One fall afternoon, as he and my father arrived together at the ball park in St. Louis for a World Series game, Rice stopped in dismay.

"Damn, I don't have my press ticket for the game," he said. "Maybe I can still buy a ticket to get in."

"Hold on," Pop said. "I think I can get you in."

He walked up to the gate attendant, displayed his own press ticket, and said, "This is Grantland Rice behind me. He doesn't have the right ticket for the game. Can you let him in?"

The man's eyes shone. "Mr. Rice," he said excitedly, shaking him by the hand. "It's a pleasure to meet you. My wife won't believe this when I tell her I met you today. Come in! Come in!"

At the entrance to the press box, they went through the same formula. Rice followed my father in, shaking his head.

"You've got a lot of friends here, Frankie," he said. "I never could have got in without you!"

Rice wrote a syndicated column called "The Spotlight" that appeared in the *Sun* and many other newspapers around the country. As its popularity increased during the thirties, he was persuaded to create a series of film shorts bearing the same title, covering golf, fishing, and other sports. This venture began to take more and more of his time, and at length he asked my father to write his column for him several days a week. I think Pop derived a certain satisfaction from seeing his prose appear regularly under the great man's name, and, of course, it provided a welcome supplement to his weekly check from the *Sun*.

After we moved closer to the city and I had entered my early teens, my father took me with him more often as he made his rounds of the ball parks, the Garden, and his office. The *Sun* stood on the northeast corner of the intersection of Broadway and Chambers Street, just across from City Hall. We usually entered by a side door on Chambers Street, walking across from the subway exit, then climbed to the second floor of the old building, along a corridor—sharp with the smell of ink, paper, and glue (glue pots adorned the desks of all the editors and rewrite men, who used it to paste up copy on yellow sheets of paper)—and into the sports department. My father's popularity among the staff was apparent; he was always greeted amiably by everyone we met on the way, from copyboys and composing-room workers to the paper's nabobs.

The sports department, like the building itself, was not prepossessing. Light entered through its tall windows, each bearing the paper's title head, *The Sun,* in Old-English type. Teletypes clattered; wooden desks and chairs were placed along the walls. Several of the other writers were apt to be in the office, working on their next afternoon's stories amid the hubbub ("Where's my goddamned hat?" "Here's the final from St. Louis—Dodgers lose!"). Eddie Murphy, who covered the Dodgers, was one of my favorites. He was a slender, light-haired man, afflicted like my father with a bum eye. He had a bright smile and a knack for witty remarks ("Overconfidence cost the Dodgers sixth place" was his), which my father urged him to sprinkle through his copy. But he apparently thought such liberties not in the *Sun's* style, and most of his *bon mots* have been lost to posterity.

The sports staff ran the gamut of outlook. The boxing writer was a silent partner of Al Weill, the manager. He covered the out-of-town bouts of the fighters in Weill's stable and, often being the only New York reporter in attendance, assured readers in the Big Town of his boy's spectacular showing if he won, or of the judges' incompetence if he lost. Boxing, in fact, was the soft underbelly of most sports departments at the time. Promoters kept some of the writers enthusiastic about their promotions through the liberal use of undercover payoffs, and since there was no way to prove corruption, the practice flourished for a long time. The only participant I ever heard of coming to grief was an employee of Madison Square Garden who feathered his own nest by listing Grantland Rice, Frank Graham, and other "name" writers as among those he was paying off. The young man's bosses, however, aware that those writers could not be bought, inquired about the destination of the expense money and learned he had pocketed it himself.

At the other end of the scale was George Trevor, who covered football. Football, for Trevor, meant Yale, and he was totally self-absorbed and often the source of either excitement or hilarity in the sports department. On one occasion he slipped his lighted pipe into a side pocket of his jacket, setting off a minor conflagration. On another occasion he took off his new seersucker jacket, draped it carefully over the back of his chair, and then absent-mindedly slid his chair back and forth over the bottom of the jacket, which reached to the floor, so that by the time he had finished writing his story, the jacket's hem was simply a ragged fringe.

One day in February, 1942, Trevor came into the office as usual to write his story. He settled himself at a desk, retreated into his thoughts, and laboriously began writing out his copy in longhand, as he always did. While he was at work, his colleagues were in a dither because of the news that the great French liner *Normandie* was afire at its berth across town. All afternoon, people rushed in and out of the office, alerting each other to the latest bulletins on the catastrophe. Trevor never lifted his head. At day's end, his phone rang. He picked it up, gasped in astonishment at the news his wife had just given him, and leaped to his feet.

"Gentlemen!" he screamed. "The *Normandie* is on fire!"

Pop was not immune to the office pranksters. Although he did not begrudge his fellows an off-color story or a vulgar remark, his own language was nearly as prim as a Victorian maiden's. A mildly blasphemous expletive was the most he ever permitted himself. One day he handed in his copy, in which he had described Pepper Martin of the Cardinals as "built like a brick smokehouse." The copy was duly set in type, but the boys in the sports department also had their friends in the composing room run off a proof with the word "smokehouse" transformed into an inelegant substitute. They encircled the offending word in red pencil, stuffed it into his mail slot with a purported summons to appear before the managing editor, and waited for him to come into the office later that day. His dismay at what he thought must have been some incomprehensible slip on his part was so great that not even the hard-hearted pranksters could keep from letting him in quickly on the deception.

A little later on, my father was himself guilty of perpetrating a different kind of "pornography." Henry Armstrong was one of his favorite fighters. He felt a genuine affection toward him, and often sat around with him in the dressing room in the gym, listening to him talk about his early days in the small fight clubs. In one column Pop's affection overflowed so that he referred to Armstrong throughout as "Little Black Sambo." This time the summons to the managing editor was in earnest. The editor of the *Amsterdam News*, Harlem's leading newspaper, had complained in print about the *Sun*'s apparent approval of a racial slur. My father was genuinely astonished. *Little Black Sambo* was a book he had often read to delighted children in his own home, and he had found both the story and the chief character immensely appealing. Later Pop carried his puzzlement to Armstrong. Henry assured him that it was a nice column, but that endorsement didn't soothe any ruffled feelings up on 125th Street, and the gaffe was not repeated.

Even more exciting for me than a visit to the *Sun*'s sports department was an afternoon at Yankee Stadium. I had long since passed the time when I preferred watching monkeys and llamas to big-league ball players. When my father was going to the ball park on a weekend or during the school summer vacation, he usually asked me to go along. If the Polo Grounds or Ebbets Field was the only alternative, I would go anyway, but Yankee Stadium was my shrine. We took the New Haven Railroad from New Rochelle to the 125th Street station, and then entered the subway for the trip back uptown to 161st Street. The train rumbled along underground for most of the trip, then began to climb, the wheels screeching as it went into a curve at the last moment and suddenly burst into daylight. And there in the early afternoon sun loomed the light-beige arena. I never came upon the Stadium like that without my heart beating a little faster. A few years later, when I first read Hemingway's short story "The Snows of Kili-manjaro," I experienced a quiver of recognition:

"Then they began to climb and they were going to the East it seemed, and then it darkened and they were in a storm, the rain so thick it seemed like flying through a waterfall, and then they were out and Compie turned his head and grinned and pointed and there, ahead, all he could see, as wide as all the world, great, high, and unbelievably white in the sun, was the square top of Kiliman-jaro."

We always made a quick stop in Manager Joe McCarthy's of-fice adjacent to the Yankees clubhouse, then walked along the dim runway and up a short flight of wooden steps (concrete or metal offered no grip to the players' spiked shoes) to the dugout. I saw the field from a strange perspective, standing below ground level and looking out to the broad green expanse where batting prac-tice was going on. It was hard at first to be completely at ease sit-ting there on the cushioned bench, especially if my father left me alone for a few minutes to have a word with someone at the other end of the dugout. Big, broad-shouldered men in pinstripes came clattering down the wooden floor, forcefully pounding a gnarled hand into a mitt ("Shaking hands with an old catcher is like stick-ing your hand into a bag of peanuts," somebody once said), turn-ing to shout friendly insults at a visiting player across the field, or acknowledging my presence with a nod and a deep-voiced "Hello, son." These were men I had—well, if not precisely wor-shiped, then greatly admired, from afar. Men like Bill Dickey, George Selkirk, Tommy Henrich, Red Ruffing, Red Rolfe, even Myril Hoag, the outfielder who, I had read in "The Old Scout," wore the smallest shoe in baseball. Now these men were all around me.

Only once was I completely discomfited. I was sitting by myself on the Yankees' bench one afternoon watching batting practice when my view was suddenly obscured by Tony Lazzeri.

"How'd you like to suit up and shag some flies out there?" he was asking me.

I was too stunned to answer. Tony stood there looking down at me, his great, broad face something like the faces of the Chinese soldiers I had seen in newsreels, but sadder.

"I'll get a batboy's uniform for you," he said.

"No," I said, shaking my head stubbornly. I had a frightening vision of being hit on the head by a fly ball and carried off the field in front of thousands of people. Dreams of glory are seldom spun by a pessimist.

"Whatsa matter?" Tony persisted. "Don't you like baseball?"

"I like baseball," I assured him.

"Then why don't you wanta get out there and shag a few?"

I certainly was not going to tell him. I simply shook my head and that was that. After a few minutes, Lazzeri, looking sadder than ever, gave up and went away. But once in a while he would see me at the Stadium and he would ask me, teasing, if I would like to "shag a few." I am ashamed to admit that, though he was my father's favorite Yankee, I was not wholly desolate when Lazzeri was packed off to the Cubs at the end of the 1937 season.

My father's column has helped me to relive that day when the Yankees came north in 1938 and I sat on the bench listening to the team's funnyman, Lefty Gomez, and watching the first appearance in New York of Joe Gordon, the young second baseman whose baseball education in Newark I had followed over the radio. Gordon had already been proclaimed Lazzeri's successor.

Joe McCarthy sat near one end of the Yankee dugout, greeting newspapermen, being pleasant to everybody . . . but never taking his eyes off the field. The young man at bat in batting practice had the number six on his back. An unfamiliar face.

"Gordon," McCarthy said. "He's a good ball player. He'll hit pretty well, too. He has a lot of power, if he can just hook it up. But watch him handle the ball. He can make a double play better than anybody I've seen in a long while."

"I knew you'd like that," a newspaperman said.

McCarthy grinned and nodded. The double play is almost an obsession with him. And not since he has been managing the Yankees has he had a good double play combination.

"He's very fast," Joe said. "Comes in on a ball fast and then

stops suddenly and gets it away. He made a play the other day that was a honey. The ball was hit far to his left and looked like a sure base hit, because it was a slow hit ball. But he charged over and stopped short and picked up the ball and just gave it to Gehrig, like this."

You could almost see him getting the ball to Gehrig at short range.

"I don't mean that he won't boot some balls," Joe said.

"But he'll boot 'em hustling, eh?" a newspaperman said.

"Yes," Joe said, "and he'll boot some easy ones, too. I don't want to say anything to him about slowing down a little. I don't want him to become deliberate. He'll rate himself after a while."

Vernon Gomez stood up and peered over the roof of the dugout. Paul Krichell, a Yankee scout, was standing in a box just back of the dugout.

"There's Paul Krichell, who scouts for the Yankees," Gomez said, loudly enough for Krichell to hear.

Krichell grinned.

"He can't recommend anybody that hasn't graduated from college," Gomez said.

Krichell, among his other duties, reports on college players.

"How did you come to overlook Hank Greenberg?" Gomez asked.

It is well known that Krichell recommended Greenberg, and the Yankees wanted to sign him, but Greenberg finally turned them down and signed with Detroit because he didn't want to sit by for years waiting for Gehrig to wear out.

"I don't know," Krichell said. "But that's nothing. I overlooked you, too."

"Maybe it was just as well," Gomez said.

Krichell came down into the dugout and sat down next to McCarthy. Charlie Conlon, the veteran photographer who specializes in action photos of ball players, also came in and sat down, and the three of them fell to talking about the ball players of a few years back.

"They don't interest me," Gomez said. "I don't care if Cobb could hit a curve ball. He can't hit me any more. They tell me

Willie Keeler could hit the ball where they weren't, but he's a dead pigeon, too. The only fellows that interest me are fellows like Jimmy Foxx and Charlie Gehringer and Greenberg. I have to pitch against them."

A newspaperman came in the dugout. He was hatless and his hair was mussed,

"Go home and comb your hair," Gomez said.

"I don't look as funny as you will in a little while," the newspaperman said. "You're going to be scalped."

"It won't be the first time," Gomez said. "You should have seen me pitch in New Orleans last week. I was over at third base backing up throws from the outfield so often I wanted to pitch from there. It would have been easier than pitching from the box and then running over there after every pitch."

Chapter Twelve
The Hero

My finest moments were passed in the dugout when Lou Gehrig came to sit with my father and me. He spoke easily, in a pleasantly husky voice tinged with a New York accent. Shy and self-effacing when he had first come to the Yankees from Columbia, he never acquired the cockiness that often accompanies athletic success; instead, a mild, almost scholarly confidence radiated from him. I cannot remember that we ever talked with each other, beyond casual greetings. That he knew my name was sufficient for me. We had our picture taken by a *Sun* photographer as we stood together on the steps of the Yankee dugout, Gehrig showing me his powerful grip on a bat while I wore his cap and remained at a loss for words. He gave me the cap, which I found to my chagrin was too small for me. I suppose he was a bullet head, whereas I was a round head.

Later on he gave my father one of his old first baseman's mitts to bring home to me. Although it was a slightly sturdier piece of leather than my father's battered fielder's glove, no self-respecting Little Leaguer would choose such an inadequate mitt today. Fortunately, I was left-handed and, of course, a first baseman, so I could wear my hero's mitt even if I couldn't wear his cap. Word of my prize spread through New Rochelle, and presently I was invited to join a celebrated local team, composed of other thirteen-year-olds, called the Wykagyl Whackers. My glove and I were assigned to first base. Under the delusion that the glove, like Zeus's shield, imparted certain powers to its bearer, the manager went so far as to write my name into the cleanup slot in his batting order. One game served to relieve him of that delusion, and I was demoted to a slot more in keeping with my earnest poke-hitting. But I did cling to my job at first base until we Whackers outgrew our uniforms and the team was disbanded.

Still at the top of his form as 1938 began, Gehrig was the cleanup hitter in the new "Murderers' Row," as he had been in the group's prior incarnation, which included the Babe, a decade earlier. The Yankees had won world championships in 1936 and 1937, and now they were on their way to another one. I might have twisted Larry Doyle's ancient remark about the Giants to fit my own case: "It's great to be young and a Yankee fan." It was certainly a pleasure to read the papers every day, or to go to the Stadium and watch the Yankees assault the opposition. Perhaps the first piece of verse I ever learned of my own volition was this modest four-liner I found one day on the sports page of a New York tabloid:

> Ashes to ashes
> And dust to dust:
> If DiMag and Gehrig don't,
> Dickey must.

This preceded an account of the latest demonstration of the Yankees' "five-o'clock lightning," when the two great sluggers had failed to keep going on a late-inning rally, but then Dickey, following them in the batting order, had won the game with a towering home run. My pride in Gehrig's performance was magnified because I knew that whenever I looked at the paper, I would find his name in the box score. Other athletes took off now and then to recuperate from fatigue or injury, or even a batting slump. But the Iron Horse went on day after day, never having missed a game since that afternoon in 1925 when he took over at first base for the injured Wally Pipp. He played in his two thousandth consecutive game in 1938, and went rolling along. He was baseball's Old Man River.

My father was at the Stadium early that season when Gehrig took one turn in batting practice and then came in and sat in the dugout.

"What's the matter, Lou?" somebody said to him.

"I have a bad thumb," he said. "I think maybe the darn thing is broken."

"Are you going to stay out of the lineup?"

"I should say not," Lou said. "It isn't as bad as that. Oh, it hurts, but I can grip a bat and handle the ball all right, and there isn't any reason why I shouldn't play. I'll tell you this: If I wasn't going to play, you wouldn't see me sitting here. I'd be on my way home—or fishing or going to a show. You don't think I could sit here and watch the fellows play, do you?"

Hero worship, like other manifestations of passion, implies a possessive streak. I knew that Gehrig had other admirers and fans, but I was sure that none of them cared about his success quite as deeply as I did. When I overheard another boy talking about what a great ball player Gehrig was, I felt a certain satisfaction, as if I were included in the praise. Not that I ever "identified" with Gehrig, in the sense that I was up there hitting home runs with him. It was enough to sit in the stands and root intensely for him to come through. But in my concern for his fortunes, I shared in the praise for him as if I were a part of his family, or at least his "entourage."

Conversely, I was vulnerable to even his slightest misfortunes. I was embarrassed for him when he struck out or fumbled a grounder around first base. One afternoon when I was at the Stadium, Gehrig drove the ball to the deepest part of left field. He had the heavy legs of a fullback, and he rumbled around the bases

like a runaway truck. As he steamed into third base, Arthur
Fletcher, the Yankees' coach, waved him right on around the bag
to try for an inside-the-park home run. But Fletcher had miscal-
culated. The throw from the outfield reached the plate well before Gehrig, and the catcher was waiting with the ball to tag him
as he came in standing up. My adolescent outrage at Fletcher
knew no bounds. He had made my hero look bad in front of thousands of people, and I was close to tears.

But something went sour in 1938. Gehrig was no longer rattling
the fences with his long drives, or covering ground at first base, as
he had done in past seasons. He was in a "slump," the writers said.
"A touch of lumbago," Gehrig himself said, dismissing his failure
to get down quickly enough for a ground ball. Although the Yankees flattened the Cubs in four games in the World Series, Gehrig
played little part in their attack. Sometimes he met the ball solidly with his bat, but merely looped it over the infield. "Is he near
the end of his career?" I heard one of my father's friends ask, and
he got no reply. Or maybe I didn't want to hear it, because I was
at a stage of my life when I still hoped that mortality was selective.

Spring training, 1939, and Gehrig could not work himself into
condition. He looked, as some of the reporters wrote in their dis-
quieting stories, like a man who had aged overnight. "I think
there is something physically wrong with him," Jim Kahn, one of
the sportswriters, told my father. "I've seen ball players 'go' overnight, as Gehrig seems to have done. But they were simply
washed up as ball players. It's something deeper in this case, I
think." The Yankees played an exhibition game in Norfolk on the
way north, and Gehrig got four hits, two of them home runs, and
hope sprang up again. My father visited the Yankee dugout when
they played an exhibition game at Ebbets Field just before the
season opened.

*The day was gray and cold and the crowd was small, and in the
dugout Joe McCarthy sat with his hands in the pockets of his
windbreaker.*

"How's Gehrig?" the reporter asked.

McCarthy shook his head.

"I see he hit two home runs in Norfolk."

"He looked a little better there."

"Two home runs and two singles," the reporter said.

"The singles were all right," McCarthy said. "The home runs were fly balls over a short right-field fence."

The Yankees were going out for fielding practice.

"Watch Lou," McCarthy said.

Gehrig looked very bad. He would go down for a ground ball hit straight at him, and the ball would go through him. Or he would come up with the ball and throw it to second base and then start for first base to take a return throw, but he would be woefully slow. Back of first base, some fans jeered at him.

"Why don't you give yourself up?" one of them yelled. "What do you want McCarthy to do, burn that uniform off you?"

The reporter turned to McCarthy.

"He looks worse than I thought he would," he said. "What's the matter with him?"

"I don't know."

"Are you going to open the season with him?"

"Yes."

Gehrig opened the season at first base for the Yankees, just as he had for the last thirteen years, but he managed only four singles in twenty-eight times at bat. The Yankees took the train to Detroit, where they were to begin a swing through the West. After school that afternoon in New Rochelle, a classmate came up to me on the sidewalk, his face twisted in excitement.

"Didja hear the news?" he blurted. "Gehrig took himself out of the lineup."

I was too stunned to feel anything much. I didn't understand exactly what it meant, but I knew that this was not the usual benching of a tired or slumping athlete. Something had come to an end. The Iron Horse's string had been shattered, after 2130 consecutive games. The last play of the game just before the team left for the West had forced his hand. It was a simple play, a bouncing ball to the right of the mound. Johnny Murphy, a Yankee relief pitcher, had moved off the mound to field the ball and make the throw to first base. Gehrig, stumbling, painfully slow, had just managed to reach the bag in time to take the throw and end the game.

"I had a hard time getting back there," Gehrig said later. "I should have been there in plenty of time. And then, when I made the putout and started for the clubhouse, Murphy was waiting for me, and he said, 'Nice play, Lou.' That was it. The boys were feeling sorry for me. In a way, and not at all meaning to, Murphy told me when to quit."

Less than two months later, the world knew what had happened to Lou Gehrig. After giving him a thorough physical examination at the Mayo Clinic in Rochester, Minnesota, the doctors discovered that he was suffering from a crippling and incurable disease of the central nervous system. Amyotrophic lateral sclerosis, the doctors called it, though since then Gehrig, because of his celebrity, has joined that small group of men who attain a different kind of immortality by having dreadful diseases named after them.

Not long afterward, my father was talking to Dr. Maurice Keady, whom he had known for years as one of the most enthusiastic of Notre Dame's football fans and who had become our family doctor in New Rochelle. When Gehrig was mentioned, Keady made a face and said, "It's a death sentence, you know. Two to four years are all he's got."

My father never told me directly, but I picked up enough to realize, gradually, that Gehrig was a very sick man. His absence hardly dimmed my ardor for the Yankees. I still went to see them play as often as I could, which was more often now because I would invite my friends to take the train to New York with me and pick up passes in my father's name at the press gate. I didn't resent Gehrig's successor. Babe Dahlgren was a wonder to watch around first base, a graceful and almost flawless fielder, but at bat he had a penchant for raising high, catchable fly balls to deep center field, where the bleacher fence seemed to stand a couple of miles away, and he thus contributed little more to the attack than the stricken Lou. But I had a new slugger to root for that season—Charley "King Kong" Keller, a muscular, beetle-browed young man whose booming hits led the Yankees' rout of the Cincinnati Reds in the 1939 World Series. Having listened to all of the Series games on the radio, I raved about Keller when my father returned from Cincinnati.

"Do you think he'll be a better ball player than DiMaggio?" he asked me.

"Well, I think maybe he will be," I said, hedging a bit.

My father pursed his lips and shook his head. "Never," he said, mildly.

I caught glimpses of my old hero through the newspapers. His picture was in the papers when Mayor LaGuardia appointed him to New York City's parole board. And here he was in Pop's column, one day in the late spring of 1940, sitting in his business suit on the Yankee bench while the Cleveland Indians took batting practice and the Yankees clowned around him.

Gomez (handing Gehrig the bone with which the players hone their bats) — You think the Mayo Brothers are good, hey? Look what they took out of my shoulder at Johns Hopkins.

Gehrig — Wait till they start to work on your head.

Gomez — They looked at that, but decided they couldn't do anything about it.

(Ben Chapman takes his turn at the plate, hits a couple and starts for the dugout.)

Gomez — Hey, Chappie! How about you and I rooming together?

Chapman — How's that?

Gomez — When we go to the Browns.

Chapman — I don't care where I go so long as I get the money.

Earle Combs — Money won't do you any good when the war comes. They'll take it all away from you.

Chapman — If they take yours, they'll have to dig it up first.

Gomez — Hey, Feller! . . . Hey, Bob! . . . Hey, Bobby! . . . Hey, Mr. Feller!

Feller — Yes?

Gomez — If you think you're fast, wait till you see a blitzkrieg.

(*Rollie Hemsley, said to have mended his roistering ways, steps to the plate.*)

Gomez — *So you reformed, hey?*

Hemsley — *That's right.*

Gomez — *They tell me you quit riding on flat cars and only ride the rods on streamlined trains now.*

Hemsley — *All I ride on now is the wagon.*

Coach Johnny Schulte — *You can't have any fun on the wagon.*

Hemsley — *That's what I've found out.*

Gomez — *So you released Punching Bag, eh?*

Hemsley — *Yes.*

Combs — *Who's Punching Bag?*

Gomez — *Johnny Broaca* [*who used to pitch for the Yankees*].

Combs — *Where did he go?*

Gomez — *How should I know? Last year even J. Edgar Hoover couldn't find him.*

(*A reporter comes in and shakes hands with Gehrig.*)

Reporter — *I'm going to call you up one of these days and make a date to go in and see you.*

Gehrig — *Fine. I wish you would.*

Gomez — *Call Gehrig up? Did you ever try it? The first girl that answers the phone wants to know what your name is. The second one wants to know how old you are. The third one asks if you've ever been arrested. By the time you got to Gehrig, you don't care whether you talk to him or not.*

(*The Indians have finished their batting practice and begin their fielding practice. Most of the Yankees move out in front of the dugout and begin to warm up.*)

Gomez (*picking up a fungo stick*) — *Want to hear something? Get a load of Keller. I drive him nuts every day hitting fungoes to him. He quits after two or three. . . . Hey, Charley!*

(*Keller looks over and Gomez holds up the fungo stick.*)

Keller — *Oh, my God!*

Gomez — *What's the matter?*

Keller — *Why don't you let me alone and pick on somebody else?*

Gomez — *What do you want me to do, hit the ball right in your hands? The hitters don't hit the ball right in your hands, do they?*

Keller — Not when you're pitching.

Gomez — Well, I'm just getting you in shape to play the out-field the way it should be played when I'm pitching.

(In the Indians' fielding practice Henry Helf has taken Hems-ley's place as the catcher.)

Gehrig — Who's that big catcher?

(Gomez looks out on the field and shakes his head.)

Gomez — I don't know.

Gehrig — What's the matter with you—slowing up? I knew you when you knew every player in the league.

Gomez — This is only the second time I've seen the Indians this year. I didn't go to Cleveland.

Gehrig — How was that?

Gomez — I pitched in that exhibition game in Akron and they sent me home. Next week I'll pitch in Butler, Pennsylvania, and they'll send me home the next day. Let's see. We play in Butler on Wednesday. . . . What are you doing Thursday, Lou?

Reporter — You play in Butler on Thursday.

Gomez — We do? All right. What are you doing Friday, Lou?

(The ball game gets under way a little later, with Gomez still going strong. By the seventh inning he is going so strong in the dugout that Umpire Eddie Rommel hears what he is saying about a decision at second base in the previous inning and chases him.)

But every moment around Gehrig wasn't loaded with gaiety. One afternoon when my father was in the dugout, George Selkirk stomped in, grumbling about his hitting.

"You'll be all right, George," Gehrig, who was sitting there in the shadows, assured him. "Keep swinging."

"Lou, why don't you grab one of those bats and go up there and hit a few for me?" Selkirk said.

"I wish I could, George," Gehrig said. "I wish to God I could."

And on another afternoon, when Gehrig was leaving the ball park with Rud Rennie, a sportswriter on the *Herald Tribune*, a group of Boy Scouts on the sidewalk began to cheer him. Gehrig smiled and waved to them. Then he turned to Rennie.

[FRANK GRAHAM, JR.]

"They're cheering me," he said, "and I'm dying."

It was late one evening in June, 1941. My parents had company, and I was upstairs alone, listening to the radio. A voice broke in to say that Lou Gehrig was dead. I walked downstairs and told my father, hoping that I would not display any embarrassing emotion in front of the guests. My announcement broke up the party, because Pop had to rush down to the *Sun* and write a new column for the next day's paper. Everyone stood around, talking in low voices, while my father got ready to leave for the railroad station.

Death had touched me for the first time. In no generation before mine would it have been possible for anyone to grow to be sixteen years old without suffering some affecting, or even shattering, bereavement. John Keats, in a letter to Fanny Brawne, had made plain one of the enduring agonies of human life: "I have never known any unalloy'd Happiness for many days together; the death or sickness of some one has always spoilt my hours." My father's mother had died at his birth, but her absence had marked his childhood. My mother had lost her father in the vulnerability of her young girlhood. The few country cemeteries I had seen showed a generous sprinkling of tiny headstones among the larger ones.

I was a product of a time and a country when medical science was pushing death out of the adolescent's world, delaying the impact on the survivors (orphanages, even then, were anachronisms in middle-class America). Death had taken no member of my immediate family, or any of my classmates. I was part of the first generation that would, for the most part, receive these intimations of mortality from public life—from the assassination of a politician, the suicide of a movie star, the death of a hero, taken, as the newspapers said, in the prime of life.

That night, I remained the great stone face until my father had departed for the station. Then I went upstairs, undressed, and lay down on my bed, under my framed pictures of prizefighters and football players and baseball players. And I blubbered a little, not because I had loved the man who was dead but because something uniquely mine was gone for good.

152

Frank Graham, Sr. —"the kid" to his family—dressed for the role of a promising young sportswriter of the post–World War I era.

The photographer came up with an ornate idea for posing the wives of the players and writers during spring training, circa 1924. My mother is sixth from the right in this tableau. (Courtesy United Press International, Inc.)

Casey Stengel, an outfielder for the Giants in the twenties, is led off the field by the police after a dispute with opposing players. (Courtesy Photoworld / FPG.)

John McGraw, "Muggsy" to his foes, accepted this wildcat as a mascot from his admirers. (Courtesy Bettmann Archive, Inc.)

Press accommodations at a Giants' exhibition game in 1923 were not quite up to the sartorial elegance of the writers who occupied them. My natty father is at the far right.

Billy Soose, the college boy who was taken in hand by a film writer and went on to win the middleweight championship of the world.

Jim Braddock autographed this placidly pugnacious portrait for me after winning the heavyweight championship.

I gazed at my hero, but whatever advice Lou Gehrig offered never paid off for me at the plate.

One of Pop's heroes, Tony Lazzeri of the Yankees.

Toots Shor was the host at a party to celebrate the departure of Frank Graham, Sr., from the *Sun* for the job of sports editor at *Look* magazine. Willard Mullin, the leading sports cartoonist of his day, drew the spurious magazine cover.

(*Above*)   I put on my old sailor suit for a gag when Roger Donoghue (at right) visited Pop and me at home. (Photo by Michael Cipriano.)

(*Below*)   My father joined one of his old heroes, Jack Dempsey, at some long-forgotten banquet.

During my brief existence as a sandlot entrepreneur I "sold" tickets for a benefit game to Dodger catchers Roy Campanella and Bruce Edwards.

Jackie Robinson on occasion conducted his radio program from Ebbets Field. Here he interviews a royal visitor, King Faisal II of Iraq, as Irving Rudd and I look on. (Photo by Barney Stein.)

Pop receives the James J. Walker Memorial Award for Meritorious Service to Boxing while heavyweight champ Floyd Patterson displays an award of his own.

Pop (right) and Red Smith, 1 and 1A, at Saratoga, where the former hoped to be buried in the infield. (*Life* magazine photo by Walter Osborne.)

(*Above*)   The Dodgers' old DC-3 before heading for spring training, carrying writers and club officials. Frank Frisch is third from left, I am second from right. When we deplaned, an airport bystander muttered, "No wonder they blew the pennant!"

(*Below*)   The Dodgers come to the dugout steps as Gladys Goodding, the Ebbets Field organist, plays the national anthem. I stand at right, holding a bulky envelope of press releases. (Photo by Barney Stein.)

Chapter Thirteen
Fight Night at the Garden

In 1939 I was a baby-faced fourteen, too immature to talk my way into a girlie show at the World's Fair that summer but, under my father's aegis, old enough to be admitted to a far more depraved spectacle: the merciless beating of an almost defenseless man by another man who was said to be his friend. I was shaken, but fascinated.

No fighter in history had made such a psychological impact on his opponents or on the public as Joe Louis. Several of his victims, pasty-faced and quivering, had to be prodded from the dressing room, like some drugged wretch on his way to the gallows, to face the awful lightning in those fists. Other, less imaginative foes climbed through the ropes with a show of bravado that soon congealed under Louis' cold stare. To catch the crowd's attention, almost every prominent modern champion has exploited a special facet of his personality: rowdiness, erudition, braggadocio, amiability, surliness, even comic volubility. The public aspect of Joe Louis, his inscrutability, was the most effective of all.

Louis was a remote, if vivid, figure, facing the world with an

unalterable mask. Perhaps the mask was a result of shyness, insecurity, indifference, lethargy. Perhaps merely stupidity. But in
tandem with his catlike speed and slashing fists, it suggested some
unfathomable intent, a merciless concentration on the deed at
hand. Exposure evaporates mystery. A few minutes with an insin-
uating host on a modern talk show and Louis would have been revealed to be as human as Muhammad Ali or Joe Namath. But in
the thirties he came to the public filtered through less leveling
media. His fights were shown on film in local movie theaters, it is
true, but without TV's hoopla, without the prefight interviews
that render the contestants as sapless as the fellow behind the
counter in the corner drugstore.

My father didn't choose any old fight for my introduction to
what was probably, at the time, his favorite sport. He got press
tickets for my mother and me to the match at the Garden between Joe Louis and John Henry Lewis for the heavyweight
championship of the world. It was an encounter between two
titleholders, for Lewis was the light-heavyweight champion, a
skillful, resourceful fighter with years of experience who had
never been knocked out. But Louis was at the very peak of his
career. His last fight had been his greatest—his savage assault on
Nazi Germany's representative of the super race, Max Schmeling,
who had mocked Louis and knocked him out two years earlier.
Louis had recovered to win the championship from Braddock and
then given Schmeling a terrible beating in the space of two minutes and four seconds. Poor John Henry Lewis, past his peak and
looking almost frail beside a genuine heavyweight, was chosen as
his next opponent.

I sat with my mother about fifteen rows from the ring while my
father took his place in the press row. It was a noisy, overdressed
crowd, furs, jewels, and diamond stick pins on display, as they
were for every heavyweight title fight, but the atmosphere was a
little subdued, almost uneasy. Enthusiasm seemed forced, as it
must have been in the Place de la Révolution in Paris when the
tumbrels clattered in with the condemned. One would have had
to be drunk, or a brute, to miss entirely the cool draft of doom as

John Henry climbed manfully through the ropes, clutching his glossy robe around his shoulders.

A brief, tense interval, and Louis was in the ring, his head hooded and obscured by a towel, his handlers kneading his shoulder muscles through the lettered robe. The announcements were intoned, lesser pugilistic lights introduced, the fighters called to the center of the ring for their instructions.

Then, uniquely in my experience in sports, I felt a moment of absolute awe. I think it was akin to the shiver of reverent terror that comes over primitive man as the tribal deity (to be propitiated, not worshiped) reveals itself in the gloom at the fire's edge. The towel and the robe were slipped from Louis, and I saw him for the first time. His glistening, light-brown body set off the rich dark red of his gloves, defining them as weapons, blaring their menace to the crowd. I could see his impassive face, turned toward his opponent across the ring in the moment before the bell rang. His mask reflected something that lived outside anything I had encountered in my own round of home, school, and friends. It seemed to hold, in one stare, all of the stereotypes of an alien race's passionless venom in which my schoolboy reading and moviegoing had steeped me. I felt no pity for the victim. When the bell rang, a part of my humanity closed down and something else arose, as it did one afternoon later when I watched a classmate drop a phlegmatic white mouse into the cage where his pet boa constrictor was waiting.

It was not an ordinary spectacle. My father's heart, though he had seen hundreds of big fights before, apparently had beaten at that moment as disturbingly as mine had.

Maybe this is being written too soon after the thing happened. Maybe it was no more than a one-round knockout of one fighter by another. But last night, in the Madison Square Garden ring, it was almost frightening.

It is all very well to say that John Henry Lewis had been on the skids for a couple of years, so that he wasn't the fighter he had been. But it is well, also, to remember that he is only twenty-five years old, and that when he climbed through the ropes last night he was finely trained and probably could have beaten most of the fighters anywhere near his weight.

And yet within three minutes—two minutes and twenty-nine seconds by the time keeper's watch—he was knocked down three times and was reeling crazily along the ropes, when Arthur Donovan, the referee, grabbed him and motioned to Joe Louis that the fight was over. In less than three minutes a finely trained athlete had been beaten into a state of helplessness. And the crowd that had gone there expecting to see a knockout was shaken by what it had seen.

When the men had entered the ring and were sitting in their corners, a reporter behind you in the press row leaned over your shoulder and said:

"John Henry looks as though he was about to go into a haunted house."

He did, too. The long road he had followed since he first put on boxing gloves . . . that had led him through the tank towns and cheap lodging houses and ramshackle fight clubs . . . had brought him at last into the ring to fight for the heavyweight championship of the world. There must have been times when he abandoned hope that he ever would get that far, but now he was there, and the Garden was packed to see him. But now that he stood at the end of that road there could have been no sense of elation within him, because across the ring from him was Joe Louis. In that long moment just before the bell John Henry must have known what was going to happen.

He jabbed at Louis and moved around him and called up all the skill that he had, but nothing he could do could save him. It wasn't a fight. It was the crippling of one human being by another. The first time Louis hit him he would have gone down, but for the fact that his back was against the ropes. He clawed his way off the ropes, and Louis followed him and hammered him again and knocked him down.

He got up, and Louis was after him, and now Donovan was peering at him closely, to see how much he could stand, and Louis knocked him down again. This time he sprawled through the ropes

and almost went out of the ring. He got up and Louis drove him
across the ring and into a corner and hammered him around the
head, and he went down. He got up and slithered along the ropes
and fell, and then Donovan grabbed him, and the thing was over.

Boxing began to absorb me as much as baseball did. For one
thing, there was no off-season for the fights in New York. They
were in the Garden almost year round, and many of the important
title fights were delayed until summer, when they could be held in
the ball parks. (Because there was no television at the time, the
ancillary rights were restricted to the comparatively slim pickings
of radio and films, and the total receipts depended heavily on the
number of bodies who viewed the battle in the flesh.) Moreover,
the Grahams built a social schedule around the fights. Every Friday evening, my mother and I would drive to Manhattan, leave
the car in a midtown parking lot, and meet my father for dinner
before going to the Garden.

Invariably the meeting place was Toots Shor's. Probably never
before or since in New York has one restaurant and bar concentrated so heavily on the upper crust of the city's celebrities in
sports and the sportier fringes of show business and journalism.
Joe DiMaggio, Frank Sinatra, Barney Ross, Grantland Rice, Mel
Ott, Billy Conn, Ethel Merman, Jimmy Walker, Jim Braddock,
Eddie Arcaro, Phil Silvers, Hank Greenberg, and dozens of others
became regulars at Toots' "saloon." The proprietor, born Bernard
Shor, came to prominence as a bouncer and strong-arm man for
the Philadelphia mob and eventually established himself in the
restaurant business. For several years he ran a place in Manhattan
called LaHiff's Tavern, which had done a thriving business with
the sporting crowd in speakeasy days but had fallen on evil times.
Shor restored it to prosperity, and it was there that he developed
the style that made him a celebrity in his own right.

He traded on that curious craving of many celebrities to be in-
sulted publicly by a hearty man of the people. He was polite,
aloof, even hostile, toward the run-of-the-mill customer, but if a
celebrity entered, he was likely to be clapped ferociously on the
back, or seized in a bear hug, while being smothered with Shorian

endearments such as "You little creep" and "You crumbum." He
was a massive man, wandering his establishment with mincing
steps, his chest and belly thrust out ahead of him like a barrel of
flour ("It's handy for bumping creeps out of the joint"). But the
decorum was such that the proverbial little old lady might com-
fortably have had her cup of tea there at any hour of the day or
night. Gutter language was never tolerated. (Shor mostly confined
his epithets to "Cripes!" and "Jimminy cricket!") Would-be
brawlers were hustled to the sidewalk before violence broke out.
("We leave that stuff to café society.") He cultivated the image of
an ignoramus. (Invited to an opening of *Hamlet,* he remarked,
"Well, one consolation, I was the only bum in the house who
didn't know how it was going to come out.")

In fact, he was proud of the circumstance that he was the only
man he knew of who was a "certified bum."

*This distinction was achieved when he was the manager and
part owner of the Tavern and living in one of the apartments over
the restaurant. One morning an income tax inspector asked to meet
with him to discuss his past returns.*

"He sits down, opens his brief case and takes out some papers.
" 'Did you file an income tax return in 1931?' he asks me.
" 'No,' I say.
" 'In 1932?'
" 'No.'
" 'Why not?' he asks. And I tell him:
" 'In 1931 and 1932 I was a bum.'
"The guy looks at me.
" 'That's right,' I say. 'I was a bum. I had no job and no
home—nothing. Put it down.'
" 'But I can't write in here you were a bum,' he says.
" 'Here,' I say. 'Give me the pen.'
"I take the pen and I write in the form:
" 'In 1931 and 1932 I was a bum. Toots Shor.'
"So the little guy says 'Thanks,' and goes out and I never hear
from him again."

Of all Shor's customers, he was most solicitous of the men who wrote about the celebrities and who might, in passing, mention the name of his restaurant. The name constantly appeared in gossip columns and on the sports pages, and, consequently, though he never paid a nickel for advertising, his Tavern won a wide reputation as a place where the sporting crowd might relax in congenial surroundings. Less exalted souls likewise frequented the Tavern to bend elbows and rub shoulders with the stars, though autograph-hunting was frowned upon.

Shor, however, had an Achilles' heel. He was a knowledgeable sports fan, but he tended to wager with his heart. A close friend and frequent host of Horace Stoneham and of Bill Terry and Mel Ott, Toots bet large sums of money on the Giants just at a time when their fortunes were declining. He also went overboard on several fighters, basing his estimate of their prowess not so much on their records in the ring as on their fidelity to his first restaurant, LaHiff's Tavern.

"I bet the Tavern a couple of times," he told my father.

He bet it once too often, and the lights went out forever in that particular establishment. Toots maintained his Philadelphia contacts, however, and a year or two later he was back with a more elegant place of his own on West 51st Street, across from Rockefeller Center. There was always one of the better tables up front for my father, cheek by jowl with the celebrities, because he was a front-rank columnist as well as a "nice little creep" and a "pal" of the proprietor. Ours was one of the first tables Toots visited on a busy night as he entered and made his rounds. There was the inevitable wisecrack in his harsh Philadelphia hood's voice, followed by a clipped bark of mirth and a blow with his heavy hand between the shoulder blades of the patrons he deemed sturdy enough to withstand it. Whatever shoulder muscles I developed as a youth I attribute to the weekly workout I gave them as I tensed to absorb that friendly slap.

Dinner itself would have been a sufficient treat for my mother, as she surveyed the celebrities, nodded to old friends, and commented on the clothes of the flashy ladies who frequented Shor's.

For her, a ticket to the Garden was just a second stage of the observations she had begun at dinner; she didn't care much about the fights, and averted her eyes when the blood began to flow. Of course, I enjoyed sitting among the big shots at Shor's, too. It was especially bracing for a teenager to be acknowledged on a first-name basis by such as DiMag, Sinatra, and Jimmy Walker.

But the moment in Shor's that stands out above all others in my memory was the night that Lew Jenkins walked into the place a couple of hours before he was to fight Lou Ambers for the lightweight title. Jenkins had come, almost literally, out of nowhere, marking himself within the space of a few months as the most exciting young fighter in the business. He had served in the U.S. Cavalry and fought with indifferent success throughout his native Texas. He was a tall, skinny fellow, with a leathery face, seamed and scarred, and his left ear had crumpled under the force of a thousand blows. He had the pale, gray-blue eyes of a dime-novel killer, and that was precisely his reputation in the ring. He may have been the hardest-punching lightweight who ever lived. He had arrived in New York a nobody, lean and hungry, but suddenly his punches began landing squarely and he ran up a string of victories in the small clubs. After a couple of quick knockouts in the Garden, he became a sensation and was matched with Ambers. And here, just as we were finishing dinner, was Jenkins trailing his manager, Hymie Caplin, into Shor's. He wore an old brown suit and a khaki shirt open at the neck; his hair was a sandy, untamed thatch; and he looked as unconcerned as if he were on his way to the movies.

"Come over here," Caplin beckoned to him. "Shake hands with my friends."

He stopped at our table, obediently shook hands all around, and a few minutes later disappeared into the night. Later that evening I cheered him as he attacked the aging Ambers with a ferocity that even Joe Louis could hardly match. He knocked out Ambers' mouthpiece with a left hook and almost tore off his head with a barrage of long right-hand punches. When Ambers, reeling along the ropes, became tangled in the strands, Jenkins darted at him with the deadly instinct of a spider striking at an insect trapped in its mesh. Even the cigar-chomping ringsiders were screaming at the referee to stop the fight when he finally pulled Jenkins off the disintegrating champion late in the third round. The storybook element of that night—the drab little man in the restaurant; the wiry, relentless predator in the ring—has stayed with me for forty years.

But every fight night at the Garden was an event of sorts to me. To my father's mild amusement and my mother's discomfort, I was always eager to wind up dinner early and get to my seat in time for the first preliminary bout. First, there was a visit to the men's room where Joe Little (once identified by columnist Jimmy Cannon as "Toots Shor's knight of the bath") handed you a clean towel and touted you on the fighter he, in his wisdom, surmised you were rooting for. Then out onto Fifty-first Street, all the traffic in midtown seeming to surge westward toward the Garden, though much of it, of course, was destined for the theaters this side of Eighth Avenue.

There was a knot of milling people beneath the marquee at the Garden by eight-thirty, the pleading cops unable to clear the sidewalk. The lobby was even more tightly packed, all of Jacobs Beach having moved en masse into its warmth. Two figures always drew my attention as I hurried through: a bronze statue of Joe Gans, once lightweight champion and now dead many years, frozen into a classic fighting stance on its pedestal, and the not quite so romantic figure of a black man standing athwart the flow of ticket holders, alive but blind and holding out a tin cup with a hand-lettered sign hanging by a string from his neck that read JA- MAICA KID—EX PRIZE FIGHTER. One of the Garden regulars compared the Jamaica Kid to the one-armed army recruiter who, Napoleon complained, was a bad advertisement for war.

Sometimes the preliminary bouts interested me as keenly as the main event. As a constant reader of *Ring* magazine, I knew at least by reputation most of the fighters who appeared in the Garden, and knew by sight, from prowling Jacobs Beach with my father, most of the managers and trainers who worked in their corners. Some of the fighters I watched in preliminaries went on to become champions—Willie Pep, Beau Jack, Sugar Ray Robinson. Robinson was dazzling, his speed, power, and grace proclaiming even to me, a newcomer to the Garden, his future greatness. And from the beginning I shared with my father the sense of mournful drama that hung over a fighter on the far side of success, pulled back down to the preliminaries from airier realms.

The other night in the Garden there was an old guy in there with a young fellow in a six-round preliminary. The old guy knew how to box and he knew all the tricks of the ring, as he should, because he has had more fights than anybody can count, including himself. But the young fellow wouldn't give him much chance to box but was in on him most of the time and was belting him around.

The old guy had plenty of heart and kept poking and banging away and trying to tie the young fellow up or slip his punches. Now and then he would make the young fellow look bad by sticking him in the kisser at the end of one of his flurries, but the young fellow would straighten himself out and then he would be punching the old guy around again. The old guy went through the ropes a couple of times, once when he was hit with a solid punch and once when the young fellow just rushed in on him and bullied him through. But both times he climbed back and the referee rubbed his gloves against his shirt to get the rosin dust off them and then motioned to him to come on and he came on, doing the best he could.

The referee was an old fighter himself and, in his day, a very rough and tough fighter and a dead game one, just like this old guy who was in there taking a beating.

More than once the referee could have stepped in and stopped the fight because the old guy didn't have a chance to win. The referee knew that as well as anybody but he wanted to see the old guy go as far as he could and didn't want to do anything to hurt him, such as putting a knockout on his record, because something . . . a miracle or something . . . might happen and he would win after all.

At the end of one round he walked over to the old guy's corner and looked at him closely and saw he was in pretty bad shape and asked him if he wanted to quit but the old guy shook him off. The old guy couldn't see very well because his left eye was closing rapidly. But he could hear him all right and he knew what he was saying and the referee didn't argue with him but turned and walked away from him. The referee was giving him a chance to win . . . or to go the way game fighters want to go.

Three or four rows behind the press seats there was a man who was yelling at the young fellow.

"Kill him!" he yelled. "Kill him! Knock his brains out!"

The fighters were whirling in and out and the young fellow hit the old guy on the chin and drove him into the ropes and the man in the ringside seat yelled:

"Don't let him live! Kill him! Kill him!"

The third round . . . the fourth . . . it didn't seem possible the old guy could last the distance. And then the fifth . . . and the sixth. The old guy's left eye was almost completely closed and he was squinting at the young fellow and trying to keep him in focus and the young fellow was banging away at his bad eye or ripping punches to his stomach or rocking him with smashes on the jaw. And then the final bell rang and the old guy walked to his corner and they put his robe on him and took him out through the ropes and the crowd cheered him for his gameness.

The young fellow, in his corner, was grinning at his seconds and they were cutting off his gloves and slapping him on the back and telling him what a great fight he had made. He had made a great fight, at that, and he is a very promising young fellow and may go a long way in the ring.

But for the moment you could take no interest in him and could only think of the old guy climbing out of the other corner. Because he was a very good fighter once. He was the featherweight champion. He made plenty of money but he couldn't hold it. It went this way and that way. On rent and food and clothes. On good times. On the horses, too, somebody said. And now he had been in there fighting a six-round preliminary with a strong young fellow and taking a beating.

And all you could think of were nights when the announcer,
with a gesture toward his corner, would say:
"The featherweight champion—Mike Belloise!"

The crowd, of course, was also part of the show. My mother's roving eyes could pick up a celebrity as he came up out of one of the tunnels—a matinee idol, a politician, or a champion of the past. Most of these grand entrances occurred after the Garden had filled up and it was nearly time for the main event, which was the reason why my mother saw no reason to arrive early. She was not alone in detecting the familiar faces, for many of the grand entrances caused a general stir in the crowd, cheers or boos erupting according to the general mood and inclinations. There were beautiful women, too, richly dressed. A sporty character was certain to swagger up the aisle with a stunner on his arm, in full view of the crowd, while wolf whistles showered down on her from the gallery. (In later years, after television intruded, these gentlemen became more circumspect, always demanding seats on the Fiftieth Street side of the Garden, with the cameras to their backs lest their wives, sitting alone in front of the tube at home, catch a glimpse of them and their companions.)

But of all the receptions accorded the famous as they walked to their seats, I think the warmest were reserved for Joe DiMaggio. You could hear the murmur when he appeared at a ramp entrance, and then the roar began to swell as more people noticed him and ringsiders stood and craned their necks, and on several occasions, as during his fifty-six-game hitting streak, the cheers had evolved into a standing ovation by the time he reached his seat.

The excitement was sharp for an important title fight or even when a great fighter was meeting a mediocre opponent. But some of the wildest nights in the Garden occurred when a local favorite appeared with his neighbors in tow. Gangs of enthusiastic fans from Brooklyn or the Bronx often followed their heroes from the small clubs into the Garden, and on nights when Steve Belloise (Mike's younger brother), Tami Mauriello, Lulu Costantino, or Al "Bummy" Davis was in action, the rafters would ring with almost hysterical cheers. Belloise was accompanied to most of his fights by a crew of well-wishers who called themselves "the Gang Busters" after a popular radio program of the time. They supplemented their cheers with a variety of noisemaking devices, including cowbells, tin whistles, and sirens whose shrillness drove everybody else daffy. Some of the most peculiar demonstrations in the old Garden occurred on those nights when Melio Bettina, who held the light-heavyweight championship for a while in the late thirties, was followed into town by his neighbors from Beacon, New York.

They must have closed the town of Beacon up last night and moved down here behind three bands and a fife and drum corps, and they marched from the Grand Central Station to the Garden, which they helped to jam from the floor to the topmost girders. And the curious part of it was that this crowd from Beacon was not made up of brash young men and their girls out for an evening of sport and noise making, but marching through the streets and into the Garden were dignified middle-aged and even elderly men and women. They were the last persons in the world you ever would have expected to see marching through the streets to a prize fight, and it must be that there is something fine in this Melio Bettina.

The preliminaries, the fans, and the celebrities contributed mightily to the Garden atmosphere, but ultimately the excitement was provided by the main event. Curiously enough, in the case of a building whose very function was to provide a container for excitement and the unruly passions, an uproar carried to its logical conclusion usually has been deplored by boxing officials, politicians, editorial writers, and other interpreters of the public conscience. Never in the old Garden was the causative agent so explosive, or the response so agonized, as on the occasion of Fritzie Zivic's encounter with Bummy Davis.

Davis had earned his *nom de guerre* scuffling in the streets of the tough Brownsville section of Brooklyn where he grew up. A rather wild look in the ring, created in part by the mop of undisciplined light hair that surmounted his chubby face, seemed to confirm Bummy's reputation as a dirty fighter. Yet that reputation rested mainly on a 154-second rampage in 1940. Otherwise, his deportment in the ring was as exemplary as that of any man who has earned his living by trying to convert the gray matter encased in the skull of an opponent into runny gelatin. His early record was simply a compilation of quick knockouts in obscure Brooklyn fight clubs. The instrument of execution was a heavy left hook.

Bummy's sin was artlessness. Fritzie Zivic pursued his craft with a devious skill that still brings a warm glow to the eyes of all who prize rowdiness in their fighters. "Being in there with Fritzie was like trying to handle a man who's got three hands," Sugar Ray Robinson once said. To poke (surreptitiously) a soggy thumb into a clear blue eye, to grasp with the left hand an unwary head and pull it down into the path of a short right uppercut, to lay open an eyebrow with a well-placed butt—these were the grace notes with which Fritzie embellished his performance. The best of Pittsburgh's five fighting Zivic brothers (Jack, Pete, Joe, Eddie, and Fritzie), he had boxed for ten years all over the country. Although he had inflicted considerable damage on local heroes with his various extremities, his own nose, in turn, had fronted such violent storms that its shape had been likened by Red Smith to a "mine cave-in."

Fame and modest fortune arrived simultaneously in October, 1940, when Zivic was matched with Henry Armstrong, who had faded considerably and by then was clinging to the last of the three world championships he had held simultaneously. Exhausted after fifteen brutal rounds and blinded by his own blood, Armstrong could not withstand Zivic's closing surge and lost his welterweight title. Six weeks later, Zivic met Bummy Davis in a nontitle bout. Like most of the other seventeen thousand people who jammed the Garden that night, I craved a dash of hooliganism with my violence and was richly entertained.

The first round was a true measure of the abilities of the two fighters. Davis, his record nourished by those soft touches in the small clubs, was face to face with a thoroughly experienced boxer. Crudely, he rushed Zivic, trying to put over his left hook. Zivic moved away and stabbed him with long left jabs. Occasionally he caught Davis, boring in, with straight rights to the head. When Bummy got inside he was literally in Fritzie's clutches. There the champion worked him over with every weapon at his command. By the end of the round, the blood bubbled through Bummy's thick lips.

Whatever had taken place in those first-round clinches proved to be more than a proud son of Brownsville could endure. At the bell for round two, Davis walked across the ring and fired a left hook that landed, according to one reporter, "about a foot above Zivic's knees." Zivic's face screwed up in pain, then settled into righteous indignation as he glanced at referee Bill Cavanagh. Cavanagh was looking elsewhere.

Davis returned to the attack. Another low blow brought a chorus of boos from the crowd. Zivic backed away, but Davis pursued him, ripping two more left hooks into his groin. Fritzie hopped stiffly on one leg, then on the other, his face contorted. Only once did Cavanagh warn Bummy to keep his punches up. Zivic fired back at Davis, rocking his head and drawing blood again from his mouth. But Bummy, in his passion, was impervious to punishment. He crowded Zivic, hooked him low, shifted his attack to the ribs, and then lowered it once more.

Most of the crowd were standing on the seats now, roaring protest or encouragement. A wadded newspaper landed in the ring, then somebody's hat. The referee kept his fascinated gaze on the fighters, like a young lab assistant observing a couple of ferocious insects. General John J. Phelan, the elderly chairman of the New York State Athletic Commission, had left his seat and now toddled through the aisles outside the ring, looking for all the world like an agitated Mr. Pickwick as he frantically wigwagged at the referee to draw his attention. Davis dug another left into Zivic's groin. Cavanagh, jolted from his rapture by the sight of General Phelan, stopped the fight late in the second round.

Or so he thought. Davis threw off the referee's restraining arms and bounced a left hook off Zivic's skull. Faced with a more orthodox attack now, Zivic quickly solved it by hooking Davis twice in the face, bloodying his nose. Handlers from both corners, as well as a squad of burly special cops, poured through the ropes and tried to drag the berserk Davis to his corner. His arms pinioned now, he aimed a kick at Zivic, who had plunged into the struggling mob. Star-crossed Bummy! Missing the intended target on Fritzie's trunks, his kick caught referee Cavanagh, who was belatedly trying to exercise his authority, in the thigh. Bummy was finally hauled, spitting and cursing, from the ring. The fight was awarded to Zivic on fouls. Even while the excited crowd streamed out of the Garden, journalists and politicians prepared to publish their outrage to the world. My father, predictably, tempered his.

It is too bad that the commission, which will throw the book at Bummy, can't give him some kind of special award for giving the crowd nearly three minutes of terrific excitement. But General Phelan was at ringside, as usual, and the General was greatly upset by the spectacle of Davis trying to foul the pants off Zivic and he finally got the attention of the referee, who stopped the fight. This met with the approval of some of the onlookers, and with the disapproval of others who, having paid to see a demonstration of mayhem, were enjoying it to the full.

The trouble with Davis, of course, is that he was born too late. He is a throwback to the days when men fought on barges and everything went. Since he never has squawked about anything, the chances are that he would not have squawked if Zivic had begun to throw punches below the belt, too. But he is a little too rough for prize fighting as it is conducted under the rules of the New York State Athletic Commission and so he is not likely to be seen around here for a long time.

But he will be missed by a lot of people around here who do not like to see their prize fighters going around in panty-waists.

General Phelan, calling the fight "the most disgraceful thing I ever saw," barred Davis from boxing in New York "for life." Unfortunately for his own well-being, Davis was offered too many opportunities to redeem himself. Drafted into the prewar Army, he was granted a pardon by General Phelan on condition that he fight Zivic again, this time for charity. In a bout notable for its strict adherence to the commission's regulations, Zivic dealt him a savage beating and stopped him in the tenth round. Later, Davis was shot to death as he charged, bare-handed, into a gang that was holding up a friend's store in Brownsville. Bummy was still trying to get across that left hook when he went down.

Chapter Fourteen
The Champ's Pal

The summer that I was sixteen I joined the entourage of the middleweight champion.

Heretofore, my ties to the athletes had been as a fan, a hero-worshiper, a nodding acquaintance. True, among my classmates I was grudgingly accorded the status of an oracle, and my word was readily accepted by at least one of the parties in any dispute about sports. Like a clergyman's child, I was thought to have a direct link with an empyrean world. Because I attended the fights regularly, played sandlot ball wearing Lou Gehrig's glove, and displayed in my room a collection of autographed baseballs, footballs, and photographs, I was thought by my peers to spend much of my time hobnobbing with the greats. I won't swear that I vigorously disabused them of that notion, but I seldom employed such conversational gambits as "Well, as DiMag said to me, 'Frank . . .' "

The story is, in retrospect, an implausible one, a caper dreamed up in Hollywood and pulled off in Manhattan against all odds. Its leads were a couple of college boys who plunged into the jungle of professional boxing, evaded every snare, and slipped out unscathed with gold, glory, and the middleweight title. Although one of the boys, Paul Moss, was by trade a film writer and agent, thereby compounding the illusion of unreality, Billy Soose was a genuine and rather dashing hero. My father, skeptical at first, cast a cold eye on prizefighters with a college education. He believed that if such mental luggage was not a fatal flaw for a fighter, it was at least a career handicap, like a politician's stammer, or a young cinemactress's disappointing cleavage. As it turned out, there were mitigating circumstances.

The story began for me in Toots Shor's. My father asked me if I wanted to come along for lunch one late-summer day; a man named Paul Moss had been put in touch with him and wanted to talk to him about a fighter he managed. There was a twist to the story, because Moss had never dabbled in the fight game before and was known to Pop only as an agent for several movie stars, including Dick Powell and Joan Blondell.

The connection between the film colony and boxing wasn't new, of course. There was a rash of movies in the thirties about poor but sensitive kids putting up their dukes and finding the good life through the manly art, and several retired pugs made a living of sorts by teaching matinee idols how to act like prospective champs. The protagonist of one of Pop's favorite anecdotes was Mushy Callahan, a New Yorker who won the United States junior welterweight title and then retired to Hollywood, where he became a boxing instructor. Among his pupils was an actor whom he had been engaged by the studios to prepare for a role as a fighter. Weeks of laborious coaching followed, and at last the actor put the question to Callahan:

"Tell me, Mushy, how am I doing?"

Callahan shrugged. "Not bad," he said. "But if I was you, I wouldn't start up nothin' with nobody."

Other actors and film writers owned pieces of fighters, as they might of racehorses, though they took no active part in their management. Al Jolson, for instance, had put up the money for Eddie Mead to buy Henry Armstrong's contract from a manager who wasn't getting anywhere with him, and Jolson's name brought the fighter some welcome attention. But dabbling in this hard sport, or lending one's name for the publicity, was about as far as it was considered safe to go. The neophyte was thought to be at the mercy of the sharks who infested boxing, and a fighter could get nowhere without the right connections.

Now Moss was walking into New York with his fighter in tow and challenging the sport's grimy establishment. My father, as I said, was skeptical.

We had lunch at a table up front. Moss, already graying, spoke so softly that one had to lean forward to catch his words out of the chummy laughter and clattering silverware that surrounded us. Billy Soose, in college and in Hollywood, had acquired a polish that was unusual in any sort of athlete at the time. He was tall and slender, in his middle twenties, with thick black hair, a fleshy but not misshapen nose, and a long scar (the result of a butt in an amateur bout) across his cheek. The two of them seemed to be likely prey for sharks.

I already knew some of the details from reading the newspapers and boxing magazines. Moss, a Penn State alumnus, had drifted to Hollywood a few years earlier, where he mingled with Budd Schulberg, Jerry Wald, and other promising young men. He wrote scripts and earned a few screen credits, then later became an actor's agent. On a visit to his boyhood home in Farrell, a steel-making center in western Pennsylvania, he met Soose for the first time. Billy, a Hungarian mill worker's son, was a skinny kid who contributed substantially to the family's support by boxing in the local amateur or bootleg clubs. Bootleg boxing flourished in those days; by listing their programs as "amateur," the promoters evaded both the regulations of the boxing commissions and the tax levied on professional sports events.

"I was surprised later on when I went to New York," Soose said, "and they gave the amateur fighters mostly watches and medals. They gave us cash in Pennsylvania."

Pop told him that there was a gag in New York about the amateur who got a watch for his first fight, and then came back a week later and they gave him the works.

Moss saw Soose fight, liked what he saw, and arranged a boxing scholarship for him at Penn State. Boxing probably outranked tennis as a sport at some colleges in those days (ca. 1935), and Penn State had one of the best teams in the country. It was not weakened by Soose's arrival. With many of his 170 amateur and bootleg fights behind him, he was challenged about as fiercely as Franco Harris would be in a prep-school football game. In two years he had sixteen college fights—and scored sixteen knockouts.

Gently needling the two men now as the lunch crowd thinned out at Shor's, my father remarked that professional boxing was no place for a college boy. Soose smiled and went on eating his pot roast. Moss, who said he had tried to talk Billy out of turning pro, nevertheless disputed the "college boy" label.

"He was a fighter before he went to Penn State and he went there only because we got him a scholarship," Moss said. "He wasn't much of a student, and we had to keep the pressure on him just to make him get passing grades. He had no competition in the ring, of course. Finally it got to a point where the other colleges wouldn't enter anybody against him, and the colleges went and put in a rule that barred any boy from competition who had taken part in the Golden Gloves or any other recognized tournaments before coming to college. That rule was aimed right at Billy. So he left school in the middle of his junior year."

Moss had tried to talk him into remaining at Penn State, but higher education seemed to Billy stale and unprofitable (a vision as likely to come at times to scholars as to athletes). Instead, he turned his persuasive powers on Moss and talked him into becoming his manager. Billy moved to Hollywood, where Moss trumped up some story about Dick Powell's having a piece of his contract; it was all a lot of hooey, but it got everybody some newspaper space. A less determined athlete suddenly discovering Hollywood might have joined the lotus eaters. There were pretty girls and fawning boobs who liked to feel his muscles. ("I never really had big muscles," he told us. "Here, feel," and it was true: he didn't.) But Soose never lost sight of his goal, which was to win a championship and make some money.

He won a few fights in California, but an injury to a knuckle nearly ended his career. Surgery partly repaired the damage, leaving a scar across the back of his right hand and a tendency for the knuckle to swell and sap some of his power after he had landed several solid punches. Although he lost a few fights, he won a great many more. The sport's ruling bodies were as much at odds with each other then as they are today, and in the summer of 1940 two men, Ken Overlin and Tony Zale, laid claim to the world middleweight championship. Soose outpointed both of them in nontitle bouts within thirty days and, as far as New Yorkers (who had never seen him) were concerned, became the division's man of mystery.

"Some people said I got a hometown decision against Overlin because the fight was in Scranton where everybody knew me," Soose told us. "The Zale fight in Chicago was different. He was a murderous puncher. He hit me in the liver in the first round and I thought somebody had stuck a red-hot poker in there. I couldn't breathe for the rest of the round. But he was a mechanical fighter, and I got to know every move he was going to make. By the third round I had him all wrapped up."

Now I had another autographed picture to hang up on my wall beside those of Lou Gehrig and Clint Frank. Soon Billy Soose was boxing in the Garden, where the press described him as the "uncrowned middleweight champion," and earning a following because of his good looks and graceful boxing style. He used his long left jab to good effect while he held his right hand high, partly as a threat and partly as a shield, picking off his opponent's punches as deftly as a first baseman plucks thrown balls from the air. He fired his right sparingly.

Soose won a lopsided fight against the inexperienced and awkward Tami Mauriello, then picked himself up off the floor to pull out a decision against the bull-like Ernie Vigh. The fight had been close and exciting, so Mike Jacobs rematched them in the Garden. At the bell, Billy walked across the ring and hit Vigh on the chin with a short right-hand punch. Vigh pitched forward on his face. For a moment it looked as if he would not get up, but at nine he managed to regain his feet, a light coating of resin dust still on his chin. Soose, his right hand useless once more, kept his left in Vigh's face for the rest of the fight and won an easy decision.

On May 9, 1941, Soose fought Overlin, who was recognized as

the world champion by the New York State Athletic Commission
and its allies. Overlin, a former sailor, was a light-punching but
clever veteran who referred to Soose scornfully as "that college
punk." Moss believed that Soose "could beat Overlin every night
in the week," but he had heard rumors about a fix that disturbed
him. Since he had no proof of any foul play in the works, he wrote
himself a "Dear Paul" letter. The letter purported to be from a
friend in Pittsburgh who claimed to have knowledge that the officials had been bribed to award the fight to Overlin. Moss slipped
the letter into an envelope he had just received from Pittsburgh
and took it to the boxing commission.

General Phelan flew into a tizzy. He summoned before him all
the officials eligible for assignment to the fight and delivered an
outraged address; threats and fulminations filled the air. On the
night of the fight the old Garden abounded in referees and judges
eager to demonstrate their purity of heart and their nonallegiance
to the cause of Ken Overlin. The fight itself was close but unexcit-
ing. Overlin retreated and clutched and twisted, and Soose vainly
tried to bring him down. A champion is seldom deprived of his
title after a fight in which there is little to choose between him
and the challenger. But this was different: the sweating officials
voted unanimously for Soose.

Soose retreated with his title and his money to Lake Wallenpaupak, a large artificial body of water created by a power company in Pennsylvania's tranquil Pocono Mountains. There he and
Moss paid $25,000 for 375 wooded acres, with a house and barn,
and set about converting the place into a training camp. Moss remarked to my father that his nephew and Billy's brother, who
were both about my age, were going to spend the summer at
Wallenpaupak and there was room for additional slave labor;
would I like to join them? I had never been away from my family
before, but I needed no urging.

One morning soon after school had closed, Moss drove the three
of us to Wallenpaupak and we settled into the old green frame
house with its splendid view of the lake. It was an exhilarating
summer. Ray Arcel, a delightful man and one of boxing's great
trainers, was in residence. We picked up some pointers about

boxing from Arcel and went around parroting his favorite anecdotes and expressions. ("When that guy hits you on the chin, you
either go down or do tricks standing up.") We palled around
with the sparring partners, who included Paul Klang, a mild-
mannered, moon-faced preliminary fighter from Brooklyn, and
Augie Arellano, a gentle, battle-worn Mexican who had also been
a wrestler. Augie couldn't knock your hat off with a punch, but he
had stubby, muscular legs on which we would sit while he lay on
his back and then raised us into the air as if we were on the prongs
of a forklift.

In the mornings we did roadwork with Billy and his sparring
partners, snorting down the dirt lane in the wake of our elders.
Later in the day we rolled into place the rocks for a stone wall and
helped to build an outdoor ring in a grove of conifers near the
house. (Soose had already torn out the loft in the big red barn
across the road and converted it to a gym.) In the evening we
three teenagers piled into the rear of Billy's long, green convertible and rode through the nearby towns, sharing in the stir that
the champion caused wherever he showed his face in those hills.
Billy displayed no trace of the cockiness or excessive pride that
puffed up his juvenile staff.

When the outdoor ring was completed, Soose and his sparring
partners worked out there every day, and the public was admitted
for a small charge. With my young friends, Gene and Buddy, I
took tickets at the makeshift gate, carried the punching bags to
the ring, rolled up the tarpaulin, tightened the ropes, and generally earned my keep before the fighters made their appearance.
Then Paul Moss had an idea. Why not have the boys entertain the
early crowd with boxing exhibitions of their own? Reluctantly, we
climbed into the ring, but before long we were slugging each
other with spirit while hardly enhancing Ray Arcel's reputation as
a boxing instructor. I looked on a battered nose as a badge of
honor and began to covet one as ardently as a Heidelberg student
might hope for a dueling scar.

In early July, Soose, Moss, and Arcel went to Cleveland so Billy
could "sharpen up his punching" (i.e., fight a stumblebum) and
they returned with a two-round kayo to their credit. "I wanted to

have more of a workout," Billy told us, "but the padding on the ring floor was so thick I couldn't move around on it. So I took this fellow out early."

A couple of weeks later Moss drove his teenage battalion to New York to watch Billy fight Georgie Abrams in a nontitle bout. The three of us sat together near ringside. It was a heady feeling, coming to New York as a part of the champ's entourage and being pointed out as such in Shor's and the Garden. Everything was perfect, except for the fight. Abrams, who was known as a "spoiler," had already beaten Soose twice, and probably could have beaten him every week if they had gone on fighting for ten years. He was stocky, ring-wise, and hard to hit, though he wasn't much of a puncher. Our cheers grew thinner, less strident, as round after round Abrams got inside, tugged and hauled our hero around, and kept him off balance. Billy's classic style was in a shambles by the end of the tenth round. Nobody got hurt, but it wasn't much of a fight, and Abrams clearly earned the decision.

Afterward, the three of us glumly nursed our Cokes and our pride at Shor's while the waiters consoled us. Billy came in about an hour later, with a slight discoloration under one eye and his composure intact, and the gentle clap he applied to each of our shoulders suggested that it was not the end of the world after all.

That fall I returned to school with added luster in my classmates' eyes. I was a friend of the champ's and apparently an expert to be reckoned with, either in discussion or otherwise. But I never saw Billy fight again. He was already outgrowing the middleweight division and, after surrendering the title, had a couple of fights in Cleveland before accepting a United States Navy commission as a part of Commander Gene Tunney's conditioning program at the outbreak of war.

I saw Billy years later at Lake Wallenpaupak. Paul Moss had died, and Billy had added to his extensive holdings along the lake. He showed me around Billy Soose's Restaurant & Bar, and later we stood talking in the parking lot. Across Route 507, on land sloping down to the lake, were his motel and cottages and, farther up the road, his marina. People waved to him as they drove past in their cars or pickup trucks. Soose, a plump cigar in his fingers, waved in return. A streak of gray ran through his black hair by then, and he had ballooned to nearly two hundred pounds. The old green house we had lived in burned, he told me, some years ago.

"I'm not rolling in money," he said complacently. "Everything I have is in the land and buildings."

He surveyed his domain once again, then invited me inside for a more substantial beverage than the chocolate sodas with which he had plied his entourage on those excursions through the Poconos in his open green convertible more than twenty years before.

"When I was a kid, we never had any money," he said. "But every year when my father's vacation came around, we scraped together enough to get away from the smoke and grime of the mill towns and rent a little shack near a lake. You know—one of those places where you even have to carry your water. This was in the middle of the Depression, but everybody we knew went away on some kind of vacation. I used to say to myself that if things ever got any better, the best business in the whole world must be the resort business."

Hollywood, I thought, could not have improved on this script, and I had been a part of it. But my nose remains as straight as if sporting blood had never coursed through my veins.

Chapter Fifteen
The Hero Recaptured

Somehow I eluded parental vigilance long enough to have a brief love affair with professional football. My father believed in those days that the sport was pure hokum. Even the Washington Redskins' Marching Band, umpah-umping its own fight song, could not convince him that football should be put on display outside the walls of academe, while its practitioners were mainly college boys gone to seed, lumbering oafs too lazy to find permanent work. (Like many people who have never gone to college, he set lofty standards for those who did.)

The defection of Jock Sutherland, who had coached those powerhouse teams at the University of Pittsburgh, at first dismayed my father, then confirmed his darkest suspicions. In 1940 Sutherland signed a contract to coach the ragtag Brooklyn Dodgers (now as long-gone a memory as the baseball team for which they were named) in the National Football League, and by the end of the season had them whipping their alleged betters. What added proof does one need, Pop wondered in his column, that the pros had been merely going through the motions for years. The dour

Dr. Sutherland had insisted his charges learn how to play the game.

Many of the foremost coaches in college football hold that the worst coaching in the sport is to be found in the professional game. This isn't precisely true, although it is true that few of the professional coaches had established reputations in the colleges before they took to the professional game. They got the jobs only because the good college coaches couldn't be interested in them and have grown up with the jobs. In the process some of them have found the way too easy. They have had too many good players and have had to think too little about the fundamentals of the game.

The college coaches, looking on, have been aware of this for a long time, even though they have been loath to talk about it publicly. This doesn't mean that they believed a good college team could beat a good professional team just because the professional team happened to be poorly coached. They granted that, because of the great superiority in playing strength, the professionals could beat the best teams the colleges could offer. The point they made was that the professionals, properly coached, could be so much better than they were.

Without intending primarily to do anything of the sort, Jock Sutherland has gone a long way to prove their point. The first thing he discovered was that the Dodgers—for the most part experienced professional football players—either had forgotten the very elementals of football or never had known them. This meant that before he could teach them any of his plays he had to teach them how to block and tackle as he wanted them to do. That was why the Brooklyn players worked harder than any other players in the league this year. Harder, probably, than any other players in the league ever were worked.

My father's lack of enthusiasm for the pro game was genuine, but it was also convenient, because after covering a college game on Saturday, he was not eager to surrender his only off day and a leisurely walk in the woods to spend Sunday at another game. He even gave the devil his due, attending the pros' playoff game one year and returning to talk with bubbling enthusiasm about the power running of a Redskins' back named Cliff Battles. What a terrific name for an aggressive football player, I thought, and I was especially inclined to find new autumnal heroes since Yale had declined into mediocrity with the departure of Larry Kelley and Clint Frank.

Bill McKenna, the football coach at New Rochelle High School, came to my aid. McKenna liked the pros—he would go anywhere to see a football game, as a matter of fact—and when my father offered him the two complimentary season tickets that the Giants sent him every year, he accepted them on the condition that I ride along with him every Sunday. I was delighted. We had excellent seats, on the forty-yard line, in the upper deck at the Polo Grounds (which was a much better stadium for football than for baseball, its narrow horseshoe shape conforming ideally to the dimensions of the gridiron). McKenna, who had turned down at least one head-coaching job at a small, prestigious college to stay in New Rochelle, was a keen student of the game and shared his observations with me as the play progressed.

The Giants, under Steve Owen, were among the league's better-coached teams. They had a lackluster offense, but they played a hardnosed defense that was unusual during a time when the pros adopted a casual attitude toward tackling. The backbone of this defense was Mel Hein, their almost perennial All-Pro center. Under McKenna's tutelage, I began to appreciate the game's subtlety and quickly found a hero for myself in the Giants' blocking back Nello Falaschi. He was the kind of a fellow who never got his name in the newspapers, though he played almost a full sixty minutes every Sunday. A blocking back in those days was just that. He never carried the ball but simply blocked for the other backs, and he did it very well. On defense he shared the linebacking assignments with Hein, and together they presented one of the league's most formidable barriers to optimistic running backs. Falaschi blocked and tackled with a jarring zest that, in retrospect, appears as one of the joys of my boyhood.

What minimal skills I had as a baseball player and boxer did not carry over into football. I played junior-varsity football at Iona

Prep for a year or so, but my accomplishments were so undistinguished that even I can't remember them. My one moment of glory on the gridiron had occurred when I was an eighth-grader, and it sprang from that prime mover of so much human achievement—pure terror. Bill McKenna was partly responsible.

Sandlot football players of my day wore cheap helmets that were little more than soft leather hats; I believe you could have folded one up and stuck it in your hip pocket. But McKenna gave me an old high-school or college helmet, hard and sturdy, that had been further reinforced during the years (as it was handed from one team to another, I suppose) by half a dozen layers of paint. When it came to me, it was painted white (like Clint Frank's helmet at Yale!), though some green stripes were faintly visible beneath uncounted layers. It wasn't a bad fit, and I could almost hold my head upright under its implacable weight.

One afternoon we played eighth-graders from another school. Because I was considered immobile in my top-heavy headgear, like an unhorsed knight in armor, I was assigned to play blocking back. Twice, as enemy tacklers broke into our backfield, they nearly dashed out their brains by colliding with my sagging helmet, and had to be helped from the field. I heard grumbling from across the line that I was playing dirty, and one outright promise that I would be taken care of.

The game continued scoreless until late in the final period. With the ball deep in their territory, our foes punted and the ball flew in a low trajectory into my reluctant hands. And here they came up the field at me, all eleven of them. I set out for the sidelines, propelled by fear, eating up the yards as if there were nothing on my head but my thin brown hair. No one laid a hand on me, and I experienced a moment of exultation as I touched the ball down in the end zone. That my run was called back because my route at one point included a detour on the far side of the players' bench did not diminish my satisfaction one jot. I was a survivor, and that was enough.

The sands of my boyhood were running out. My hermetic world of fantasy, of athletic derring-do, was about to be broken up by the most convulsive event in the world's history. Not at one stroke, for it lingered on in shreds and tatters, but the decisive moment, the day that will live in infamy, is marked in all the history books. Appropriately, I was watching some of my heroes at the fatal moment. And that reminds me, by way of introduction, of one of my father's stories.

In the early-morning hours after Harry Greb had outpointed Mickey Walker at the Polo Grounds in 1925, the two fighters were reported to have met again outside a New York speakeasy and resumed hostilities, this time without benefit of padded gloves. The story was reported all over town, usually by someone who boasted of having been an eyewitness. At the end of a couple of weeks, it became apparent that if all of these night owls had actually been on the spot, the unsanctioned Greb-Walker brawl would have been the best-attended sports event in history.

This attendance record stood unchallenged until December 7, 1941. In succeeding years the number of people who have assured their neighbors and friends that they first heard the news of Japan's attack on Pearl Harbor while they were watching a football game at the Polo Grounds has steadily mounted. I think I have heard it hundreds of times. Well, I was there—Scout's honor—and as a public service, this account may help to refresh the memories of the untold millions who sat beside Bill McKenna and me on that long-ago day.

Under ordinary circumstances, that game, the last of the regular season, would have been anticlimactic. The Giants had already clinched the Eastern Division championship. Their opponents, however, were the resurgent Dodgers, and under Jock Sutherland's stimulation there was a hope (quickly snuffed out) that an interborough rivalry akin to that in baseball was in the making. New hopes fluttered in the hearts of the Brooklyn faithful, engendered chiefly by Clarence "Ace" Parker, a triple-threat halfback from Duke. Supporting Parker were Clarence "Pug" Manders, the league's leading ground gainer in 1941, and a lineman aptly named "Bruiser" Kinard.

If the Giants held formal claim to the division title, they had not proved it to the Dodgers' satisfaction. Ace Parker had led Brooklyn to two straight victories over the Giants, one in the final

game of the 1940 season and another after the Giants had won
their first five games in 1941. The Dodgers were finishing a strong
second in the division this year under Sutherland, as they had the
year before.

To reach the New York sports pages that weekend, a reader had
to pass over some pretty glum dispatches. Great concentrations of
Japanese troops had been observed in Indochina. Menacing notes
flew between Tokyo and Washington, and Australia had the jit-
ters. Nevertheless, 55,051 people (other than the uncounted
phantoms) pressed into the Polo Grounds to watch the game. Before it started, the Giants assembled docilely on the field to watch
a ceremony honoring their illustrious running back Alphonse
"Tuffy" Leemans; December 7 was Tuffy Leemans Day before it
became Pearl Harbor Day.

A moment before the speeches began, the first Japanese planes
dropped their bombs on Pearl Harbor. No report was audible at
the Polo Grounds. The ceremonies concluded, and the two teams
began knocking heads. Although there was no score in the first period, the players assaulted one another with uncommon ferocity,
and the wounded began to pile up around the Giants' bench.

The Giants, in fact, were being trounced, much to my discomfort. Parker, passing occasionally, slanting off the tackles more
regularly, kept them off balance. Manders was all over the field.
In the second period he intercepted a pass, spun up the middle for
a first down on the Giants' four, then took two more cracks at the
Giants' line, finally hitting right guard to score from the three. In
the third period, Leemans, who was to gain only 18 yards rushing
all day, tried to change his luck with a forward pass. The ball
tipped off Len Eshmont's fingers into the arms of Manders, who
returned it 65 yards for a touchdown.

Meanwhile, a steady hum of curiosity could be detected under
the roar that distinguishes an assemblage of professional football
fans. We heard an urgent call for Colonel William J. Donovan to
get in touch with his office, the words faintly ominous as they
were barked out over the public-address system. There were several other calls for military and government officials. The boys in
the press box saw the bulletin about the Japanese attack come in

on their ticker, but the fans, who were obliged to follow a game in those days without the benefit of transistor radios to acquaint them with what they were watching, were left to speculate on the nature of the crisis. Perhaps the management feared that an announcement during the game would cause an exodus before the stocks of beer and hot dogs had been consumed.

On the field, the slaughter continued unabated. A threat mounted by the Giants early in the fourth period came to nothing when Manders intercepted one of Hank Soar's passes. A few minutes later, the Dodgers, set in motion by Parker's 19-yard run, drove 59 yards for a touchdown. Manders scored from the two. The Giants finally scored with 23 seconds to play, when Soar passed 38 yards to Kay Eakin.

The final score was 21-7. Three Giants—George Franck, Mel Hein, and my hero, Nello Falaschi—were taken to the hospital; half a dozen others were put under doctor's care. The Dodgers remained in second place, but they had softened up their old tormentors to the extent that the Giants were pushed over, 37-9, by the Chicago Bears in the league's championship game. I have never talked to anybody who saw that one.

Bill McKenna had no radio in his old Chevy, so our ignorance about the nature of the day continued until we arrived home.

"We're in the war," my father announced as we came through the door.

His face was funereal as he looked briefly but searchingly at his oldest son, who was sixteen years old. But his son's mind was still on that pounding the Giants had taken at the Polo Grounds.

I was soon aware that my world had gone topsy-turvy. The trickle of athletes into the armed services at the beginning of 1942 would become in time a rushing cascade. Baseball, for the moment, was losing its very young players and its bachelors (Hank Greenberg and Bob Feller were among the first to go that year), though most of the established stars remained with their teams throughout the season.

For the first month the war seemed remote. No one I knew well had become involved yet, aside from a few older men who belonged to the National Guard. My father, however, was already touched by events, hearing news of some of the officers he had known when they were connected with the athletic programs at West Point and Annapolis and who were now in action in the Pacific. I think that what really brought the war home to me was the most dramatic gesture yet taken by any American athlete since Pearl Harbor. Joe Louis, fittingly enough, announced that he would defend his championship against Buddy Baer at Madison Square Garden and donate his entire purse to the Navy Relief Society. Some of boxing's fast-buck men did not share the public's admiration for Louis, and they considered such generosity a grave defect in judgment.

The fight, which went off on schedule on January 9, slightly more than a month after Pearl Harbor, stirred unusual interest in New York. Even though this was Louis' twentieth defense of his title and a rematch, the champion created excitement as a matter of course. Buddy Baer, Max's kid brother, was an attractive challenger. He stood six feet six and a half, weighed two hundred fifty pounds, and, unlike most ring giants, punched with stunning force. In Washington the year before, Buddy had knocked Louis through the ropes, lasted until the seventh round, and escaped with both his life and his prestige: he had been disqualified when his handlers, charging a foul by Louis, refused to let him continue. To the reputation of the fighters add the emotional mood of the country and the quasimilitary nature of the event, and one can account for the match's appeal.

On the day of the fight, New York's newspapers painted for their readers a frightening picture of the world. An American army was trapped in the Philippines. The Japanese had smashed through British defenses north of Singapore. The besieged Russians fought the Nazis along the Eastern Front from Leningrad to Sevastopol. An Axis submarine was reported lurking off the coast of New England. Turning to the sports pages, the readers found little relief. Grantland Rice's column in the *Sun* was dedicated to the proposition that football offered a boy the best training for war. It was reported that baseball players would pay inflationary prices for their gloves and shoes in the spring. The Yale Club had canceled its historic squash tournament because of a shortage of good-quality rubber balls.

That night, a crowd of 18,870, paying $189,701, packed the Garden while boxing made the best of Louis' glory. The Stars and Stripes hung everywhere. The arrival of the champion and challenger in the ring was heralded by spirited bugle calls, played by a sailor and a marine in dress uniforms. A telegram of thanks from Frank Knox, the Secretary of the Navy, was read to the crowd. Wendell Willkie, the recently disappointed challenger for a weightier title, made a speech that proved to be longer than the fight. He rushed to a climax with "As for you, Joe Looey, and you, Max Baer, I know you will put up a great fight!"

The crowd momentarily set aside its good manners to inform Willkie raucously of the challenger's last name. Willkie apologized and concluded by hoping that after the battle the two boxers, and everybody else, would unite to fight the Japanese. Lucy Monroe appeared in the ring, wearing a blue gown adapted to the occasion with a red-and-white sash, and sang "The Star-Spangled Banner." The crowd, edified and combative, roared in anticipation. In the absence of Nazis and Japanese, any victim would do. Buddy Baer jogged in his corner and tried to look calm.

The bell rang. Baer rushed Louis, using his bulk to push him into the ropes, and flailed at Louis' side. Louis twisted away and jabbed Buddy twice, then rocked him with a two-fisted attack. Baer fought back ponderously, cutting Louis' mouth, but the champion did not back off. Punching swiftly and accurately up at his target, he took the steam out of Baer. The fans were standing now, aroused by an aggressive and savage Louis they hadn't seen since his fight with John Henry Lewis.

Baer sagged, then clutched at Louis, but Joe pushed him away again. They stood in mid-ring, frozen in a classic pose for a moment; then Louis followed a jab with a short right to Baer's chin, and Buddy's long legs folded under him and he sank slowly to the floor.

Baer rolled over onto his hands and knees. At first he had trouble locating Louis; then he turned to face him and got to his feet at the count of nine. Louis knocked him down again. Buddy struggled up, turning uncertainly to meet Louis' rush. He alternately punched back at his tormentor and clung to him, but nothing slowed Louis' attack. Louis threw a right uppercut and Baer went down on his back, his hair flying as his head struck the canvas. He was still trying to stand up when the referee counted ten. The time was 2:56 of the first round.

A few minutes later, Louis sat hunched on a rubbing table in his dressing room, eating an apple and telling the reporters in a soft voice that he would donate his next purse to the Army Relief Society. Baer, sucking an orange through puffed lips in his dressing room, said that Louis' next opponent "better go in there armed with a baseball bat." The fans, streaming out of the Garden onto Eighth Avenue, compared this with Louis' other great fights. And more than one cynical old fight manager mused on forty percent of $189,701, and wondered what their world was coming to.

Later that year I experienced a moment of intense pride. An event occurred that determined the course of my life in the most profound of ways, by planting a seed in a youthful, unformed mind. My father became an author—an author of not just another book but of one that gave pleasure to thousands of adolescent readers and brought him years of modest but satisfying royalties.

Delos Lovelace, an assistant managing editor of the *Sun*, had written a biography of Knute Rockne for young readers. In 1941 Lovelace's publisher suggested he write a similar biography of Lou Gehrig. He declined, recommending instead that my father be given the assignment. And so, after months of work, relying heavily on his own memory but also talking to Gehrig's family and friends and poking through old newspaper files and records in the Yankees' office, my father brought forth in 1942 a book entitled *Lou Gehrig: A Quiet Hero.*

There had been other biographies and autobiographies aimed at young baseball fans before this—Christy Mathewson's *Pitching in a Pinch,* for instance—but mostly they amounted to what someone has called "the Victorian miracle of a Pygmalion metamorphosis in reverse," taming a living man into a marble statue. Perhaps *because* Gehrig was singularly deficient in panache, élan, or what you will, my father wrote what he liked to describe afterward as "the story of a little German boy from Manhattan who grew up to play first base for the Yankees." Here, at somewhat greater length, was Andy Blue, or Davy Lane, in pinstripes.

His book also created a sort of cottage industry for baseball biographies that has not yet expired. Apparently boys from ten to eighteen years old were able to get something from the book, and some of them even identified with its hero. Certainly what many of them got from it was a book report. Kids who had absolutely no interest in history, geography, or fiction suddenly found a book they were able to plow through and say something about. Librarians stocked up on *Lou Gehrig.* "It was the instant solution to all my problems with boys who were nonreaders," an elderly librarian told me a few years ago. I have been assured by at least a dozen men that this was the first book they ever read all the way through in boyhood. A part of my father's "leisure" for years consisted of answering letters from teenagers who announced they were writing a book report about *Lou Gehrig* and could they please have, as soon as possible, the answers to questions such as "Did you know Gehrig personally?" "How did you get started writing?" and "Have you written any other books?"

I suppose that before the book's publication, I had seen my father as a kind of animated recording device, a lovable but anonymous scribe who set down mechanically for the *Sun's* readers the exploits of people who led exciting and glamorous lives. Now, for the first time, I began to realize that he was a personality himself, a man whose life was every bit as interesting, and probably more satisfying, than the people he wrote about. In my daydreams I had always been the Yankees' first baseman, or a triple-threat halfback at Yale, or the middleweight champion of the world. But now, slowly, the focus of my daydreams began to shift; sometimes another scenario would take over, and for a few minutes I would become the writer of a popular newspaper column or the author of a book as good as *Lou Gehrig: A Quiet Hero.*

The book had a more immediate meaning for me, too. I found pleasure in reliving some of my old hero's days of glory, pleased and rather surprised to read in a book the descriptions of events I had witnessed (or closely followed in the newspapers). Then, in the closing pages, I came close to Gehrig as I never had when he was alive and a hero, feeling an adolescent's awe in the presence of death as my father portrayed that massive, heavily muscled man going through his last days, the flame sputtering out. He told of Gehrig's job at the parole board, which he filled conscientiously to the end; of long talks at home in Riverdale with his old friend Ed Barrow, the general manager of the Yankees; of his no longer being able to drive his car ("with its license plate LG 1 that every traffic cop knew and saluted as it passed"); and of the candlelit suppers alone with his wife, Eleanor. As I came to the final chapter, my eyes were as misty as those of any child of a century before when an elder read aloud, from the last installment of *The Old Curiosity Shop*, the death of Little Nell. This is how my father brought his story to an end:

Another spring . . . the ball season on again . . . and now Lou rapidly was growing weaker. There were days when, although he got up in the morning, he didn't feel like going to his office, and Eleanor would call up and say he wouldn't be in that day. And Lou would read and pore over the papers on his desk upstairs in the square room they called his office. Or play the phonograph . . . or sit by the window, looking out toward the parkway . . . and thinking . . . of what?

Of baseball, probably. For now, slowed down to a halting walk, tiring after the least exertion, unable to go regularly to his office in town, it is likely that his mind dwelt frequently on baseball. For baseball had been so very much a part of his life that it had seemed, at one time, almost to be his life itself.

All that he had had sprung from baseball. The tangible things. The security he had provided for his mother and father, the homes in which they had lived in New Rochelle and Larchmont, his boat on the Sound, his fishing tackle, his car. Those trips he had taken to the Orient and around the world. Those trophies in the library. His niche in the Hall of Fame.

And the intangible things. The love of Eleanor, whom he never

would have met if he hadn't been a ball player. The memories of
their years together. Of sunny days fishing in the Florida keys and
frost-bite days on the Sound. Memories of the days when he was
storming the American League towns with the Yankees or playing
in a packed Stadium at home. Of games won and lost . . . and
world series . . . and trains whistling through the night.

Of the friendships he had made and cherished and of how much
it had meant to him to know Ed Barrow and Joe McCarthy and the
Babe and Christy Walsh . . . and Bill Dickey.

There had been little else in his life but baseball, and most of
that little had sprung directly from baseball. Christy Walsh, his
business agent, had syndicated newspaper articles under his
name, had arranged for him to sell his endorsements of bats,
gloves, caps, and breakfast foods, even had made a motion picture
star of him once. A recollection of that always made Lou smile.
"Rawhide," the picture was called. It was the story of a city-bred
cowboy and it was very bad indeed, and Lou knew that as well as
anybody and it was at once the beginning and the end of his motion picture career. Once, too, he had embarked on an off-season
venture as a customer's man for a brokerage firm but he was no
more a customer's man than he was an actor, and he knew that,
too.

The air was soft. There were blossoms on the trees and the
shrubs were green and there were flowers about the doorway. In a
few days it would be June. Wonder if, as he looked back across the
years, he realized what a fateful month June had been in his life?
He was born on June 19, 1903. As a schoolboy he had hit that
home run at Wrigley Field in June of 1920. In June of 1923 he
joined the Yankees and saw his name in a major league box score
for the first time. On June 1, 1925, he had begun his streak of consecutive games, and on June 2 he had become the regular first
baseman. On June 3, 1932, he had hit four home runs in a game in
Philadelphia. And now, in a few days, it would be June again. . . .

Eleanor didn't know that he knew he was doomed. But he did.
And she never let him know she knew their days together were
numbered and that the numbers were dropping fast.

191

"There," a fellow in the press box had said on Lou Gehrig Day at the Stadium, "goes the gamest guy I ever saw."

The gamest guy had found a mate as game as he.

On the night of June 2, there was a sudden change in his condition. What Eleanor first thought was drowsiness after a day propped against the pillows on his bed reading and listening to the radio was, she quickly realized, a coma.

The doctor was at the house in a few minutes. Mom and Pop, shaken and frightened, were driving over from Mount Vernon. Ed Barrow, roused from an easy chair in his home in Larchmont, was being whirled across the parkways by a driver who, that night, gave no thought to speed cops.

Shortly before ten o'clock, Lou opened his eyes and looked at those grouped about the bed. He seemed surprised to see them there, for they had not been there just a . . . a . . . moment before. And then, as though he had fallen asleep again, he died. Death had brought no pain. Only bewilderment.

In newspaper offices and radio stations across the country, the report of his death came as a shock, as it did when it was announced to the public. Within an hour, messages of sympathy were pouring in on the bereaved parents and widow, and cars lined the streets about the house. The Babe and Mrs. Ruth arrived in tears.

In Detroit, Joe McCarthy stepped out of a taxicab in front of the hotel where the Yankees were staying and the manager of the hotel said to him:

"Gehrig died tonight."

Joe was shaken as though he had been struck in the face and as he walked into the lobby and saw some of the players gathered there, he saw that they knew, for they were gray and stunned. And in his room, that he had shared so long with Lou, Bill Dickey cried.

By order of Mayor LaGuardia, flags flew at half-staff in New York the next day, as the city, and the nation, mourned the death of this young man. Thousands of persons filed past his bier as he lay in state in a little church in Riverdale. The newspapers carried editorials citing his gallantry and deploring his untimely death. From the White House, from the Governor's mansion at Albany, from the homes of children who played on the sidewalks as he once had done, came expressions of grief.

He died as he had lived. Bravely, quietly. To his mother, to his wife, to all who knew and loved him, to the millions who sorrowed at his death, he left the shining legacy of courage.

Chapter Sixteen
From the Mailbag

The Great Lakes Naval Training Station fielded a powerful baseball team in the spring and summer of 1943. It was managed by Commander Mickey Cochrane and included a number of players, like Big John Mize, whom I had last seen wearing major-league uniforms. Sitting in the stands behind first base at the station's ball field, I watched these newly inducted sailors play exhibition games against several teams from the American and National leagues and beat all of them except the Yankees, who squeezed out a one-run victory. Probably the season's most dramatic moment at Great Lakes came about when Cochrane (chiefly a nonplaying manager because George "Skeets" Dickey, Bill's kid brother, was the regular catcher) delegated himself as a pinch hitter in the ninth inning against the Reds and drove in the tying and winning runs with a line-drive single down the right-field line.

But one day Great Lakes took on a team from the Negro leagues—Kansas City, I believe. I had seen bearded men, and aging, fat-assed actors, and even women play baseball, but never a black man, and now I sat with my colleagues from boot camp and watched these anonymous itinerants, who were not allowed to play in organized baseball, overwhelm the big leaguers, 15–2. It made one wonder.

My departure from a comfortable home and a warm family life to enter the Navy had been precipitous, and a little unnerving. Not that I had been hauled away kicking and screaming. I knew that upon graduation from high school in June, 1943, when my eighteenth birthday would have passed, I would be fair game in the draft and have little chance to choose my own branch of service. In March, two weeks before my birthday, I left high school and joined the Navy.

For my three years in uniform, I was to be prey to homesickness. And why not? I grew up in a home where all the amenities were practiced. The first commandment there was *consideration* for others—for parents, for brother and sisters, for the neighbors. ("Turn down the radio. It might bother the people next door.") Tantrums were vulgar; vulgarities were—well, they were vulgar, too. I was never aware of a parental squabble, and we children, if not especially close, seldom exploded in open warfare; it was as if we had made an unspoken pact to purify ourselves of unseemly passions to live in the presence of placid, smiling, saintly Jim, who was so much a part of the family, and yet so much apart from us, and who as he grew older seemed to have no other substance than his hospitality and consideration. Even Minnie began to fit in. Her grandiose notions shriveled with her bulk, and toward the end she was a vaporous thing, hunched at the table over her food, from which she extracted tiny particles that were to be put in an envelope and sent to J. Edgar Hoover, whose toxicological laboratory apparently would confirm the infamy of Emma Akins. But what was left on her plate, Minnie ate with obvious relish.

If this was not a home in which one evolved a thick skin and sharp elbows, it was at least a place where one could dream, whether of prewar Paris boulevards or five-o'clock lightning in a roaring ball park or golden-voiced Royal Mounties wooing girls in a boreal landscape, and so I have never looked back on the scenes of my boyhood with condescension. Now all of this, the dignity and consideration accorded each individual in my home and the bogus blood-and-thunder of my world of sports, was about to be torn from me, and I was on my own.

My father was apparently in no frame of mind to make his accustomed rounds the day I left for the induction center, because the column he wrote for the next afternoon's *Sun* (and which he sent me at the end of the week in an envelope stuffed with other clippings from the sports pages) was composed at home off the top of his head. It dealt with one of the novelties of the time: baseball's spring-training camps were pitched in the North that year because Commissioner Kenesaw Mountain Landis was determined that there would be no picture of big, strong athletes lolling on the beaches while other mothers' sons were marching off to war.

There are strange datelines on the stories from the training camps this year. Bear Mountain . . . Asbury Park . . . Lakewood, N.J. . . . Medford, Mass. . . . Cape Girardeau, Mo. . . . Lafayette, Ind. . . . Hershey, Pa. . . . There are no palm trees in the background this year, no blazing sun, no azure skies. But the young men will do all right. They have been pampered to some extent in recent years, but they're sound and tough enough. Training in the North isn't going to harm them any more than it harms the college kids who train in the North every year.

There were not enough seats on the trains leaving New York that day for the Midwest, and our eventual destination at the Great Lakes, so the authorities lodged us recruits in rooms at the Seaman's Institute, then a gloomy old stonepile near the East River. Weighed down by the building's aroma of evangelism and the unaccustomed proximity of strangers, some of whom seemed to me as outlandish as Queequeg, I felt a little like Ishmael at the Spouter-Inn before he set out in pursuit of the Whale. The next day I boarded a grimy coach at Grand Central and, twenty-six hours later, alighted at a siding near the naval station. I went into boot training as an apprentice seaman.

My old heroes did not desert me. Herolatry was not a common sentiment in American sports during the war, but I tried to keep up with what was going on, and while I was reading whatever sports page I could lay my hands on, I felt my ties with home were being renewed. My father sent me a copy of the 1943 *Baseball Register*, published by *The Sporting News*, which came with a blue-spangled, red-and-white cover on which a sprightly Uncle Sam, bat in hand, posed in front of a large baseball autographed by Bob Feller, Hank Greenberg, Hugh Mulcahy, and other stars who had already entered the service. Inside were pages of the lifetime records of contemporary players and many of the immortals. A rich bonus was a history of the World Series by Fred Lieb, a veteran baseball writer, which was accompanied by dozens of photographs and the box scores of every Series game ever played, back to the dawn of history, which in this case was 1903.

To my delight, I found myself in the center of a somewhat sporty scene at Great Lakes. Mickey Cochrane's stalwarts were there, the equals of almost any team the major leagues were able to muster against them. When the Yankees arrived for an exhibition game, I visited with Dan Daniel, Will Wedge, and other newspapermen who covered them on the road. Then, as the tempo of the war speeded up, our boot training was cut short. After a brief leave at home (which did not coincide with my high-school graduation, so that a classmate had to accept my diploma on the appointed day), I went on to torpedo school at Great Lakes. My new lofty status as a second-class seaman allowed me to apply for passes and visit Chicago, which I did frequently in the company of a new friend.

Mickey Genaro had been assigned to me, as it were. He was a retired club fighter, with the scars and a mangled nose to prove it, and he had entered the Navy as a noncommissioned officer in the physical-training program. At this remove it is not possible to calculate his exact rating, because he was always threatening to punch some pompous officer in the kisser and thus spent much of his time ripping off or reaffixing the stripes on the arm of his uniform. Ray Arcel, during his years as a trainer, had come to know Genaro and admired him for his loyalty and resourcefulness. When Ray learned that I was at Great Lakes, he wrote Mickey and asked him to keep an eye on me.

[FRANK GRAHAM, JR.]

Mickey took his assignment seriously. He was an engaging little man who must have juggled his favors because he had influence, well beyond the powers of his rating and his record of deportment, in all the offices of the stark, windswept base. He not only wangled more than my share of overnight passes for me; he also supplied me with the fare to Chicago in the form of long-invalid railroad tickets that he had sent to the laundry along with his dress whites, thereby rendering them illegible to the scrutiny of the most suspicious conductor.

When Ray Arcel came to Chicago with Lou Nova, I holed up for the weekend with Mickey at the Morrison, an enormous hotel in the Loop that was frequented by the fight mob. Nova seemed to have been put on this earth to break the hearts of his handlers and supporters. He was a husky Adonis, gifted with a solid punch, who assumed a classic stance in the ring and on occasion looked like a world-beater. Twice he had knocked out Max Baer in exciting fights. But he had certain weaknesses, including a tendency to believe in the flights of fancy indulged in by his public-relations men. At one time he had been exposed to the teachings of a student of the occult who called himself the Omnipotent Oom and instructed Nova in the science of an awesome weapon called the Cosmic Punch. As explained to the press, the trajectory of this punch, thrown from the Dynamic Stance, coincided with the earth's rotation on its axis, or some such phenomenon, and thus landed on the recipient's chin with exponential force.

Bolstered by this weapon, or at least by the lift it gave to his confidence, Nova had entered the ring in 1939 against Tony Galento, who knew nothing of cosmic influence and punched Lou soggy. Having recovered to become the leading heavyweight contender (mostly by attrition) in 1941, he engaged Joe Louis in what was certainly the most torpid championship bout I have ever seen. For five rounds he backtracked warily, locked into his Dynamic Stance. In the sixth round Louis spied a chink in the defense and, firing a single right-hand punch, sent Nova into the trance that Oom had tried to induce by less violent methods. Now, after some further ups and downs, Nova was in Chicago to fight Lee Savold at Wrigley Field.

198

For a fleeting moment I was again part of a fighter's entourage. I lounged with Nova and Arcel in their hotel room, ate with them in a Loop restaurant, and strolled up Michigan Boulevard with them in the evening (horrifying the male-chauvinist pugilist when I gave a smart salute to a passing officer in the Waves). I suppose Nova, with his sulks and his fatuous notions, was a severe trial to Arcel, but I found him a likable companion. He resented the public's image of fighters as mental cripples, but he could be funny about it. He told me of a recent experience when he was a spectator at a fight in the Garden. A man who was walking up the aisle with his son spotted Nova and brought the boy over to shake hands with him.

"I'd never seen the man before," Nova said, "but I thought I'd make him look like a big shot in front of his kid. So I laid it on, you know, telling him it was good to see him again, and letting the kid know that I thought his old man was a great guy. They got my autograph and started to walk away. And I heard the guy say to his kid, 'See, I told you he was punchy.' "

That weekend Mickey Genaro was never far away, carrying out his duties as my chaperon. He reminded me to shine my shoes, made certain that I drank nothing stronger than beer, and pointed me to bed before the clock struck midnight. On Sunday morning, saying "Your mother would like it," he insisted that the two of us attend Mass, which I knew was even more of a novelty for him than for this youthful infidel.

Yet all was forgiven when Mickey secured me a pass allowing me to come to Chicago during the week and watch the fight. It was mercifully brief. Lee Savold, a stolid, unimaginative fighter, was nonetheless equipped with a paralyzing left hook. Just after the bell opened the second round, Savold hit Nova on the chin with his unheralded right. As my stricken friend began to fall, Savold dispatched him with the hook, and Lou took the count on his face near his own corner. I caught an early train back to Great Lakes.

My father wrote his last column for the *Sun* at the beginning of August. The Gehrig book was a modest success. Not even his unwillingness to blow his own horn, to ask from the paper some of the publicity and salary that were now his due, could obscure his standing as one of the country's most respected sports columnists—at that moment, probably the best. When *Look* offered him the post of sports editor with a considerable increase in salary, he made what must have been a painful decision to leave the newspaper business. Still at Great Lakes, I looked forward to his last column and was faintly disappointed when I read it. I don't know what I expected: a glittering tour de force in which the highlights of twenty-nine years on the *Sun* were trotted out for the reader's inspection, perhaps, or at least a column devoted to one of the two New York baseball teams that had attracted him since he was a child. But instead he chose to write about Branch Rickey, who had recently left the Cardinals to take over as president and general manager of the sagging Dodgers. I look on that last column now almost as if it were an omen, a cryptic note directed at me, though it would be some years before that new regime in Brooklyn would shape my own life.

Branch Rickey, breaking up the Dodgers and asking waivers on his shop-worn heroes, finds a ready claimer in the Giants. This is a sharp reminder that the Giants, who once ruled the National League, find themselves in a plight so desperate that they must swallow their pride and take what they can get.

There was a time when, if any Dodger athletes were to be waived out, the traffic was in the other direction. It was a time to which old-line Giant fans, always more than slightly contemptuous of Brooklyn, must look back with longing. Meanwhile, Rickey is moving so fast there are likely to be few familiar faces in the Brooklyn dugout when another spring rolls around.

Remodeling the team, Rickey is also making over the entire set-up that Larry MacPhail [the team's former president] left behind him when he turned his back on Ebbets Field and headed for the Army. That was, to Rickey's mind, a very curious set-up indeed, and not at all to his liking. It was spectacular and had been extremely successful, as ball games were won and a pennant was flown from the flagstaff at Ebbets Field after the victory of 1941.

*Some of the daffiness with which baseball had been marked in
Brooklyn in other years crept back again, but this time it was a
controlled daffiness that made fans all over the country love the
Dodgers for the thrills they gave them.*

*But that was all achieved in MacPhail's way, which is not
Rickey's. It will be interesting to see the kind of team he will put
together to replace the one that is vanishing so rapidly. His
progress will be retarded, naturally, by the man-power shortage, so
that it is unlikely he will have a rip-roaring array by next spring.
But it will be there one of these days.*

After additional training on the West Coast, I spent eighteen
months as an aircraft torpedoman aboard an escort carrier, U.S.S.
Marcus Island, in the Pacific. On the whole, our ship was incredibly fortunate. We ferried planes to Guadalcanal, took part in
antisubmarine patrols, and supplied air cover for the invasions of
Palau, the Philippines, and Okinawa. We played a strenuous part
in the Battle of Leyte Gulf, keeping our own fighters and torpedo
planes in the air all day and taking aboard planes from other car-
riers that had been sunk or disabled. Through all the destruction
we passed relatively unscathed.

Yet those violent hours were few on the *Marcus Island.* I found
myself with long periods of idleness. There was an excellent little
library aboard, presided over by the chaplain's assistant, and since
it was light on froth, I was easily channeled into "literature."
There, for the first time, I read Dostoevsky, Mann, Faulkner,
Katherine Mansfield, Sherwood Anderson. When I wrote home
about my new enthusiasms in reading, my father sent me books,
and I weeded my wardrobe to the barest minimum to accommo-
date my own traveling library in my seabag. Clifton Fadiman's
Reading I've Liked made an even larger bulge in the bag than Nat
Fleischer's *Ring Record Book.* There were two new books by my
father, which became my prize possessions: *The New York Yankees: An Informal History,* and *McGraw of the Giants.* Occasionally on a shelf at home now I run my hand over the
mildew-spotted cover of a collection of Hemingway's short

stories, a reminder that it waited for me in a mailbag for months on some damp tropic isle while I was on an escort mission aboard the *Marcus Island*.

But of everything that came in those mailbags, I waited most eagerly for the immensely fat little envelopes that my father dispatched several times a week to an unknown point in the South Pacific. In each there was a breezy letter from him (always signed "Pop," in soft, black pencil), recounting a trip to the Stadium, a visit to the racetrack, a testimonial dinner for a sporting luminary. There was news of the family: a dinner party my mother had given, the doings of Mary and Judy at school, some tutor's optimistic attempts to teach reading and writing to Jim, a comical remark by Emma Akins. And what gave the envelopes their bulk was the sheaves of newspaper clippings packed around the letter. Now that my father was no longer writing a daily column, he included those of his erstwhile colleagues that he thought would interest me, along with a selection of miscellaneous news items that might have formed a data bank for anyone engaged in writing a history of American sports during World War II.

Yes, presumably the front pages were telling the people at home that American troops had stormed Monte Cassino, that Allied heavy bombers were pounding Frankfurt, and that the Russians had the Nazis on the run in Bessarabia. But the sports pages survived, President Roosevelt had given baseball a "green light," and somehow the big leagues scraped together enough players to keep going. They delayed spring training for a week or so to enable their prospective players to remain a little longer at their jobs in defense plants; like certain insects that mimic twigs to escape the notice of predatory birds, some players passed themselves off as defense workers in the hope that their draft boards would overlook them.

But the mainstay of the big leagues was the reservoir of 4-Fs—males of draft age who had been rejected on physical grounds by the Armed Forces. Not since harem attendants had gone out of style were men's physical deficiencies so highly prized. Ulcers, hearing defects, and torn cartilages were coveted by team owners. Philadelphia was among the best-stocked teams in the American

League, for it owned a pitcher named Russ Christopher who had heart trouble, and a three-toed outfielder named Hal Peck. But the St. Louis Browns picked the ultimate plum. Pete Gray had lost his right arm in a childhood accident but learned to hit and play the outfield with his left, and he performed quite satisfactorily (besides being the Brownies' leading gate attraction) in 1945.

The names that I memorized from afar will stay with me always, like childhood ditties. The White Sox activated Clayland Maffitt Touchstone, who had pitched sparingly for the Boston Braves in 1928–29 without ever winning or losing a game. Forty-two years old in 1945, he pitched in six games for Chicago and preserved his virginal record. And there were the others: Frankie Zak ... Dominic Dallessandro ... Clyde Kluttz . .. Whitey Wietelmann ... Leon Treadway ... Tony Criscola ... Mike Milosevich ... Ruffus Gentry ... Tom Sunkel ... Roberto Estelella ... Mike Garbark ... Ace T. Adams ... John Dickshot ... George Binks ... Japhet "Red" Lynn. One could go on till one babbles.

But there were other names that appeared almost as footnotes to the wartime pennant races. Branch Rickey remained the pioneer, refusing to pare his scouting staff while other teams withdrew into wartime austerity. The Dodgers thus had almost a free choice (at ridiculously low bonuses) of the finest young players coming out of high school during the war. They signed Duke Snider, Carl Erskine, Clem Labine, Gil Hodges, Rex Barney, and Carl Furillo. These were among the names that were to shine in baseball's—and my own—golden tomorrow.

Chapter Seventeen
The Road to Brooklyn

Ever since the day that Tony Lazzeri had put that question to me ("How'd you like to suit up and shag some flies out there?") and I had chickened out, I knew in my heart that I was not of the stuff from which heroes grow. When I entered Columbia in 1946, I did so as a commuter and a nonparticipant, with no thought even of trying out for the college baseball team. W. H. Auden remarked somewhere that Don Quixote went mad because he set out to imitate what he admired. I was constitutionally incapable of madness, and I returned from the war with only one virtue—an unclouded awareness of my ineffable ignorance and mediocrity. The abundant evidence I saw that so few of my fellows shared this virtue gave me, now, a new vice—a pronounced superiority complex.

I became a college student and a *Sun* man almost simultaneously. In a sense, I was crawling back into my womb of orchestrated strife after a prolonged dose of the real thing. What bothered me most about my wartime service was not fear of violence but the open-ended aspect of the war. Would it last for ten years? Or more? When would I be able to return to my own world and its comfortable heroes? At times I could not imagine how it would all end, just as I could not imagine the weapon that abruptly put an end to it. In a reaction to communal living, then, I turned my back on my old determination to attend Yale and selected Columbia because it was within commuting distance. And I applied for a summer job at the most familiar of working places, the *Sun* building at 280 Broadway.

My grandmother, Minnie, had died shortly before my discharge from the Navy, but otherwise the family was intact. It was settled in a new home in a fancier section of New Rochelle, just down the street from the home and the showy rose garden of the erstwhile Fordham Flash, Frank Frisch, who was then managing the Pittsburgh Pirates. The uncertainty that had troubled my father during the war years was at an end. His son was home again, and he was back on a newspaper. The magazine business had bewildered and sometimes probably enraged him: writing copy and captions to fit an art director's preconceived layouts could have been borne, but not the weekly staff meetings where editors from the arts and fashion departments made suggestions for the next issue's sports page.

He saw a light at the end of the hall and got out. With the modest success of his books, his editor at Putnam's suggested that he retire to his study and confine himself to writing books for a living. The literary life at last! In prospect it was appealing, but in practice it proved to be a torment. He wrote a history of the Dodgers, and then widened his horizons by tackling a biography of Al Smith. Somehow "the Happy Warrior" 's family got in on the ground floor here, with agreements from the publisher that let them, in effect, look over my father's shoulder as he was writing the book. There were familial demurrers and tactful suggestions, so that at one point he cried out in a letter to me, "And yes, I neglected to put in that Aunt Tillie went to the bathroom, too!"

He washed his hands of the whole affair, and the finished book appeared without his having even glanced at the galleys. At his lowest point, there came a call from William Randolph Hearst, Jr.

Damon Runyon, one of the writing stars of the Hearst newspaper chain, had heard that Frank Graham wanted to get back into the newspaper business, and he urged its editors to sign him to a contract. It was an echo of that day thirty years before when Runyon, who had barely a nodding acquaintance with my father during all that time, praised him highly to Joe Vila at the *Sun.* Pop promptly "inked his pact," as they say on the sports pages, and enthusiastically went back to writing a daily column, this time for the New York *Journal-American.*

It was at this time that he cemented his friendship with Red Smith. They had known each other during those years when Red was working for the St. Louis *Star* and the Philadelphia *Record.* In 1946 Stanley Woodward, the sports editor of the New York *Herald Tribune,* was determined to put together the best sports department of his time, and the first man he hired, having followed his work in the out-of-town papers, was Smith.

"Red turned out to be a better writer than he had ever been before," Woodward wrote afterward. "The young man who moves up from a small paper to a big one will find this is very often the case. In Philadelphia, Red worked in a department that was understaffed, and as a result he was forced to write too many words every day. No matter how good a man is, his writing will suffer if he is overworked. In New York, where our larger staff took some of the burden off him, Red was able to put in the little extra time on his column that soon made all the difference in the world."

Smith himself described the primary function of a sportswriter as well as anyone has. "People go to sports events to be entertained," he said, "and they probably read the sports pages for the same reason. So I try to entertain them. I try to avoid saying things in a hackneyed way—the way that they've been said over and over again by other people."

Red has always been as adept at entertaining his colleagues on the sports beat as he has in his column. One morning, after a hard night on the town, he appeared for breakfast in the hotel dining room, ashen and bleary-eyed.

"Your eyes look awful, Red," a friend commented super-fluously.

Red sat down and unfolded his napkin. "You should see them from *this* side," he said.

He and my father became traveling companions, going almost everywhere together. If one was seen at the ball park or a fighter's training camp, the other was sure to be somewhere close by. At the racetrack they were referred to as an entry—"1 and 1A." My father revealed absolutely no jealousy toward this rising star, boosting him to anyone who would listen, while Red treated his senior running mate with humorous irreverence.

In a hotel lobby one day, my father was accosted by a sometime acquaintance who began to assure him that he was still writing the best column in sports and that there was no one else who even came close to him. Smith stood silently by until the man had bestowed his final compliment on my father and walked away. Then Red jerked his head in the direction of the departing figure and inquired, "Who was that illiterate bastard?"

Pop specialized more in the leisurely anecdote than in the one-liner, but every once in a while he came up with a very nice shot. One of the most frequently quoted since his death concerned Bob Meusel, a tall, dour man who played in the outfield with Babe Ruth on those formidable Yankee teams of the 1920s. Meusel was an uncooperative interviewee, seldom giving a newspaperman the time of day. Then, as it grew apparent that his career was in a sharp decline, he changed his tune. He became—as far as it went within his limited capacities—a hail-fellow-well-met. Pop was not impressed.

"Meusel began to say hello," he noted, "when it was time to say good-bye."

The best-known sentiment that this oft-acclaimed nice guy passed on to posterity, however, was not his own. It was uttered at the Polo Grounds by Leo Durocher, who was then managing the Dodgers, on the night of July 5, 1946. Apparently my father was the only writer present who took the trouble to record Leo's soliloquy.

Red Barber, the Dodgers' radio announcer, was needling Durocher about the home runs the Giants had hit the day before.

"Home runs!" Leo said. "Some home runs! Line drives and pop flies that would have been caught on a bigger field! That's what they were!"

"Why don't you admit they were real home runs?" Red asked. "Why don't you be a nice guy for a change?"

Leo had been reclining on the bench. Now he leaped to his feet.

"A nice guy!" he yelled. "A nice guy! I been around baseball for a long time and I've known a lot of nice guys."

He walked up and down the dugout, then whirled and pointed toward the Giants' dugout.

"Nice guys!" he said. "Look over there. Do you know a nicer guy than their manager, Mel Ott? Or any of the other Giants? Why, they're the nicest guys in the world! And where are they? In last place!"

He walked up and down again, beating himself on the chest.

"Nice guys! I'm not a nice guy—and I'm in first place. Nobody helped me to get there either, except the guys on this ball club and they ain't nice guys! There wasn't anybody in this league helped me to get up there. They saw me coming and they—"

He stamped on the floor of the dugout.

"That's what they gave me!" he yelled. "Nobody said to me, 'You're in third place now, Leo. We want to see you get up to second.'"

He picked up a towel from the bench and held it high and patted it and said, "Nobody said, 'You're in second place now, Leo. We'd like to see you in first place.'"

He threw the towel back on the bench.

"No, sir! Nobody wanted to see me up there. All the nice guys in the league wanted to knock me down, which is the way it should be. But in spite of them, I got up there. I'm in first place now and—"

He waved a hand toward the Giant dugout.

"The nice guys are over there in last place. Well, let them come and get me!"

The Dodgers were at batting practice and Eddie Stanky, the second baseman, was at the plate.

"Look at that little—!" Leo said. "Think he's a nice guy? The hell he is! He'll knock you down to make a play, if he has to. That's the kind of guys I want on my ball club."

He spoke warmly now.

"Look at him," he said. "The little—. He can't run, he can't hit, he can't throw, he can't do nothing. But what a ball player! I wouldn't give him for any second baseman in the league. Or for any two second basemen."

The bell rang and the Dodgers were streaming into the dugout. A reporter who had been sitting on the bench got up.

"All right, boys," he said. "Make room for some nice guys."

"Not in this dugout," Leo said.

He waved toward the Giants' dugout again.

"The nice guys are all over there," he said. "In last place."

It was more than an expression of Leo's philosophy. It was a sound forecast. The nice guys finished last.

I tagged along with my father when I could, even to the racetrack, in which I had very little interest. On a trip to Joe Louis's training camp in the country, I saw Damon Runyon for the first time. Runyon suffered from cancer of the throat, and surgery had removed part of his larynx, so that he could no longer speak. He carried on conversations with the aid of a pad and pencil, scribbling a question or a comment on the pad, showing it to the other party, and then tearing off the sheet to clear the pad for the next comment. As he crumpled up sheets of paper and tossed them on the ground, onlookers scrambled for the souvenirs, like pigeons in the park dashing in to retrieve crumbs from a man who is eating a sandwich. There must have been a lively trade in these holographs along Broadway.

The *Sun*, when I joined its summer staff as a copyboy, was in its death throes, though I was blissfully unaware of it. It had always been there, and it would go on and on, like—well, like the Brooklyn Dodgers and *Look* magazine and Stillman's Gym. The *Sun's* receptionist, who sat at a desk in the hallway, was said to be in his nineties. His presence there might have been dismissed as a quaint touch, but most of the men in positions of responsibility walked in a funny, curled-over way. Keats Speed, white-haired and aristocratic, was palsied, and could just about maneuver the few steps from his small office to the city room. Changes had occurred, both inside and outside the *Sun* building, but the men who ran the place didn't seem to be aware of them. A few years ago Ariel Durant, in *A Dual Autobiography,* which she wrote with her husband, Will, recalled the poverty of her childhood in New York. She and her mother peddled newspapers in Grand Central Station before World War I.

"I learned to tell, from a glance at an oncoming commuter, what paper he would want," she wrote. "The *Sun* appealed to the leisurely aristocrat with his spats and cane; the *Tribune* to the conservative businessman; the *Times* to alert and enterprising men of affairs; the *Telegraph* to the sporty man with tilted hat; the *Morning Journal* to the average man or woman. When, years later, I heard that the *Sun* had faded out, I saw the event as symbolizing the passing of the type that had loved it—men who felt themselves to be Anglo-Saxon gentlemen who had inherited the manners and culture of England."

The *Sun* hadn't noticed that that sort of codger was among the missing. There were other gaps in its perception. One day, when my father and I were visiting a man who was an editor on the *Sun,* I spoke of my plans to take a graduate course in journalism after earning my bachelor's degree.

"No need for that," the man told me. "We prefer to teach you to do things *our* way on the *Sun.*"

When I went to work there at twenty-one dollars a week, one of my colleagues confidentially pointed out a young man on the rewrite desk who had attended the Columbia School of Journalism. Having been tipped off in advance, the rewrite man had never mentioned this indiscretion to his superiors. They seemed to be well pleased with his performance and marveled at how quickly he picked things up.

Copyboys were no longer urchins. By the late 1940s, most of

the copyboys were college students—young fellows like Dave Anderson, now a sports columnist on the *Times*, and Les Woodcock, who joined the original staff of *Sports Illustrated*. Yet, as a matter of immemorial custom, each copyboy took his turn once a week in fetching the morning mail from the post office some four or five blocks away. On the appointed morning the well-dressed young scholar would descend to the basement, commandeer a large cart, heap it with mailbags, and set off across Broadway, pushing the contraption ahead of him through the gutter. Several of the more self-conscious copyboys always took a lengthy detour, sticking to the back streets and proceeding in mortal fear of an encounter with a college classmate strolling to a plush job in a downtown law office or brokerage firm. One of our number, not wholly in jest, suggested that we go on strike for higher pay, shorter hours, and the right to pee in the streets like the horses.

I spent three summers preparing myself to be a *Sun* man. I ran copy in the city room, clipped newspapers in the morgue, and prepared box scores in the sports department. The only really interesting work I did was in the society department, where I shared an office with Paul Stewart, the society editor, and occasionally with last year's leading debutante whom the *Sun* in its senility had hired (along with Milton Berle) to spruce up the paper with an offbeat column. I was occasionally permitted to write a brief account of a minor wedding, but the most fun I had was researching the background of our big newsmakers in a long card file that had been compiled over the years by Stewart. It provided good reading, especially when I came across some dirt on the family backgrounds of a couple of my socialite fraternity brothers at Columbia.

If the work in the sports department was generally boring, the office itself wasn't. There was banter and horseplay, and in the afternoons the teletype machine chattered incessantly with the play-by-play of the three home teams' games. Unfamiliar faces bustled in and out of the sports department all day long, though it was some time before I became aware that the racing handicapper doubled as a bookmaker. Through much of the summer of 1948, I worked around a large metal cut of a sentimental cartoon (boy waving to ball player who is being wafted heavenward, wrapped in clouds) that was to be run on the day of Babe Ruth's approaching death; a celebrity's cancer is a convenience for a newspaper's makeup men, who can then plan their pages well in advance.

In January, 1950, while I was in my senior year at Columbia, the *Sun* folded. Technically, it was absorbed by the *World-Telegram*, but since the latter was the buyer, most of the old *Sun* men who were not ready for retirement found few openings available. Certainly there were none for an overage copyboy, even though I was to have assumed a slightly more prestigious position in June. For a while it appeared that I was bound for the bushes.

One Friday night in early spring, after the fights at the Garden, I returned to Toots Shor's to nurse a few beers and be uplifted with a nod from DiMag or Jim Farley or Horace Stoneham. Or maybe I would listen to some lewd tales from the mouth of Abe Attell, former featherweight champion of the world and a prime mover in the Black Sox scandal of 1919; Abe was full of amusing practical jokes, too, which included surreptitiously pinning a phallic-shaped cork to the trouser front of self-important drunks at the circular bar. But this time I sat with Lou Niss, who was the sports editor of the Brooklyn *Eagle*. We talked about the problem I faced, with graduation only a couple of months away.

"Why don't you come over and see me," Niss said. "I think I've got a job for you."

There was no job on the *Eagle* itself, as I had suspected. But there was an opening at an annual salary of three thousand dollars for a young man who would serve as executive secretary of the Brooklyn Amateur Baseball Foundation. This, I learned from Niss, was a nonprofit organization sponsored by the *Eagle* and the Dodgers to provide playing fields and equipment for sandlot players in the borough. The equipment was stored in a dusty room at the *Eagle* building on Johnson Street, while the executive secretary hung his hat in the Dodgers' scouting department on Montague Street. I accepted the offer, and stuck a tentative foot into each of the two worlds that had always beckoned me.

Chapter Eighteen
Prospects and Snake Oil

I moved into an alcove in the Dodgers' scouting department where almost at once I was confronted by a crisis of faith. Like any zealot, I was a vessel of intolerance. I had refused until now to entertain kindly thoughts of other gods, consigning the players on fifteen major-league teams to limbo if not damnation and finding virtue only in those who wore the Yankee pinstripes. Suddenly I was a Dodger. Here I was, earning a regular salary out of a fund accumulated from an exhibition game the Dodgers played for that purpose, sharing a set of ground-floor offices at 215 Montague Street, Brooklyn, with an immortal who was Lou Gehrig's chief rival as the greatest first baseman who ever lived. The seeds of doubt were planted, a note of complexity stirred like a worm in my simplistic sports world, and that, as any dogmatist knows, is the beginning of the end.

George Sisler, who was the Dodgers' chief scout for player talent, occupied a desk in these offices. Although he mingled on easy terms with us nonentities, I was acutely aware that he dwelt apart from us, in a rarer atmosphere, because a bronze plaque bearing his likeness and a recital of his triumphs hung in baseball's Hall of

213

Fame, at Cooperstown, set among those of Ty Cobb, Babe Ruth, Honus Wagner, Walter Johnson, Christy Mathewson, and what was then a handful of others. Sisler had been a marvelous defensive first baseman and a deadly hitter. In 1920 he batted .407 for the St. Louis Browns, and in 1922 he batted .420; no American League player (and in the National League only Rogers Hornsby) has since equaled those averages. Like Gehrig's, his career had been snuffed out by illness, though happily Sisler survived. Spectacled, gray-haired, he flashed a shy, Midwesterner's smile and moved about the office with an odd, flat-footed gait. After spending some time in his company, I no longer bristled when I heard his skills compared with those of Gehrig.

Here, as at the *Sun*, I had no reason to regret that my parents had failed to find a different forename for me. My father had written the team's history, and thus he was as familiar to the men who worked for the Dodgers as if he had been a columnist on the *Eagle*. The relationship did me no harm in Brooklyn. I hastily dipped into his book, which I hadn't read since I was a torpedoman second class at the old destroyer base in San Diego. Then, bits of forgotten lore came back to me. For example, the Dodgers had taken their name from the inhabitants of Brooklyn back in the 1880s, who, the streets having been made hazardous by the introduction of street cars, had begun to refer to themselves as "trolley dodgers." One season, early on, they played as the Brooklyn Bridegrooms because six of their stalwarts had recently married. And, later, they took the name Robins (and hence "the Flock") in honor of their longtime manager, Wilbert Robinson. But the name "Dodgers" kept recurring and even survived the team's transplant to Los Angeles.

The Brooklyn Amateur Baseball Foundation was conceived as a public service to Brooklyn's youth, and I suppose it was. But lurking at the back of everyone's mind in the Dodgers' office was the hope that somewhere on all of those fields in Brooklyn and Queens, where boys played with bats and balls provided by the foundation, there was a budding star who would leap at the chance to play in Ebbets Field. Until then, the hope had been largely frustrated. One part of the program as originally worked out by the Dodgers and the *Eagle* was a game, or series of games, grandly designated as "Brooklyn Against the World." An annual clash at Ebbets Field, it pitted a team of the best sandlot players in Brooklyn against one composed of players from many cities across the country, each boy having been selected by a local newspaper. It was an expensive and time-consuming chore to juggle all the cities involved, and by my time the "World" in this equation had been reduced to Montreal, where the Dodgers had a farm team whose officials could assemble the best native talent for the game. Thus we played up the "international angle."

The program's most successful product so far had been a smallish left-hander from Queens named Edward "Whitey" Ford. Perhaps the Dodgers' scouts were looking only for large pitchers in those days, but, for whatever reason, Ford slipped through their net and signed with the Yankees, for whom he became a star. The best the Dodgers had done was to uncover a talented but eccentric and rather off-putting right-handed pitcher named Billy Loes, who joined the parent club in 1950, the same year I arrived in Brooklyn. Loes was a reincarnation of Lardner's Alibi Ike, and to explain away his setbacks, he crowded his professional world with bugaboos of a very special sort. Malicious puffs of wind goosed ordinary fly balls over the fence. Blinding shafts of sunlight deflected themselves unnaturally, like the planes in a Picasso painting, to transfix him at the moment of truth. Atmospheric conditions of a peculiarly sinister nature flattened out his fastball and straightened his curve. In short, his failures could be traced less to his stuff on any given day than to demonology.

I kept my ears open on various excursions to sandlots in Bay Ridge, Coney Island, and the Parade Grounds, jotting down the names of any players whom word of mouth heralded as a prospect. These I brought back to Montague Street, where I handed them to Arthur Dede in the scouting department. Dede was one of the sweetest men alive, everyone's idea of a gentle, twinkle-eyed, wisecracking grandfather. None of us minded that his jokes were pure cornball; it was the manner and not the substance of his patter that brought out the laughs. He had been a catcher for the Bushwicks and other semiprofessional teams of the World

War I era and, responding to some long-forgotten emergency at Ebbets Field, had played in a single game for the Dodgers in 1916. If I brought back a sandlotter's name to Dede, he would check it out in one of the drawers of index cards he kept in the office. Each card noted a boy's name and background, and rated his various physical abilities (running speed, throwing arm, batting power) against a big-league norm. Those that measured up were certified as "prospects." I remember that he had one drawer of cards labeled "Prospects Only in Time of War."

When the Dodgers were on the road, the scouting department often invited genuine prospects to come to Ebbets Field for tryouts. I attended these sessions as often as my other duties permitted, for they were both instructive and entertaining. A third member of the scouting department was John Carey, a slender Southwesterner whose undistinguished pitching career had been ended in the minors by a sore arm, and whose dry, sardonic humor was the counterpoint to Dede's exuberance. Aspiring young pitchers would throw to Dede while he yelped in purported agony as their best fastballs nestled into his big catcher's mitt. When the hitters were given a chance to show their prowess, the batting-practice cage was wheeled into position at home plate. Carey pitched, Dede donned the mask and chest protector, and Sisler stood behind the cage and made notes on the aptitude (power, quickness of the bat, etc.) of the young men to whom Carey served up a succession of fat pitches. Just as a brawny high-school boy, watching his drives bounce off the right-field wall, began to make out the cheers of a phantom crowd, Carey would pull the string on a pitch. In his eagerness, the boy would wind up with his bat twisted around his neck, off-balance and goggle-eyed, several seconds before the ball reached the plate.

"Gotta learn to wait for the pitch, young man," Dede would cluck sympathetically as the chastened prospect left the cage.

One morning a foul tip ricocheted off a bar of the batting cage and struck Dede in the back of the head, sending him to his knees. Carey and Sisler rushed to his side, sized up the situation, and bent over him in mock solicitation. Sisler, with a broad wink, ordered the groundskeepers to locate a stretcher. While the prospects stood around dumbfounded, the stretcher was brought forth, and Dede, one eye open and the other screwed shut, was rolled aboard it. Sisler solemnly placed the old catcher's mitt and mask on his stomach, whereupon the groundskeepers lifted their burden and carried it, in cadence with Carey's hummed funeral march, to the Dodgers' dugout. Dede rolled off, took a drink from the water cooler, and then walked back to his position. I heard a prospect murmur something about "daffy Dodgers."

Although I was not, strictly speaking, on the Dodgers' payroll, everyone in the office treated me as if I were one of the team. There was a definable sense of camaraderie, an evangelical fervor and a solemn purposefulness, in the office. It seemed to radiate from a presence. I had not yet been granted a close view of that presence, having caught only a glimpse of it seated in the president's box, which hung from the bottom of the upper deck behind home plate, and so I was startled to learn that I had come within the circle of its recognition.

"Mr. Rickey would like to talk with you one of these days," Harold Roettger, the team's public-relations director, told me. "He's had his eye on you, and he is very interested in your work."

That one tidbit was sufficient to keep me going for months. The reverence in which Branch Rickey, the Dodgers' president, was held by his underlings may be difficult to comprehend in this irreverent age, but his hold on them was almost magnetic. "There goes the greatest man since Jesus Christ," one of them is said to have gasped after attending a hortatory organization meeting in his office. Words flowed from this teetotaling old ball player and hard-hearted businessman as from a drunken poet. His country lawyer's apparel, his hirsute, intimidating brow, his self-aggrandizing aphorisms ("Luck is the residue of design"), the very resonance of his voice, and the penetration of his glare seemed to be aimed only at the subjugation of the yahoo. But the sophisticate who sneered at him as an old fraud was, during a ten-minute tête-à-tête, likely to be charmed out of his britches. Not for nothing was 215 Montague Street known to the press during Rickey's tenure there as "the cave of the winds."

Among the few treasures I have kept from my years in Brook-

lyn is a copy of a seven-page memo, marked PERSONAL AND CONFI-
DENTIAL, that fell into my hands when I inherited an old filing
cabinet after the Rickey regime had moved almost intact to Pittsburgh. Rickey was writing to his chief aides on June 23, 1949,
shortly before leaving on a ten-day vacation. ("This is the first vacation I shall have taken since I have been in Brooklyn," he noted.
"I have had in mind that this trip is the only one I shall attempt in
the next six years.") In his memo he gives his evaluation of the
state of the Dodgers and their five leading farm teams, with instructions and suggestions for his staff during his absence. The
document is so redolent of the old man's style and approach to the
game that I think I shall bequeath it to Cooperstown. I reproduce
a section of it here, pertaining to his opinion of the Dodgers'
pitching staff:

All last winter, and this spring too, I believed our pitching
staff would be strong enough. Right now I think it is the weakest
part of our team.

Branca may be out of the class of great pitchers.

Newcombe yesterday in Cincinnati had nothing, struck out
one man, pitcher Blackwell, I guess it was. Until the 8th inning
not a single batter on the Cincinnati Club missed on his swing.
Eight balls were hit like bullets by Cincinnati hitters,—right at
somebody. Newcombe was lucky not to lose the game by a big
score.

Palica has as much stuff as anybody but is easily the most
damaging liability we carry anywhere.

I cannot help believing that Banta, if pitched regularly, would
be a big winner for us. It will not surprise me if our manager
finds a place for him regularly, perhaps in place of Branca.

Hatten is Hatten, unpredictable and undependable.

Rex Barney should win from now on.

Roe is good.

As I see it, we need another starting pitcher a whole lot more
than we do a relief pitcher. You know how I feel about relief
pitchers. I don't believe in them. On our club right now, as on
most clubs, they are simply necessary evils.

And further, this decision has boiled down, so far as I am concerned to a choice between McGlothin and Erskine, and at the
present minute, I am for Erskine. I am in no doubt that if one-

218

third, or just a small part of the patience and effort had been used with Erskine as was used in the case of Rex Barney, Erskine would be probably the ace pitcher of our staff.

We don't need Mickey Owen and I am asking waivers on him on this date. If the player is claimed, I propose to let him go. If he is not claimed, then I wish you to apprise the Commissioner of the player's status. If Major League waivers are secured on Owen, then I would like to give him outright release to the Hollywood Club.

If we were to secure waivers on Owen, then I want to force, if I can, the Hollywood Club to take Owen, either as an additional player or if not that, then in the place of Al Unser. The Hollywood Club is quite evidently high on Unser but this fellow, fine chap that he is, cannot catch anywhere. He is simply not a catcher. He can't receive and he can't throw. I would not have him as a catcher on any club above Class B. Obviously, therefore, it is necessary to do a selling job at Hollywood in order to make the Owen-Unser deal. So far as I am concerned, Hollywood can be authorized to give Unser unconditional release. On any other club in the Pacific Coast League, he would help Hollywood.

I am leaving town this coming Sunday. If you meet with emergency, you will act with authority within the general scope of this outline.

The Dodgers had pulled themselves together that year and (with help from young Carl Erskine, who won eight games and lost only one after being brought in from Montreal) captured the pennant. They were favored to win again in 1950. This was Rickey's team, a fulfillment of the promise that my father had written about in his last column for the *Sun*, seven years before. Alone among baseball's executives, Rickey had detected a golden opportunity to steal a march on his rivals and tap the two virgin sources of talent that were then available. He had kept his scouting staff intact during the war years, skimming the cream of the young talent while other teams waited for a "more stable situation," and he had been the first to realize that color barriers soon must fall and had snapped up the best young players in the Negro leagues. These canny decisions enabled the Dodgers to dominate the National League in the first decade after the war.

Rickey was a meld of flamboyant style and puritanical standards. As a youth, he had promised his mother never to play ball on the Sabbath, and to the end, whether as a player, manager, or executive, he invariably joined the Creator in resting from his labors on Sunday and absenting himself from the ball park. His puritanism carried over to pay scales, for he prized "hungry" ball players, though he himself grew more affluent as time went on. Naturally, a faint aroma of snake oil could be detected about his person by more cynical observers, and he was an inviting target for the kind of skits produced for the annual baseball writers' dinner in New York. Arthur Mann, a journalist who also fancied himself a thespian, was generally recruited to play the part of Rickey in those skits. (When the Dodgers hired Mann as a sort of assistant to the president, it was snidely suggested by the writers that Rickey was trying to take the sting out of their annual theatricals.)

In any case, the signing by the Dodgers of Jackie Robinson, the first black player in organized baseball, and the subsequent deification of Rickey by the liberal community as a great humanitarian, stirred a measure of skepticism among the baseball writers. My father shared in these suspicions of humbuggery, and described the aftermath in his history of the Dodgers.

Skeptics in the newspapers hinted that Rickey had no real interest in the future of Robinson or any other Negro player, had signed Jackie only under the pressure of interracial groups, and secretly hoped the boy would not make good in Montreal [the farm team to which he was first sent], thus solving a vexing problem to Rickey's satisfaction; or that since the admission of Negro players to the big leagues was inevitable in the reasonably near future, Branch simply had been shrewd enough to beat the gun in the hope of capitalizing on his shrewdness. At the Baseball Writers' dinner in New York that winter, Arthur Mann, cast as "Rickey," sang a parody, of his own composition, on "The Battle Hymn of the Republic." To the refrain, "Mine eyes have seen the glory of the opportunity," Rickey was alternately limned as an emancipator and a slave driver, first liberating Negroes who chorused, "Glory, Glory, Massa

*Rickey," then lashing them with a bull whip which he pulled out
of a carpetbag. It was, everybody agreed, the best song the writers
ever had had in their show, and Rickey laughed as heartily as anyone present. It is doubtful, however, if he really enjoyed it.*

It must be said that Robinson and the other beneficiaries of
Rickey's revolutionary stroke did not share in this cynicism. Robinson always spoke of Rickey with respect and affection, and dis-
liked Walter O'Malley, who succeeded Rickey as the Dodgers'
president and who never lost an opportunity to malign the old
man. That Rickey did not consider Robinson a unique experiment
can be proved by his efforts to acquire other players from the
Negro leagues. One of the players Rickey signed shortly after
Robinson was Roy Campanella, already a veteran player. In the
same file with the Rickey memo I discovered a sheaf of letters
written by Campanella in September, 1946, to Bob Finch, one of
Rickey's assistants. They made up a series of reports that Campanella had apparently been assigned to send Finch after a scouting tour of the Negro leagues. In a neat hand, alternately script
and block letters, on plain white paper, Campanella reported:

> Concerning Doby, he can hit, run and throw very good. Hits
> with a lot of power, but needs to learn how to pull. I've seen him
> hit home-run in Ruppert stadium, Newark also Shibe Park, Phil-
> adelphia. He has a nice personality, good habits and is intelli-
> gent.
>
> At present I am watching a right hand pitcher of the Elite
> Giants. His name is Joe Black, 22 years old, attends Morgan
> College in Baltimore, Md. He spent three years in service pitch-
> ing for Tommy Bridges team and was the only negro on the
> team. He has an exceptionally good fast ball, good change, good
> curve ball. Very good disposition. He's very apt to catch on. I
> will send you a report later on this week about him.
>
> The young boy Gillam has the making of a good player. He is
> one of the youngest players in the league. He is very apt and has
> good habits.
>
> P.S. The home-runs Doby hit were in the left-field stands.

FRANK GRAHAM, JR.

Four other players whom Campanella mentioned in his reports never emerged from obscurity, but a .571 average of success is as commendable for a scouting report as for most other aspects of the game. Here Campy showed another facility as well, putting to use "apt," "disposition," and other key words from the scouting jargon popularized by Rickey adherents. While I was with the organization, I heard that the Dodgers had permitted Cleveland to sign Larry Doby because Rickey, though he wanted more than his share of the brightest talent from the Negro leagues, did not want a majority of blacks on his team. (For years there was a rumor that no big-league team would ever play more than four blacks at a time, but the taboo on a black majority was quietly broken one day in 1955, I believe, when Walter Alston fielded a lineup that included Don Newcombe, Campanella, Robinson, Jim Gilliam, and Sandy Amoros.) The Dodgers, of course, signed Campy's two other finds: Joe Black produced one glorious season as a relief pitcher at Ebbets Field, being largely responsible for the pennant in 1952; and "Gillam," as Jim Gilliam, had a long and distinguished career as a player and coach with the team.

As the Dodgers stumbled toward second place in 1950, I concerned myself with Brooklyn Against the World.

A strong Brooklyn team was assembled, as scouts visited diamonds throughout Brooklyn and Queens, and a final tryout by invitation only was held at Ebbets Field. (As a note to social history, it can be recorded that there was not a single black or Hispanic player on the team. I can vouch for an absence of prejudice in the final selection, for no qualified players from these minorities could be found in the two boroughs, or in Montreal, for that matter, and thus in 1950 Brooklyn Against the World was lily-white.) Perhaps half a dozen of these players eventually signed professional contracts, though none made it to the big leagues.

The selection of players was the most straightforward of the arrangements to be made for the games. Sandlot baseball in Brooklyn was a byzantine affair, with all sorts of ambitions and jealousies and plots lurking in the background. The kids just wanted to play ball; their elders, the middle-aged men who were

222

their coaches and league officials, had more devious games to play, and a shattered winning streak was as nothing compared to a deflated ego. Since most of the tickets for the game at Ebbets Field were to be sold by the leagues themselves, one of my duties was to sign out blocks of seats from the Dodgers' ticket office and then persuade each league to accept and peddle a generous number of them. There were squabbles over how many tickets each league ought to be responsible for, and over whether a league had been allotted inferior seats. Once the tickets went out, they seemed to disappear into a thousand pockets, as they were divided among players and coaches to sell to their friends and neighbors. Because I had signed for at least fifteen thousand tickets, at two and three dollars apiece, I spent some hair-raising moments just before game time trying to account for either the tickets or the money. That I did not go to prison speaks well for either the honesty of the sandlotters or the disorganization of the Dodgers' ticket office.

Meanwhile, I had become entangled in the meshes of another problem. The highlight of the pregame festivities every year was the crowning of a Sandlot Queen, who was elected by the twenty or more leagues involved in the program; each league's vote was proportionate to the number of tickets it had sold for the game. I assumed that the issue was cut-and-dried that year because Arthur Bellone, the self-styled "Commissioner of Sandlot Baseball" (his jurisdiction really only applied to those leagues that played their games in the vicinity of Brooklyn's Parade Grounds) had a daughter named Peggy, blond and photogenic, whom he had put forth as a candidate. Peggy Bellone was an appropriate queen in every respect.

I had not reckoned on the ego of Milton "Pop" Secol, the president of an independent entity called the Ice Cream League. Pop Secol ("Say it fast," he always advised new acquaintances in his raspy voice) suddenly proposed his wife for the crown. While Ma Secol was a pleasant woman of a certain age, she was no match for the comely Peggy; nor would her picture make such a splash on the sports pages of local papers. A born salesman, of tickets as well as of ice cream, Pop Secol made an unprecedented effort in

Ma's behalf, and I welcomed the boost he gave to the game's attendance. Yet everyone was in a bit of a sweat until Arthur Bellone exercised whatever clout he could muster, and the other leagues pooled their votes to bring his daughter home a winner.

The game at Ebbets Field was a modest success. A respectable, if not capacity, crowd showered wolf whistles on Peggy Bellone as well as on Ma Secol, who took a bow as the runner-up, and cheered on a one-sided victory of the home forces over the "World," as represented by the gallant sandlotters from Montreal. In turn I took the Brooklyn team to Montreal, where E. J. "Buzzie" Bavasi, the general manager of the Dodgers' farm team and later vice-president of the Dodgers, proved a generous host. He arranged dinners and sightseeing tours for the players, and the trip would have passed without incident had not my charges located a vendor of water pistols and briefly disrupted a boat excursion up the St. Lawrence River.

The highlight of my first year in Brooklyn occurred at the banquet we staged at the Hotel St. George for the sandlot players and their families. Branch Rickey, Burt Shotton, and the Dodger players appeared for speeches and bows. Rickey delivered a fiery speech that made headlines the next day, castigating the players for their lackluster performance that season.

The moment I had been waiting for arrived when the banquet was over. As stars and hopefuls alike filed out of the ballroom, I was told that "Mr. Rickey" wanted to talk to me. When I approached the dais, he descended, greeted me with a firm handshake, and fixed me with his penetrating stare.

"Young man," he intoned, "I have been very, very lax. My behavior toward you has been unforgivable—absolutely unforgivable. I have been meaning to arrange for a meeting with you for months, but somehow the time has gotten away from me. Now, let's go over here so that you can tell me about your work."

Wrapping a fatherly arm around me, he steered me to a table in the corner of the ballroom and insisted that I sit down before he took a seat opposite me. I was already in thrall, not even troubled by the prospect of having to stammer out in such august circumstances a description of the mundane little tasks at which I spent my days. But I need not have worried. No opportunity to open my mouth presented itself, for there was no break in the flow of words that fell in plangent tones from Rickey's lips. I cannot recall a word that he said at the table, but who asks for syntax from the incantatory surge of the sea? At the end of—what? five minutes? twenty?—he suddenly excused himself because of the lateness of the hour but demanded that I present myself to his secretary the first thing the following morning so that an appointment could be made for us to continue our meeting. As he pumped my hand in a departing handshake, he seemed to want me to understand that he would not draw an easy breath until we had completed our discussion of every aspect of my work and my plans for the future.

My head was still whirling as I went to his office the next morning. His secretary met me pleasantly enough but informed me that Mr. Rickey had just left town for a ten-day business trip. It would be eight years before he and I exchanged another word.

That year rushed to a conclusion in a swirl of confusing and sometimes dispiriting events. The Dodgers lost the pennant to the Phillies in the tenth inning of the final game of the season when Dick Sisler, Philadelphia's first baseman and a son of the immortal George, hit a three-run home run into the left-field stands at Ebbets Field. Shortly afterward, Rickey announced that he had sold his share of the Dodgers to Walter O'Malley and would take on the task of transforming the Pittsburgh Pirates into a winning team. Many of the Dodgers' executives and scouts, including Sisler, joined the exodus, and one of them let me know that I was among the invited. But New York was still the center of my universe, and I elected to throw in my lot with the staff that O'Malley was beginning to put together in Brooklyn.

At the end of the year I accepted an offer to join the Dodgers' public-relations department. Never-never land had been shaped for me through an intermediary until then, filtered through my father's perceptions and craft. Now I was at the source, where I would have a hand in passing on the tidings to others.

Chapter Nineteen
The Creeping Terror

In *The Boys of Summer*, that unsparing account of man's passage from youthful glory into troubled middle age, Roger Kahn remembered a shining moment:

"At a point in life when one is through with boyhood, but has not yet discovered how to be a man, it was my fortune to travel with the most marvelously appealing of teams."

Roger Kahn's team was the Dodgers of those special years, a team that will always be associated with Jackie Robinson. The Jackie Robinson Brooklyn Dodgers. Those words still are as plucked strings even to men and women who can no longer be stirred by paeans to the flag, motherhood, or apple pie.

Kahn again: "Robinson could hit and bunt and steal and run. He had intimidating skills, and he burned with a dark fire. He wanted passionately to win. He charged at ball games. . . . He bore the burden of a pioneer and the weight made him strong. If one can be certain of anything in baseball, it was that we shall not look upon his like again."

Enough in itself to brand a team remarkable, and yet Robinson was surrounded at Ebbets Field not by a supporting cast but by a

226

dozen other players of exceptional skills and personal qualities. Harold "Pee Wee" Reese, the team captain who did not lead but who forged a camaraderie among the others by the example of decency and quiet humor. Gil Hodges, soft-spoken, gently teasing, as powerful as Gehrig and, like Gehrig, doomed by a flaw in a body that seemed fashioned of pig iron. Edwin "Duke" Snider, moody, spoiled, like so many athletes from Southern California, but with the grace and potential abilities (briefly realized) of a DiMaggio. Roy Campanella, raconteur and con man, who could dismantle the National League during his astonishing streaks of power-hitting. Billy Cox of the incomparable glove, and Carl Furillo of the incomparable arm. Carl Erskine, slightly built but gritty, whose only shortcoming (in manager Charlie Dressen's eyes) was that he would not risk the maiming of another player by throwing a knockdown pitch at him. Don Newcombe, who didn't "win the big ones," they said, but who won a great many little ones for the Dodgers. And scrappy bench warmers like Tom Lasorda, Dick Williams, and Don Zimmer, who went on to become big-league managers. It was a team that moved Marianne Moore to indite a poem to its members and that encouraged Philip Roth's Portnoy to weave pleasurable daydreams set in Ebbets Field. Yes, Roger Kahn made a good case that this was "the most marvelously appealing of teams."

Yes, but: sometimes, during the years I worked for the Dodgers, my father would come to Ebbets Field and visit the dugout, as he had done so often at the Polo Grounds and Yankee Stadium. Though he had put on pounds and a hint of jowls, he was still youthful-looking, still "the kid" sitting back in a corner, attentive to what was going on about him. But little was going on about him, or so it seemed in the *Journal-American* the next day, where his column failed to soar beyond the level of his colleagues'. It imparted information, the descriptive prose was typically accurate and apt, though the spontaneous banter and the *air* of the dugout that had characterized his *Sun* columns were missing.

"I'm no longer a part of the dugout fixtures," he explained to me one day with a helpless little shrug. "These players are all several decades my junior and I'm an elder statesman, a personage, to them. When I walk into the dugout, they interrupt whatever it is they were doing or talking about, and they smile and shake hands. 'Hello, Mr. Graham,' Reese will say. 'How are you today, Mr. Graham?' Robinson will say. And that air of informality, that sense of ease or even of disdain that players feel for the younger writers, just evaporates. The players try to make me feel welcome, but I only feel more of a stranger."

The most appealing team for Frank Graham was not Jackie Robinson's Dodgers but John McGraw's Giants or Babe Ruth's Yankees. He admired Robinson, though I think he was a little wary of him; he was genuinely fond of Reese, Hodges, and Campy. Yet this team was not, could not be, a part of his experience, a stage in the rites of passage toward his maturity, as it was for Roger Kahn—and for me.

Like a player who has been traded from one ball club to another, and at once sloughs off old loyalties to give his all for a team he had battled and reviled only the day before, I was an unrepentant turncoat. In the Yankees' dugout I had been a boy, gazing silently on my idols, happy to receive the handout of a nod or a "Hiya, son" as one of them clattered by on his way to the bat rack. Now I was on my own, a genuine Dodger, needing neither a pass to enter the ball park nor my father's presence to violate the security of the dugout and clubhouse. (Even headier was the experience on a road trip when I went by the team's chartered bus from the hotel to the stadium, alighting with the players and sometimes being mistaken for one of them by a fan; I learned to brush aside a proffered pen and autograph book as grumpily as any rookie infielder.)

If there was a night game scheduled at Ebbets Field, I went straight from the office to the ball park without dallying for dinner in one of the restaurants on Montague Street. There would be an opportunity, I knew, to have a sandwich and a beer in the press club sometime during the evening, and I was eager to be among the early arrivals on the field. I bustled up out of the BMT subway with my briefcase (which was packed with press releases, Dodger yearbooks, and perhaps a set of photographs of the players a friend had asked me to have signed) and passed by the ticket booths and entry gates at the rotunda, exchanging greetings with police lieutenants and peddlers of pirated scorecards on the way.

The press gate was guarded by Jim Clark, a cranky, shriveled-up ancient who was said to have worked at Ebbets Field since its opening in 1913; he was a veritable Cerberus, pugnaciously barring entry to urchin and powerful politician alike, if he could not recall the face, but swinging wide the gate for me as if I were old Charlie Ebbets himself. Friendly greetings and respectful salutations from other ball-park employees marked my progress to the clubhouse, for I was "front office." If the metal door (the word DODGERS slanting across it in bold script) was locked, a sharp rap on its surface drew the clubhouse attendant, paunchy, slack-jawed John Griffin, to screen the intruder. Through the widening crack I detected his dirty T-shirt and the big, floppy, comical hat (perhaps a cast-off sombrero) that had become his trademark. A nod, a grunt, and I was in the sanctum.

"Duke Snider signs baseballs!" Charlie DiGiovanna, the bat-boy, called as he set out a box of Spalding balls near the door for the players to autograph when they found a spare moment. "Preacher Roe signs baseballs! *Everybody* signs baseballs!"

The "batboy" was a man, and had been one for some time, with a family of his own; but he liked the job, and the players liked him, and since he was partly invalided by the heart disease that would kill him before long, he stayed on and on. Short, stocky, with a wide grin and beetling brows (for which the players nicknamed him "Charlie the Brow," or the variant "Charles de Brow"), he was possessed of a special skill for which all of the players valued him highly. Signing baseballs that were to be given to big shots and their kids was an irksome chore for the players. The balls sat around in their boxes for so long that if they had been tomatoes, they would have rotted. When, after a suitable interval, large, uninked gaps remained on the balls, DiGiovanna picked them one by one from their boxes and carefully forged the appropriate signatures. Many an aging Dodger fan now preserves in his rumpus room a baseball whose stitched cover is densely scribbled all over with the various signatures of Charlie the Brow.

Today the Players' Association would form a grievance com-

mittee just to complain about the clubhouses in Ebbets Field—
dingy, poorly ventilated spaces crowded with stools and open
lockers. The only amenity apparent was an old swivel chair someone had scavenged for Reese, which the shortstop lounged in before and after a game. Looking up, he greeted me in his soft
Kentucky voice and took several letters from me. This was a time
before players' agents were in vogue, and business matters were
usually channeled through the front office; Pee Wee showed little
interest in the letters I had for him, and readily agreed to my offer
to answer them.

One of my few onerous duties with the Dodgers was to try to
wheedle the players into making an appearance at one of the
banquets, testimonial dinners, or "sports nights" that seemed to
be taking place every evening somewhere in Brooklyn or Queens.
In the players' contracts was a vague clause requiring them to
make some promotional appearances at affairs of this kind during
the year, but it was observed mostly in the breach. In case of an
emergency (perhaps a civic function in which Walter O'Malley
was interested), I could persuade one of my "class guys," Reese or
Robinson, to attend, but it had better have the highest priority.
Unfortunately, Snider was in constant demand for these appearances, and he and I played a cat-and-mouse game. Bearing an invitation, I would warily circle the Duke's locker, which was one
of the few set up in the middle of the clubhouse, waiting for an
opportunity to approach him. He studiously ignored me. Finally,
when I had used up fifteen minutes or so, he looked in my direction.

"What have you got for me?" he asked, wearily.

"Well, there's this church in Bay Ridge that has a father-and-
son night next Saturday. They said they would pick you up and—"

"No," Snider said, turning away to finish buttoning his uniform
shirt.

And that was that. I would set off across the room to try to harass a rookie into accepting the engagement, and if it was early in
the season and the rookie was still unsure of himself, I might be
successful. Otherwise, the father-and-son crowd would have to
make do with some funny stories from the parish priest.

[A FAREWELL TO HEROES]

About then I would see the clubhouse man, John Griffin, leading a poodle on a leash, and I knew that Dressen had arrived in
the manager's office. When Ruth Dressen, Charlie's wife, came to
the ball park, she turned the dog over to him for safekeeping, and
he in turn left it in Griffin's care. It made an arresting sight: the
tiny poodle, exquisitely coiffed and elegantly spangled and berib-
boned, tiptoeing daintily ahead of the lumbering Griffin, his jowls
unshaven, his lips saliva-flecked where a cigar had rested, wearing
one of his outlandish hats.

"That's the only dog I ever saw that looks like a whore," Reese
remarked one evening.

I walked through the vestibule that was the coaches' dressing
room into the manager's modest office. Squat, sad-eyed, his thin
hair slicked back, Dressen seemed to cry out for sympathy. A boy-
ish ego contended endlessly in him with a dark suspicion of inferiority, and no matter how well he was doing one always had the
feeling that he was going to end up with egg on his face. A born
loser who sometimes won. Even his brashest pronouncements
seemed pathetic rather than offensive. "Stay close to 'em," he
urged his team in the dugout one afternoon as they trailed by a
run or two in the closing innings. "I'll think of somethin'." I admired him. All he wanted out of life was to be known as a smart
baseball man, and he worked at it twenty-four hours a day,
dreaming up clever moves as an adolescent creates fantasies,
eager to go anywhere and talk to anybody if it might help his ball
club.

Dressen's office was frequently infested by pompous little men
of the kind who are forever clinging to the nipples of the illustrious: in this case, a stockbroker, a florist, a manufacturer of shoe
polish. They were no asset to him, except insofar as their unde-
viating approval shored up his ego, but Charlie felt comfortable
in their company. More congenial to me, at any rate, were the
baseball men who dropped into the office to exchange a word
with the manager. Two of my favorites were veteran scouts for
the Dodgers, Andy High and John "Red" Corriden, who lounged
in easy chairs that were set back in the corners and spoke to
Dressen about the players (Johnny Podres, Sandy Amoros, Don

231

Zimmer) they had been following in the Dodgers' farm system. Many times I was reminded again of that long-ago afternoon with my father in Joe McCarthy's office at Yankee Stadium when Oscar Vitt extolled the virtues of a minor leaguer named Joe Gordon.

It was but a short step from public relations into show business for me. One of Brooklyn's more characteristic institutions was Nathan's Famous, a hot-dog establishment that had been founded some years earlier in Coney Island by an immigrant merchant named Nathan Handwerker. His son, Murray, ambitious and thoroughly Americanized, approached me with the idea of putting on a "Coney Island Night" between the games of a twinight doubleheader. Nathan's would pay for the clowns, stilt walkers, tumblers, and pretty girls who cavorted for the crowd, and the eatery would get its name mentioned on the public-address system. It was an agreeable and innocuous promotion, and even the ball players returned early from their clubhouse siesta to take in a part of the show.

Murray told me later that the occasion did much to rebuild his own confidence. A year or two earlier, while his father, the imposing Nathan, took a summer holiday in Miami Beach and Murray was minding the store, he was approached by a man who had somehow come into possession of a dead whale. The man talked Murray into renting the remains and installing them in a vacant lot next to the hot-dog stand, on the theory that the crowds lured there would consume large quantities of hot franks and cold sodas. All went well for a day or two, but when a heat wave descended, the stench drove the pleasure seekers to distant parts of Coney Island. Neighboring businesses complained to the police, who branded the embalmed whale a public-health hazard and ordered Handwerker to dispose of it at once. The family patriarch, who had built his business on choice meat and not on hoopla, returned home in the midst of the uproar.

"Pop let me know what he thought about cockamamie promotion stunts," Murray told me. "And he was even madder when he found out how much it cost me to have a man cut up the whale and tow it out to sea. Business didn't recover for weeks."

In the lull before game time I generally took the elevator to the base of the upper level, from which hung a long, shallow structure that held both the broadcasting booth and the president's box. I'd look in on the three radio and television announcers, Red Barber, Connie Desmond, and Vin Scully. Barber, a dapper little man with a knack for turning hill-country sayings into personal trademarks (one of them, "The Catbird Seat," became the title of a witty short story by James Thurber), was a perfectionist. Once in his booth, he was all business, and he expected those around him—the other announcers, the engineers, and the ball club's publicity department—to keep to his standards. By the time I arrived at Ebbets Field, Barber still had traces of his old charm, but he had levitated onto a slightly higher plane of existence than his fellows, having forsworn alcohol after a nearly fatal stomach disorder and embraced the Lord.

"The night I almost died I suddenly woke up, and there was the angel of death sitting at the foot of the bed," he told me once.

Barber moonlighted occasionally as a lay preacher after that, and if any of the wit and charm carried over from his baseball broadcasts, he must have brightened many somber evangelical evenings.

Just before the game began I stepped next door into Walter O'Malley's private box. O'Malley's wife, Kay, a sweet, unfailingly cheerful woman to whom he was devoted, often accompanied him to night games. (Many years earlier, after their marriage plans had been made, she underwent surgery for the removal of her larynx, but Walter gallantly refused her offer to release him from the engagement.) He grew orchids as a hobby at their home in Amityville, Long Island, and it seemed that the guiding impulse of his life was to provide a secure future for his family.

O'Malley never forgave Branch Rickey for what he believed was a blow to that security. The two men were among the four owners of the Dodgers, each of the owners having agreed to give the others a chance to meet any outside offer for his share of the ball club. Rickey, according to O'Malley, saw a chance to make a killing and paid a contractor to make him an inflated offer. O'Malley, who had been eager to buy a controlling interest in the club, was obliged to meet what he considered the outrageous price of a million dollars for Rickey's one-fourth interest, as well as to pay off Rickey's debt to the contractor who had made the specious bid. In bitter jest, O'Malley assessed a fine of one dollar for each time a member of his front office uttered Rickey's name in his presence.

He was a portly, jowly, florid man, with a raspy voice, and he circulated with a kind of bonhomie that no one ever confused with charm. Socially, he had a tin ear. Complimented sincerely by Pee Wee Reese one evening after an agreeable but hardly sumptuous victory celebration, he could only reply, "Well, it *should* have been nice. It cost me an arm and a leg!"

Whenever his insensitivity graded into cruelty, it carried a flavor of the nastiness visited on a less privileged classmate by boys at a wealthy boarding school. (The adolescent Walter O'Malley had attended a military school in Indiana.) On one occasion, having accepted the resignation of a middle-level aide who had found a job elsewhere at a more civilized salary, O'Malley bade him a perfunctory farewell and, almost as an afterthought, handed the man a couple of letters to drop in the mailbox for him on the way out. Humiliation was a part of Walter's game, and, like every other thing he took seriously, he was very good at it.

I write the above with a troubled conscience. From the time he hired me, O'Malley never treated me with other than good-natured courtesy, and sometimes he included me in small dinner parties with his cronies and board members at one of the private clubs to which he belonged. I was not in any doubt about why I shared in the glow of whatever personal warmth he was able to muster outside his family circle. "Never offend a man who buys his ink by the barrel" is ingrained wisdom for small-town merchants and politicians who need to be wary of the press, and O'Malley was too much of a big-city merchant and politician to browbeat a columnist's son. Still, I enjoyed his company and the politicians' chatter of his gatherings.

Now, as Erskine threw his final warmup pitch to Campanella and the visiting team's leadoff man approached the plate, I bent over the O'Malleys in the private box. Kay smiled brightly.

Walter asked me if any special "groups" were in the park that night. When I replied that a dozen busloads of fans had come from Patchogue for the game, he told me to call the public-address announcer on the press-box phone and have him pass on the information to the crowd. This was always followed by: "And let the boys in the broadcasting booth know about it."

Then on to the press box high above the field, near the roof of the upper deck, for an eagle's-eye view of the field and a stroll along the rows of writers hunched over their scorebooks at the extended common desk. Most of them had been on the field before the game, but Gus Steiger, of the *Mirror*, had been delayed by business details (he sold baseball caps on the side), and Mike Gaven, of the *Journal-American*, in a funk, had refused to join "all these jockstrap sniffers" (meaning his colleagues) in the clubhouse and dugout. I made sure this pair knew the names of the starting pitchers for the next day's game, how Billy Cox's pulled leg muscle was responding to treatment, and what reserve outfielder had just been optioned to Fort Worth.

I went into the press club for a sandwich and a chat with the attendant, Bill Boylan. Babe Hamberger, a ball-park factotum, looked in to ask me to get him a set of "glossy prints" of the players for a friend who wanted to hang them in his new bar and grill. There was a phone call for me. Lou Nova was calling from a nearby bar: he'd asked for the complimentary ticket I had left for him at the gate and the unimpressed Clarkie had told him that there was nothing in the box under his name. I took the elevator downstairs and found that Clarkie had filed the ticket under "L." After meeting the disgruntled Nova with apologies, I took him to the press room to cut up old touches over a beer. He was pushing his theatrical career, he told me, and had hired Carnegie Recital Hall to give a dramatic reading of Alfred Noyes' "The Highwayman" for friends and press. (He shadow-boxed to the metrics and the beat of the horses' hooves.)

With the Dodgers trailing, Erskine had been taken out for a pinch hitter, and I walked down a series of ramps to the clubhouse to check on the condition of his arm. Tight, but nothing to worry about. The curve just wasn't breaking tonight. I watched an inning or two from the seats in the right-field corner, just over the clubhouse, and chatted with one of the ushers.

The game was over. I ducked down a flight of stairs marked NO ADMITTANCE and into the clubhouse again, just ahead of the players clattering in on their spikes. A glove was slammed into a locker, and someone was already in the hissing shower.

"Lucky bastards."

"Get 'em tomorrow, guys."

"Billy Cox signs baseballs!"

"Fuckit."

For much of that season of 1951 the Dodgers were strangers to defeat. They grabbed an early lead in the pennant race and moved steadily ahead, flattening the opposition with their terrific power. Campanella ... Robinson ... Hodges ... Snider ... Furillo. Andy Pafko, brought to Brooklyn in a midseason trade: not since the Yankees fielded their aggregations of window breakers before the war had the fans seen such an explosive ball club. And the fielding—superb. That the pitching staff was apt to be a little threadbare was forgotten in the euphoria. A couple of guys would get on, and Campy or the Duke would belt one. Or Charlie would think of something.

By August 11 the Dodgers led the second-place Giants by thirteen games. "Eat your heart out, Leo!" the Dodgers screamed at their onetime manager, Leo Durocher, when they battered his Giants early in August. It was great to be young and a Dodger, I thought. I looked forward to the World Series against the Yankees, from whom the bloom, as far as I was concerned, had gone forever. There were still some great ball players over there, even DiMaggio playing out his last season, but they were mere mortals now. They were—well, just heroids.

But, as chess players say, "Before the ending the gods have placed the middle game." Several of the Dodgers fell into batting slumps. Campanella, who had been hitting with deadly effect and was on his way to winning the league's Most Valuable Player award, was hit in the ear by a pitched ball; after being taken to the hospital, he was lost to the team for two weeks. Billy Cox, the

marvelous defensive third baseman who had a terrible fear of flying, refused to board a plane with his teammates after a long
game in Pittsburgh and found it impossible to reach Brooklyn by
the usual train ride in time for the next day's game; Dressen assigned Bobby Morgan, an unremarkable fielder, to cover third
base that day; when Morgan failed at one point to come up with a
ground ball hit just to his left, two runs scored, and the Dodgers
lost a close one. Without the usual support of booming bats and
expert gloves, the Dodgers' pitching staff began to reveal its
weaknesses, and the team's imposing lead crumbled.

The Giants, though not a great team, were ideally suited to
prey on a floundering behemoth. Nearly three years earlier,
Durocher had taken over a disorganized and largely dispirited
collection of players at the Polo Grounds and set out to build "my
kind of team." Two of the players he brought there in a trade certainly met Leo's qualifications—the pugnacious Eddie Stanky and
the grimly efficient Alvin Dark (whose raven brow and squinting,
deep-set eyes made him look, said Leonard Koppett, of the New
York *Post,* like everybody's idea of a Confederate cavalry officer).
There was also a trio of pitchers who were what a schoolteacher
might have called "late developers"—Sal Maglie, Larry Jansen,
and Jim Hearn—who were only now coming into their own after
years of trying to put all of their skills together. Leo believed he
needed only a spark to set his team ablaze, and he found it early in
the season on the Giants' farm team in Minneapolis, where Willie
Mays was tearing the American Association apart. As soon as
Willie joined the Giants, the unbridled enthusiasm of his play and
the high-pitched "Say, hey!" of his pregame clowning infected
the team. The Giants seemed at first to have little chance of
catching the Dodgers, but they were no longer a joke.

Then, as August faded into September, the pennant race tightened. The Dodgers won a few and lost a few, while the Giants'
splendid pitching helped set them off on a winning streak. Dressen fumed, the players raged and taunted the Giants, but still they
came on. "The Creeping Terror," Bill Corum, my father's fellow
columnist on the *Journal-American,* called them as they cut into
the Dodgers' lead. By the final day of the season the two teams

were tied for first place, and I stood in the press box at old Shibe Park in Philadelphia (the seats all taken by writers, who had come to town in droves) and watched my new heroes with a shaken faith I had never experienced when the Yankees were my team.

The Giants had quickly snuffed out the Boston Braves earlier in the afternoon, clinching at least a tie for the pennant. The Dodgers *had* to win, or all of us faced an interminable train ride back to Penn Station. The Phillies took an early lead, but the Dodgers struggled back and sent the game into extra innings. Don Newcombe, who had shut out the Phillies the night before, was pitching in relief, and he held them back again, this time until the twelfth inning, when they filled the bases with two out.

Eddie Waitkus, the Philadelphia first baseman, came to bat. He hit a low line drive between first and second that was apparently the game-winning single, but Robinson threw himself at the ball, his glove outstretched. As he crashed heavily to the ground, stunned by the impact, the ball disappeared from view. It was one of the most thrilling moments I had experienced in sports, as I watched Robinson lying motionless on the grass, the other players rushing toward him (Reese arriving first), and then the umpires and players rolling him over—and there was the ball, still clutched tightly in his glove.

Frank Merriwell never would have left it at that, and neither did Jackie. Revived, he remained in the game, to come to bat in the fourteenth inning and hit a low, savage drive into the left-field stands. (Robinson's home runs were not grandly Ruthian, just line-drive singles that happened to clear the wall.) The Dodgers won the game and set up a postseason playoff against the Giants.

The teams split the first two playoff games, and met in the showdown at the Polo Grounds under a forbidding sky where rain seemed to lurk behind the dark clouds. Surprisingly, on that famous day, October 3, 1951, there were more than twenty thousand empty seats in the ball park. Perhaps fandom was exhausted.

Both managers went with their best, Newcombe and Maglie, and in the first inning Robinson singled sharply to drive in a run. For the next seven innings the most notable fact was the bumbling performance of Bobby Thomson. Ordinarily an outfielder, he was converted to a third baseman by Durocher when Mays came to the Polo Grounds and fitted himself into a strong outfield with Monte Irvin and Don Mueller. In the second inning, Thomson tried to stretch a single into a double without being aware that the runner already on base had decided to stop at second. The Dodgers ran Thomson down and tagged him out. When the lights were turned on to relieve the gloom in the fifth inning, someone in the press box said, "Now maybe Thomson will be able to see where he's running!"

Thomson tied the score with a sacrifice fly in the seventh inning, but in the top of the eighth, the Dodgers bounced two hits off his uncertain glove and took a 4–1 lead. A few Giant fans booed Thomson, but their indelicacies were submerged in cheers from the clusters of Brooklyn fans. Newk was pitching just fine.

Newcombe had often been accused of wilting under pressure, but there was no dog in the man during that pennant race. His fastball had kept the Dodgers alive, and he pitched heroically on the final day. Then, bringing a three-run lead into the bottom of the ninth inning, he began to tire. Dark punched a single to right field. Mueller, an artful batsman who was nicknamed "Mandrake" for the uncanny accuracy with which his dribbling grounders slipped through enemy infields, bounced a single past Hodges. Two men on. Newk reached back for one more fastball and got Irvin to hit an easy pop foul to Hodges near first base.

But it was Newk's last gasp. Whitey Lockman doubled to left, driving in a run, and now the score was 4–2 and the Giants had the tying runs in scoring position. There was an interminable delay as Mueller, who had sprained his ankle sliding into third base on Lockman's hit, was carried from the field on a stretcher. Dressen, meanwhile, was on the dugout phone to his bullpen coach, an old catcher named Clyde Sukeforth.

"Who's ready out there?" Dressen asked.

"Erskine's bouncing his curveball," Sukey told him, "but Branca's fast and loose."

"Send in Branca," Dressen ordered, sealing the Dodgers' doom. Ralph Branca, a dark-haired, heavy-legged young man, took the long walk in from the bullpen (no fancy carts in those days) and faced Bobby Thomson. His first pitch, a low-inside fastball, was a strike. Now he wanted to waste one, throwing high and inside to drive the hitter back from the plate, or perhaps even get him to swing at the bad pitch. But the pitch was not quite high enough. Thomson swung and drove the ball toward those inviting stands down the left-field line.

"Get down! Get down!" Cox shrieked at the ball as it flew high over his head at third base. The ball sailed on and into the stands, and a few minutes later I saw Branca, face down on the steps in the Dodgers' clubhouse, sobbing like a child.

Not knowing what else to do and agreeing that misery loves company, I accepted Walter O'Malley's invitation to ride back to Brooklyn in his limousine with several other members of the front office. O'Malley put himself forth as a hearty comforter of the distressed, but inwardly he was raging. I have no doubt that he blamed Dressen for the catastrophe, and on that day he wanted to fire him. But he had fired Rickey's manager, Burt Shotton, less than a year before, and now that Dressen was his man, O'Malley could only lose face by dropping him so hastily. Instead, it was Clyde Sukeforth who left the Dodgers abruptly to find a haven with Rickey in Pittsburgh. Dressen would get one more chance— in fact, two more.

Chapter Twenty

Transition

arly in my Dodger days I had, in effect, already closed myself off from a future in baseball. The issue was forced by a question put to me by Buzzie Bavasi, whom I had met in Montreal and who was now one of the two vice-presidents of the ball club under Walter O'Malley (Fresco Thompson, the director of the farm system's operations and a former ball player, was the other). I was still living with my parents at the time, and since Bavasi also lived in Westchester County, he sometimes drove me home after a night game.

"The publicity department is a dead end in baseball," he told me one night. "If you're going to get anywhere in the organization, you've got to learn all the phases of the operation."

Buzzie brought an almost adolescent enthusiasm to the front office. A pretty good college player, he had taken a job in the Dodgers' organization before the war as business manager of the team at Valdosta, Georgia. When war came and both ball players and ball-park employees were in short supply, he handled all the chores of management and maintenance—the proverbial boss-as-

241

ticket-taker—and even went on the air to let every young man within radio range know that the team needed players. In an emergency he put on a uniform and played a few games. He returned to baseball after service in the Army and climbed the organization ladder, reaching the top when O'Malley called him to Brooklyn.

"It's the best way," he told me. "I'll find a minor-league club for you, and you can go out and run it for a couple of years. It's a lot of fun to have your own ball club—I wouldn't have missed it for anything—and you'll learn a helluva lot about the game."

I was not seriously tempted. I had never thought of baseball as a business (and, in view of what the Dodgers were paying me, I certainly didn't think of it as one then). Rejecting Bavasi's advice, I became aware that the game existed for me chiefly in my imagination, like the interplay of pieces on the board in the mind of a blindfolded chess master. Baseball was simply old records and pulsations and the tatters of romance that my father had pulled from chaos itself and pieced together on his typewriter into enchanting coherence. Perhaps I had rearranged the pattern a little to suit myself, but I dwelt in the same rabbit hole. Contracts, tickets, and construction bills were not a part of that mise-en-scène.

I wanted to go on seeing it from my old perspective because I know that my lot was eventually with the observers, the chroniclers, not with the athletes and business managers. For a while I would remain in the setting as the team's publicity director—and enjoy every minute of it—though eventually I would follow my father's path and find a way to write about the worlds that interested me. That path began to open in the summer of 1951 even before the Dodgers' collapse. My beginnings as a professional writer stemmed from an unexpected friendship and a tragedy that had nothing to do with baseball.

On my way to the press box at Ebbets Field one afternoon, I was joined in the elevator by a tall, blond young man whose headphones and coil of wire told me that he worked with the broadcasting crew. I knew at once that I had seen him before, but not in that guise. We exchanged nods, and as the elevator jolted into motion, so did my thoughts, carrying me back to the previous winter.

"I saw you box up at White Plains," I told him, and identified myself as the Dodgers' publicity man.

"Oh, sure," he said, his face brightening. "I'm Roger Donoghue. Your father wrote a column about me."

The years right after World War II, when television was still in its embryonic stage, provided a bonanza for the small fight clubs. The new medium had not yet solved the technical problems involved in following a sports event in which the participants were scattered (or tumbled) over a large playing area, but a prizefight, confined to a compact square, was just the thing. When large arenas could not supply enough fights, the television cameras went into the small clubs so that viewers were able to turn on the tube almost any night of the week and watch two young men earnestly belabor each other for ten rounds, or fewer. Thus, in addition to the champions, a number of boxers whose names in other times would hardly have become known beyond their own neighborhoods suddenly acquired a wider fame. Roger Donoghue came along at the tag end of this era, but with a graceful carriage and Irish good looks to go with his baleful left hook, he was a TV producer's delight.

I knew from reading the papers that Donoghue had become resident tiger at the Westchester County Center in White Plains. There he pulled in capacity crowds while drubbing the succession of "opponents" served up to him by the promoters, and my father agreed that he was raw material for his kind of column: the kid from Yonkers as a throwback to local heroes of the past, peddling tickets to friends and storekeepers around the neighborhood and being followed by carloads of noisy partisans to the small clubs where he fought. We drove to the County Center for Donoghue's next fight. Someone had erred this time because the opponent was a stubby, mahogany-skinned spoiler who wrestled him around the ring, smothered his punches in an adhesive grip, and came away with a draw after eight unspectacular rounds. But my father had been after the atmosphere, which, with a liberal infusion of nostalgia, constituted a representative Graham column.

Donoghue's career was interrupted by a back injury he suffered when he lost to Lou Valles, a more experienced fighter, in a Brooklyn club. (His manager, Bob Melnick, had not wanted to accept the match, but the twenty-year-old Donoghue, riding the crest of youthful confidence, had insisted and thus learned the not-always-enlightened adage that the manager knows best.) Ambitious, quick to pick up other skills, he used the contacts he had made as a popular TV fighter to find a temporary job as a technician with the Dodgers' television crew while his injuries healed. He was already back in training, arranging his hours in the gym around the schedule at Ebbets Field.

Now, following our meeting in the elevator, Donoghue and I became close friends. We traveled back and forth to Westchester together, and since we both knew a lot of night spots in our home county as well as in Manhattan, we often stopped for a beer or a late snack. He was funny and generous (as either a boxer or a TV technician, he was making more money than I was), and he was delighted by the wildly various life that had unfolded itself before him. Everyone interested him—other fighters and their managers, television people, newspapermen, actors, bartenders, musicians, mobsters, girls; the only interest we didn't share was baseball, which bored him. (He sat beside Red Barbor in the broadcast booth, headphones on, turning over an hourglass each time the sands ran out so that the announcer remembered to give his listeners the score every three minutes. "I'm good at handling egg timers," Roger assured me.)

But I never held his disdain for baseball against him, for we were too busy being young men about town, opening new doors for each other. His welcome in bars and restaurants he knew and in homes to which I introduced him was hardly commensurate with his accomplishments until then. Yet, with all the confidence and the dreams, he had the gift of making other people laugh with him.

"I'm laid up for an operation," he would announce to the gang at the bar. "They're taking a strip of canvas out of my back."

244

(Snorts and chuckles.) "They call me the Candle Kid—one blow and I'm out!" (Roger leading the guffaws.)

In the middle of August, just as the Dodgers were beginning to wobble, he gave up his job at Ebbets Field and signed for a fight at an outdoor arena in White Plains. The opponent was Georgie Flores, like Donoghue not yet twenty-one but without any of Roger's skills. Only three weeks earlier he had been knocked out by an ordinary fighter in another small club, and this fight promised to be what the boxing mob calls a "pig-sticking." I went to the arena with Roger, wished him luck in the dressing room, and took my seat in the press row, courtesy of a friendly promoter. The fight went as everyone expected it to, providing a strenuous but not hazardous workout for Donoghue after his layoff. Flores came to him and made a scrap of it, but Roger used his longer reach to good effect, gave him a bad beating, and was pounding him without a return in the eighth round when the referee stopped the fight.

Roger was sweaty but happy when I reached the dressing room. He had made a thousand dollars for the evening and had been punching sharply at the end. Across the room Bob Melnick was talking to Billy Brown, the assistant matchmaker at Madison Square Garden. When Melnick came over to talk to his fighter, he wore a wide grin.

"We're in the Garden," he said. "August 29."

Roger turned and pumped my hand in a fit of excitement. "We're on the way, Frankie," he said.

His first bout in the Garden would offer him a showcase for his skills. He was to fight the eight-round semifinal before the welterweight-championship bout between Kid Gavilan and Billy Graham, and his purse would come to fifteen hundred dollars.

"Who am I fighting?" he asked Melnick, almost as an afterthought.

"Flores again."

The exuberance drained from Roger's face.

"Jesus, I don't want him back," he said with a pained look. "Get me somebody else. I've earned somebody better than him."

"Look," Melnick said, explaining life to his fighter as managers

245

have been doing for decades. "This fight wasn't on TV, so nobody is going to know about it. But now you'll be in the Garden. The right people will be there for a title fight, and they'll see you against a guy who'll make you look good."

"I don't want Flores back."

"I'm supposed to be the manager, and you're supposed to be the fighter," Melnick reminded him. "Tell me, who picked Lou Valles?"

So Donoghue said all right. Flores was being set up for a third terrible beating within thirty-seven days, but if his manager and the boxing commission had no objections, why should anyone else protest?

The Garden was nearly full when the semifinal began on the night Gavilan and Graham fought for the title, for both of them were popular fighters in New York. I had a seat on an aisle, near the ring. Roger was jittery about his first appearance in the Garden, and some of his nervousness had rubbed off on me. I had hoped it would be a brief fight, but it wasn't. Roger outboxed Flores at long range through the early rounds, though Flores kept coming, soaking up the punches, a perfect example of columnist Jimmy Cannon's definition of a club fighter: "A kid who never takes a backward step on the way to the insane asylum."

Roger seemed to tire in the seventh round, and Flores rallied. He got in some solid punches, forcing my friend back and winning the round. I felt sick. I remembered the night I had come in from Lake Wallenpaupak with my young pals to watch Billy Soose fight a man he was expected to beat in the Garden, and how dejected we had been at the outcome. If Flores finished with a rousing offensive, there was no way to tell how the judges would score the fight.

Then it was the eighth round and Flores rushed at Roger, flailing at him, bulling him across the ring. The crowd behind me was beginning to cheer for the underdog. Roger pushed him away. They were boxing at long range in the center of the ring when Roger fired a classic right hand that caught the arm-weary Flores on the point of the chin. The water in which Flores' seconds had drenched him between rounds flew from his matted hair in a bright nimbus of spray. His knees buckled; he hung there as if on wires for a breathtaking moment. Roger stepped in and hit him with a left hook. Flores fell straight backward, his arms limp, his head sharply striking the ring floor.

It was the last thrill boxing ever gave me. As soon as Flores began to fall, I was out of my seat and partway up the aisle, my fist clenched in high excitement. "Kill him, Roger!" Is that what I called out? Perhaps, in the aftermath, the recollection is a little too neat, but that was the sentiment behind my mindless cry.

Flores' handlers dragged him to his corner. They propped him on his stool and threw more water on him while the boxing commission's doctor briefly looked him over. When Donoghue went to his corner, Flores seemed to nod and mumble something to him, and both fighters left the ring to polite applause. The crowd settled down to watch the introductions that preceded the main event.

Roger had said he might join me at Shor's after the fight, but he did not appear. Hardly anyone around the circular bar that night mentioned the knockout, because of the uproar that had followed the main event. Billy Graham, who fought the slickest fight of his career, had apparently won the championship by a wide margin; but, inexplicably, the judges awarded Gavilan a split decision. There was an awful row, and my father was late finishing his column. As we were leaving, Toots Shor came over and told us that Flores had collapsed in his dressing room. Some of the newspapers were posting a death watch at St. Clare's Hospital, where Flores lay in a coma.

I saw Roger a day or two later. His face was drawn and grimly set and there were no jokes.

"I was scared when I got to the hospital," he said. "His wife— just a kid—was there with her folks. I walked across the lobby to say something to her. God, it seemed like a long walk, and when I tried to tell her I was sorry, the words sounded like nothing. She's only eighteen years old and she's got a new baby. But she was very nice. She said it wasn't my fault."

That was the worst moment for him, but there were others nearly as bad while Georgie Flores died piece by piece. They cut into Flores' skull and found that there was nothing they could do for him. Roger spent most of the next three days at the hospital. Reporters asked him a lot of questions for which he had no answers. Once he sat on the steps in front of the hospital to find a breath of air in the suffocating, late August night. Some of Flores' friends came up the street and one of them walked toward Donoghue, holding a pop bottle like a blackjack, but the others pulled him away.

The International Boxing Club, which had taken over the promotion of Garden fights from Mike Jacobs, paid for the funeral, which took place at a plush uptown mortuary a few days later. Melnick advised Roger to attend. As Roger was getting into a friend's car after the service, some photographers saw him and asked him to walk out of the mortuary again so that they could take his picture. At first he refused, but Melnick told him he had better go back.

"For years I've watched fighters and managers in their corners between rounds," he said afterward. "The manager talks, and the fighter nods his head. He never shakes it. He never says no to the manager. So I went back and had my picture taken."

I saw little of Roger during the next month. He was occupied with the dismal details that surfaced in the tragedy's aftermath, scrambling pathetically to make up for other people's mistakes. He ran a benefit softball game for Elaine Flores and arranged to give her his purse from his next fight. He appeared on a television program to raise money for the baby. Finally the producers of *Strike It Rich* called Melnick and asked him to get Donoghue to appear on their program with the widow. Melnick said no; Donoghue had done all he could, and he wouldn't let him be turned into a freak. Finally he was persuaded to let the announcer tell the audience that Roger had called and wanted to match Elaine Flores' winnings on the show.

Meanwhile, I was sharing a whole borough's more trivial agony. A day or two after Bobby Thomson struck his climactic blow, Roger called and suggested we get away for a week.

"I have some relatives in Lake George," he said. "We can drive up there and stay with them. We'll both feel better after a vacation."

We left from Yonkers, where Roger lived in an apartment with his family. I knew, or thought I knew, about private tragedy, but until the moment I walked toward the car with our bags, I had never been aware of the pain that strikes at the heart under the impact of public censure. To be drawn into the glare of general notice and branded a fraud, an incompetent, a degenerate, or a *killer*—this can stab deeper even than most personal bereavements, because it is not tempered by happy memories or the certainty of a goodness that shines beyond the grave. The enormity and omnipresence of this communal scorn withers one's elemental sense of worth.

"You're Roger Donoghue," a little boy said as he passed us on the sidewalk.

Roger smiled down at him. "Yes, son."

"You're Roger Donoghue. You killed a man."

The smile dried up. Roger stiffened and walked on toward the car, while the boy had turned and was following us.

"You killed a man! You killed a man," he chanted. "I'm going to tell *everybody*."

"You don't have to tell them, son," Roger said as he got into the car. "They already know."

Yet it was a good week in the foothills of the Adirondacks. We hiked and drank beer and ate hearty meals that were served up to us by Roger's hospitable relatives. We visited the tavern run by Bob Pastor, the heavyweight who had been Jimmy Johnston's pride and meal ticket and who had twice fought Joe Louis. We even went roller skating; it turned out that Roger had been a champion figure skater before he decided to put on muscle and take boxing lessons in the back of Bob Melnick's poolroom.

Though he still talked of boxing, some of the certainty was gone from his voice. It occurred to me that we were both in transition, both taking what we could from heady experiences that would always be a part of us, but would never be wholly us. I was older, and already had a practical idea of what I wanted to do. Roger sometimes talked of becoming an actor, or a writer, a *somebody*. I think he knew by that point that he was never going to be a champion boxer. Once or twice we talked about writing some things together, pooling his ideas and experience and my writing skills (skills that, though embryonic, were generally thought to have been passed on to me through heredity).

But the plan was put off for a while. Roger went back into training; Melnick had lined up several fights for him. I faithfully attended his fights, but I no longer got my kicks from seeing one man beat up another. One night Roger fought a tough little guy named Vinnie D'Andrea at the St. Nicholas Arena, on Manhattan's West Side. The first round was a war. Donoghue knocked him down, but D'Andrea got up, and in a wild melee, both of them wound up on the floor. Melnick began to minister to Roger on his return to the corner.

"I don't need any help," he told his manager. "But I got a look at Frankie Graham's face at the end of the round, and I think he's having a heart attack."

Not long after that we entered on the literary life. We wrote an article called "How a Kid Gets a Fight" and sold it to a monthly called *Boxing*. Although only Roger got a byline when the article appeared in print, we divided the fee, which came to $150, and I pocketed my first earnings as a writer. My father reminded me that he had made his first sale to a magazine of the same name forty years earlier. We sold several more articles to the magazine, and though they also appeared under the Donoghue byline, my confidence was established: someday I would be able to make a living as a writer.

Roger had only three fights after Georgie Flores' death, and he retired after losing an eight-round decision in another semifinal at the Garden. He became a successful salesman for a New York brewery, and more than a decade later, after Emile Griffith fatally beat Benny "Kid" Paret in a Garden bout, we collaborated once more, this time on an article for the *Saturday Evening Post*. (It appeared, under Donoghue's name, in the same issue with my notorious and bylined article about Wally Butts!) In it we traced the succession of circumstances in which the Griffith-Paret tragedy paralleled that of Donoghue and Flores: the indifference of officials and managers to a fighter rendered susceptible to serious injury by several recent beatings.

Roger, still a fan and still loyal to the game, argued in our article against politicians and other reformers who had called for a prohibition on boxing. By that time I felt in sympathy with the reformers. I went along with my collaborator's argument, though, because I believed then, as I do now, that a ban on boxing is as impractical as one on breweries or prostitution. It was simply that the fun went out of it for me the night that Georgie Flores walked into the most beautiful right-hand punch I ever saw.

Chapter Twenty-one
Shoptalk

Sex kept a low profile on the Dodgers during my time. This was not because puritanism reigned, or because the boys weren't interested: it was instead a reflection of management's uneasiness in a changing society. Sex in baseball was no longer merely sin, a good-natured romp by the Babe zooming away in a pal's roadster with a couple of broads clutched in his beefy paws. It was not even the youthful DiMag as part of a threesome in Shor's, the blond chorine at his table making small talk with the beard while the center fielder preserved his public image. No, Walter O'Malley knew that sex had become a hazardous substance with the intrusion of two alien elements, race and a crusading press.

On the surface it was as it had always been, and as it would become again in the sixties. Raunchy clubhouse chatter: "No, nobody ever died from eating it—but they say that fellow over in Jersey City is very, very sick." Gossip to the effect that a pitcher on the Reds was a transvestite (a southpaw, of course), prompting a dugout wit to this flight of fancy: "Sure, I'll bet he goes around at night dressed up as a Chicago Cub." And, though the Dodgers' stars were happily married men, there were for some of them the occasional discreet lapses from domesticity that an athlete's much-admired flesh finds hard to resist. Others were models of virtue, proving novelist Peter DeVries' contention that "a man should be greater than some of his parts."

Yet new elements had entered the picture. Baseball's color line had been crossed less than half a dozen years before, and the country's big integration battles lay a decade in the future. Meanwhile, the Dodgers had handled the race situation reasonably well. If a borderline player who was white occasionally groused that "they" were beating him out of a job, the relationships among the established players were free of tension, and Dressen was color-blind in the best sense. The uncomfortable moments generally had their origin outside the team's circle. A redneck's epithets were the usual bilge and could be ignored, though harder to take were the groups of vacationers milling around the players in a hotel lobby: "Autograph this for my kid, Pee Wee. He idolizes you." But then: "Hey, Jackie, sign this for my maid. She thinks you're really terrific."

To be guarded against at all cost was an "incident," O'Malley believed, especially one that might be triggered by interracial sex. A spicy part of the game for a long time had been "baseball Sadies," women who hung around the ball park and hoped to attract a player's roving eye. Ebbets Field had its share of them, including a pair of pliant young things who were known among the players as "the Hook" and "the Nook," but no one in management ever considered them as anything more serious than a threat to a rookie's virtue. Then, at the end of a long road trip, we arrived in Pittsburgh to find the Hook and the Nook on the scene with another woman. They were observed in the lobby talking to a black player, and word reached Dressen that they had telephoned the player's room.

The wires must have hummed between the Schenley Hotel and Montague Street, because Dressen called a special meeting of the team before the next afternoon's game. He was highly agitated, stung to near eloquence, and he emphasized diplomatically that the ladies in question were off limits to *all* players. He threatened

to assess a five-hundred-dollar fine against any player who was
seen even talking to them. That evening, noticing the three baffled temptresses hanging about the lobby, the writers mischie-
vously invited them and a couple of us Dodger noncombatants to
an impromptu party in one of their rooms, Aside from a few
minor outbreaks of bawdiness, decorum held sway, but one of our
number reported the party to O'Malley.

Jittery about the whole affair, O'Malley later called in those of
us on the staff who had attended the revels. After satisfying himself that nothing untoward had occurred, he dismissed us with a
lecture on the perils of encouraging women of "that sort" to associate themselves with the ball club. The men writing baseball
today were not always fine gentlemen, like those who had covered
the game in the past, he said, with a meaningful look at me; there
were troublemakers among the younger writers, and one of them
might get a story into the papers about such goings-on, blowing it
up out of all proportion.

His relationships with the press, whether race was being discussed or not, were of great concern to O'Malley from the time he
gained control of the Dodgers. Dick Young, who covered the
team for the New York *Daily News,* the paper with the largest
circulation in America, had formed an intense dislike for both
Branch Rickey and his manager, Burt Shotton, He pilloried them
day in and day out, carrying into battle the paper's entire sports
section, throughout which Rickey was alluded to as "El Cheapo."
The rancor was no asset to the Dodgers, and O'Malley, appointing
Buzzie Bavasi a vice-president, assigned him to turn things around
at once. In our office the glad-handing Bavasi was sometimes
called "vice-president in charge of Dick Young." He worked hard
at his assignment, adopting Young as a bosom companion and
feeding him information about the ball club to which the other
writers were not a party. This state of affairs did not make my job
any easier, but O'Malley was willing to put up with a little sul-
lenness on the other morning dailies to appease the volatile
Young.

Ironically, Dick Young needed no help in beating his rivals. He was as competitive in his own way as Jackie Robinson: dogged, resourceful, and single-minded, never content to accept the handout of routine news. Following the 1952 season, the Dodgers naïvely smuggled Carl Furillo from his home in Pennsylvania back into Brooklyn for a delicate operation on one of his eyes. Grit had lodged in a cornea during the season, handicapping him badly at bat. O'Malley was concerned about Furillo, because cutting into any part of an athlete's anatomy presents obvious pitfalls and he wanted to hide the matter from the press until he had received a doctor's report. That afternoon, to keep the Dodgers' name in the papers in a period of little news, we pulled together a story about three rookies who had signed their contracts for the coming season.

I called each of the writers at his office, but Young was not satisfied to occupy himself with the news that Pete Wojie was in the fold. He called Gil Hodges, who lived in Brooklyn the year round, hoping to turn their conversation into a story. Hodges, he learned, was not at home. He finally reached him later in the day and casually asked where he had been.

"I was at the hospital visiting Furillo," Hodges said.

"Oh. Is he sick?"

"Well, he just had an operation on his eye. Seems like everything's going to be all right, though."

The next morning, while the other papers printed hot-stove trivia, the readers of the *Daily News* digested an exclusive account of Carl Furillo's surgery. Eventually, the event held historical significance as well, for the next season a clear-eyed Furillo raised his average by almost a hundred points to lead the National League in batting. The other writers, of course, believed that this was simply an outrageous example of Bavasi feeding Dick Young inside information.

By all odds, the most important paper to the Dodgers should have been the *Eagle;* as the only surviving major daily in Brooklyn, it was the home sheet. Yet the *Eagle,* like the *Sun* before it, was moribund. When I joined the Dodgers, its baseball writer was

Harold Burr, an endearing oldster with a great, beaky profile and a pair of rickety legs that threatened to fold under him at every step, physical features appropriate to his paper's insignia and condition. I had known Harold since the time I was a small boy sitting with my father in the various press boxes around town, and he had always had a pleasant word for me. He was a bachelor and a gentleman. Now, during the off season, he came to my office in the afternoons to pick up whatever scraps of news I had for him and then doze off in an old wooden armchair while I made my calls to the other papers. At the end of the day I shook him gently awake. He got to his feet, his legs and cane fluttering as he tried to pull himself together, and then wobbled back across Court Street to tap out his story for the next afternoon's paper.

When spring came, Harold resumed his seat in the press box. After the season's opening game at Ebbets Field one year, he handed his completed story to a telegrapher, closed his typewriter, and remarked hopefully, "Well, only a hundred and fifty-three games to go." Like Evelyn Waugh's Gilbert Pinfold, he was always surprised and disappointed when he glanced at his watch to discover how much time still lay before him.

Younger journalists than Harold Burr, of course, wrote as though they had one foot in the grave. As Ed Fitzgerald, the editor of *Sport*, said of a highly respected sportswriter whose daily column was a potent soporific, "There's no anecdote so hilarious that he can't find a way to blunt it." In other writers, the juice of life continued to flow. Roscoe McGowen, a white-haired and fastidious man, was a study in frustration because he was unfortunate enough to cover the Dodgers for the New York *Times* before that paper had emerged from its era of excessive primness. Thus McGowen held on to his sideline of writing regularly for *The Sporting News*, a national weekly.

"The pay isn't very much," he explained, "but it gives me a chance to put a little color into my work, the kind of thing that gets penciled out in the *Times*. I write for the *Times* for a living, but I write for *The Sporting News* for my own satisfaction."

I was beginning to look as closely at writers as I had at the athletes, for lo! there were witty and colorful characters among the ink-stained wretches. Some I had known since childhood, and now I took a new interest in them when we met at Shor's or around Grantland Rice's lunch table at the Chatham. Bugs Baer, though in declining health, was still a very funny man both in print, as a Hearst columnist, and in the flesh. A hustler once exhibited in New York a suit that he claimed Lincoln had worn when he was shot. Baer went to inspect the garment. "If this story is true," he announced, "then Lincoln was killed by moths."

Tom Meany, who had covered the Dodgers as a newspaperman before becoming a magazine writer, was another wit. Like a character in a medieval morality play, he seemed to have been named for a personality trait. "Meany would shaft his grandmother if he thought he could get a laugh out of it," a colleague said. I was having lunch with him in Shor's one day when Ernest Hemingway walked in, flanked by two columnists on the New York *Post*, Jimmy Cannon and Leonard Lyons. Both were inexhaustible monologists, and after they had taken their seats, we could see that the great man was having difficulty holding his own. Meany finally nodded in their direction.

"Over there," he growled, "are three writers of varying skills but of equal self-esteem."

Beyond the men themselves, I wanted to know about their craft. Perversely, during the years I attended Columbia and worked for the *Sun*, I had been chiefly interested in batting averages and the latest results from the small fight clubs. Now I craved shoptalk among writers. For one thing, I was getting more practical experience than I had at either Columbia or the *Sun*. I wrote press releases and all the copy for the Dodgers' yearbook and other club publications, and was sometimes asked to file brief, anonymous stories for small newspapers. On a trip through the West, when one of the writers covering the team badly mangled an index finger while trying to open a beer can, I eagerly filled in for him for two or three days and sent off a story to his paper under his byline after each game. (Dick Young and Bill Roeder, of the *World-Telegram*, looked over my copy before I sent it, perhaps to satisfy themselves that I had not scooped them.)

I listened in fascination to words of wisdom dropped by writers who had tapped what was then a flourishing free-lance market with the large, general-circulation magazines. Al Hirshberg had made the leap successfully from a Boston newspaper to frequent bylines in the *Saturday Evening Post.*

"The way to hit the *Post,*" he confided in me, "is to write the best story you can, then go over it and dull it up a little here and there. Works like a charm."

While Young and Roeder maintained their standard of excellence, new blood was coming into the Dodgers' press box to provide coverage worthy of a unique collection of players. When Harold Burr died, he was succeeded on the *Eagle* by Dave Anderson, my fellow copyboy from *Sun* days who would later help to bring the *Times* sports section to life. Roger Kahn arrived on assignment from the *Herald Tribune;* he went on to magazine work before he struck it rich by ghosting a best-seller called *Calories Don't Count* and earning every old Brooklyn fan's gratitude with *The Boys of Summer.* Gay Talese, though not a regular, came to Ebbets Field on assignment from the *Times* occasionally; impeccably dressed even then, and chafing like Roscoe McGowen under his paper's editorial restraints, he was a young writer (and here I paraphrase Nabokov's description of a similar prospective superstar) in whom his envious colleagues could not help but notice a streak of superior talent as striking as the stripe of a skunk. Kahn, Talese, and I spent hours together, talking about life and letters, unaware that in a few years we would go on from baseball to tackle such weighty matters as, respectively, diet, massage, and eared grebes.

The writer who still interested me the most, of course, was my father. Younger, better-educated columnists had come along, new literary styles flourished on the sports pages, and sometimes he seemed to flounder as he struggled to keep his place with the best of them. Max Kase, the *Journal-American*'s sports editor, wrote a regular feature called "The Brief Kase," which was a collection of gossip and short notes. When he and my father were talking on the phone one day, Max mentioned the feature.

"If you come across any notes, send them to me for 'The Brief Kase,' " he said.

"If I come across a note," Pop replied, "I'll make a column out of it."

There was a certain kind of sports column at which he was still the master, frustrating the attempts of his most skillful colleagues to render anything like its spare portrait of a man in his working habitat. On the *Sun* he had written his column at the ball park, or had gone down to Chambers Street late in the afternoon to type it out at the paper's office. Now he usually wrote at home in the evening. He took a rye on the rocks up to the extra bedroom on the second floor and closed the door. First he pushed aside the clutter of mail on his heavy wooden desk (he was a wretched correspondent as far as his "fan mail" went, but zealous about writing to any member of the immediate family who happened to be away). Then he stuffed his pipe with tobacco or unwrapped one of the long Optimo Kings he favored. (Years before he had been pleased to learn that John Dillinger shared his preference for this brand.) He composed slowly but steadily, the pounding of the Corona carrying to all parts of the house. When I got home, I always looked in on him, for he would have been offended if anyone came in without exchanging a greeting.

"Hi, Pop, I'm home."

"Hello, Pop." We were "Pop" and "Little Pop" to each other.

"How is it going?"

"Godawful. Pity the poor readers tomorrow."

"I'll bet. Can I freshen your drink?"

"You may take it downstairs, but ask Mary to fix it. She makes a *man's* drink."

Interruptions seldom irritated him. He even encouraged Jim to keep him informed of the progress of any game he was listening to on the radio. Jim would mount the stairs tirelessly, arms flapping in excitement, brow knitted as he tried to retain the information he wanted to impart to his father. If the event was a pitchers' duel or a Rangers' hockey game, the trips were blessedly spaced, but he had to be restrained when the Knicks were playing.

"The old men know when an old man dies," Ogden Nash wrote, and my father was joining the circle. The strong men, the heroes of his own youth and prime, were passing. He read the obituaries and attended the funerals. When Jimmy Johnston died, I asked him if he wanted me to go to the funeral with him. "No," he said. "You'll have enough funerals to attend in your lifetime." Some of his friends had lived to a ripe age and their deaths were to be expected, occasions for columns that were sentimental but rich with laughter. Sometimes there was no place for laughter. He grieved when Tony Lazzeri, age forty-two, died alone in the night in a cheap hotel room.

The best columns were a mixture of nostalgia and a fortunate encounter with a hero, still as large as life, from the past. On a visit to Sugar Ray Robinson's training camp, he met Tony Galento.

Tony, with a fat cigar in his face, was sitting near the ring.

"I'm glad to see you," he said. "You never wrote bad about me, like some of them other bums did."

"Only," the other said, "when you did everything to Lou Nova, short of pulling a knife on him."

"Nova," Tony said. "You see him around?"

"Once in a while."

"I heard he was still in New York," Tony said. "He's a funny guy."

"What's funny about him?"

"Well," Tony said, "I seen him in New York a coupla months ago. It was at a party and we was standing near each other, but I didn't see him until some dummy that didn't know we ever fought says to me:

" 'You know Lou Nova?'

" 'Sure,' I says.

"That's when I see Nova. I say hello to him and stick my hand out, but he says to the guy:

" 'Tell your friend that I will not shake hands with him.'

" 'What's the matter with you, you bum,' I says.

"Then Nova says to the guy: 'I will not shake hands with him because he stuck his thumbs in my eyes.'

"How do you like that?" Tony said. "He was sticking his thumb

in my eye all through the fight and I only stuck my thumb in his eye once. That was when I hit him with that left hook that dropped him."

"That was in the third round, wasn't it?"

"The fourth," Tony said. "I belted him on the chin and, as he was falling, I stuck my thumb in his eye. I didn't mean to, but it served the bum right after what he done to me."

Tony waved his cigar at the two fighters in the ring.

"You don't see many good fighters around anymore," he said. "When I look at the heavyweights, I wish I was young again. When I was fighting it was like a jungle. You licked one tough guy and there was another one winding up to take a belt at you. Now there is nothing around but a bunch of bums like the ones Marciano beat to become the champeen."

"The last I heard of you," the other said, "you were a wrestler. Are you going to continue wrestling?"

"No," he said. "It was all right. I didn't mind it and the money was pretty good, but my friends advised me to give it up."

"Why?" the other asked.

And Tony said, "They don't think it is dignified."

Yet, though his past remained populous and always green, my father did not think it was the only world he could still inhabit. He may have felt like an "elder statesman" in the dugouts, but he was comfortable at the racetracks, where the trainers, owners, and stewards were growing old with him. He found there the history, the competition, the colorful characters, and the fund of anecdotes in which, for him, the word "sport" was all wrapped up. I could not follow him there, because the sport itself, the race, had never interested me. It was all a blur, a jumble at the far turn, with an interminable wait until the next race. My favorite racing story was the one that Joe Palmer recounted in his column in the *Herald Tribune* about a man who shared my apathy toward horses. This fellow was visiting an old friend in the horse country of Virginia, and the talk at that evening's party was endlessly about horses. He had nothing to contribute to the conversation.

Finally the hostess, aware that he seemed isolated from the others, came over and sat beside him.

"And what sport are you interested in?" she asked.

A gleam flashed in the stranger's eye. "I like to shoot," he answered.

"What do you like to shoot?" the woman asked.

"Horses," he said, bitterly.

Pop laughed at the story, too, but inwardly he must have shuddered. Heaven, he knew, was to be around the horse barns on a misty morning when the exercise boys were guiding their mounts back from the track after a strenuous workout and the coffeepot was perking on the little stove in the track cottage; crusty observations and stories of old times were in the offing. He enjoyed a race, but it was racing's way of life that he loved—the colors, the talk, the tree-shaded grounds and the gracious old homes in horse country. He loved it beyond life. The only word about last things I ever heard him utter was the wish that he could be buried in the infield at Saratoga.

He never talked about his own craft of writing. One would have thought that he came to it innately, as a bird that is breeding for the first time weaves a nest of the same materials and design that its species has made for centuries. And perhaps he did. "How does one become a writer?" he was asked sometimes. "Read good writers" was his reply. "Then put down a word of your own ... and another. And after a while you will find that you have a story."

Not much to go on, but certainly more than the oriole that weaves its hanging pouch with all the confidence of an old salt stringing a hammock. What my father really passed on to me, I know now, was not craft but old-fashioned virtue. Do the best you can. Be as honest with the reader as you must be with yourself. Be a professional, with all the responsibilities that the word implies. Earn and keep the respect of your fellow professionals, for if you are a faker, they are the ones who will find you out first.

He would be a tough act to follow.

Chapter Twenty-two
Madder Music,
Stronger Wine

Acrimony and uncertainty, states of mind by no means strangers to Brooklyn, seemed epidemic in the fall of 1953. For the second year in a row, the Yankees had beaten the Dodgers in the World Series, and the cranky postmortems that were rampant in the borough could be picked up by the least sensitive ear in the Dodger offices. Defeat had not been quite this galling in 1952. Shaken by their last-moment extinctions at the hands of Dick Sisler and Bobby Thomson in the two previous seasons, the Dodgers had held themselves together and staved off the Giants ("The Jints is dead," Charlie Dressen had crowed), chiefly on the superb relief pitching of Joe Black. All of us on Montague Street were delighted simply to be in a position where our friends bothered us for Series tickets.

But in 1953 a powerful and confident Dodger team won convincingly in the National League and appeared ready to bring Brooklyn its first world championship after so many "next years." The Yankees, given a lift by Billy Martin's record-breaking twelve hits, shot down Dressen's team in six games. Some of the mail was quite vicious.

I worked late in my office on the afternoon of October 14, a week after the Series, composing Walter O'Malley's answers to the letters of disgruntled Brooklyn fans. Carrying a sheaf of letters, I went to O'Malley's office to get his signature. With him, seated around his desk, were Dressen, Buzzie Bavasi, and Fresco Thompson.

"You'll be around for a while, won't you?" O'Malley asked as I put the letters on his desk.

Within half an hour the intercom summoned me back to his office, where the party had been reduced to three. Dressen had disappeared.

"Call a press conference for eleven tomorrow morning," O'Malley said. "Tell the papers it will be of major importance."

"Dressen's signing?" I asked.

O'Malley grinned the grin of a prep-school boy who was about to do something horrible to the class boob. "A switch," he half whispered, wagging a forefinger.

I went back to my office and called the sports desks of the daily papers and wire associations. The newspapermen, momentarily expecting news that Dressen had been signed to a new contract, assumed O'Malley's remark about "major importance" was the usual bunkum designed to lure a crowd of writers over the bridge for a routine announcement. Dressen was then, aside from Casey Stengel, the most successful manager in baseball, with two pennants and a photo-finish second place during his three seasons with the Dodgers. Yet he was working on a one-year contract that paid him $32,500. Several of his players were earning more, and at least two of the men who had managed National League also-rans in 1953 had recently signed long-term contracts with their ball clubs.

Next morning, as we assembled the chairs, ice, and whiskey that are the necessities of a press conference, several dailies on our desks were confidently reporting the story in advance. A head on one sports page read DRESSEN SIGNS TODAY: 50 G PACT FOR CHOLLY. When the writers and photographers had crowded into his office, O'Malley inserted a cigar into his holder, tripled his chins as he bowed his head in a moment of introspection, and made his announcement. Dressen was not coming back to Brooklyn.

The writers scattered to other rooms in search of phones, then reassembled to ask questions of O'Malley and Dressen, who was also present. Slowly, the story came out. Dressen had set forth his demands to O'Malley in a letter. The idea of writing a letter was conceived by Ruth Dressen, who reasoned that in a "discussion" her husband might be talked out of his demands by the persuasive O'Malley. She had composed the letter in longhand while Charlie hovered over her shoulder. The demand was, in effect, that his new contract cover three years at $50,000 a year.

"The Dodgers do not believe in long-term contracts," O'Malley told the reporters. "Dressen is free to sign a one-year contract to manage the Dodgers. In fact, I have one here in my desk drawer, and if Charlie says the word now, I'll take it out and he can sign it and manage the Dodgers next year."

Dressen sat hunched in his chair, looking like a man whose pair of deuces had just been called and his fate decided, manfully sticking to his (or his wife's) decision. None of the reporters challenged the existence of a contract in O'Malley's desk drawer. The press conference closed with Dressen insisting that he had earned a three-year contract but that he would accept one for two years, and O'Malley generously if inaccurately telling him "the door is still open" to sign the one-year contract.

"I won't second-guess Ruth now," Charlie told a reporter.

He left Montague Street believing that he had twenty-four hours of grace in which to mull over his decision. But the door had already been closed. O'Malley went into seclusion with his orchids in Amityville. Although Dressen repeatedly called the Dodgers' office during the next couple of days, his calls were not returned. Two weeks later, when he realized what had happened to him, he signed a three-year contract to manage Oakland, which was then an independent minor-league franchise in the Pacific Coast League. He also directed a few bitter remarks in O'Malley's direction.

"I am sure that Mrs. Dressen will be very happy in Oakland," O'Malley told the press.

Meanwhile, I had made a fateful decision of my own. I was married at the end of the month, and after a honeymoon in northern New England, Ada and I moved into an apartment on the top floor of an old building off Washington Square. When I returned to the office, I caught up on the dailies, which were in the throes of a guessing game begun as soon as it became obvious that Dressen had been mousetrapped. Pee Wee Reese was frequently mentioned as the new Brooklyn manager, though I learned from Bavasi that he had never been seriously considered. Buzzie had called him, asking the rhetorical question "You're not interested in the job, are you, Pee Wee?" Pee Wee took the hint and gracefully declined; the Dodgers were not interested in a playing manager, and Reese was too valuable to the team at shortstop to consign permanently to the bench. Other names appeared as candidates in the papers, among them Frank Frisch, Rogers Hornsby, Joe DiMaggio, Tommy Henrich, and even Leo Durocher. Near the bottom of the list, buried with such names as Lefty O'Doul and Bill Terry, was that of "Wally" Alston, the manager of the Dodgers' farm team at Montreal.

What must have been one of baseball's best-kept secrets was Bavasi's selection of Alston. The two men had been together for a long time, as business manager and manager of, respectively, the farm teams at Nashua and Montreal. Buzzie, supported by Fresco Thompson and other officials in the minor-league organization, convinced O'Malley that Alston could manage in Brooklyn. A press conference was called for Tuesday, November 24, almost six weeks after Dressen's removal.

When I arrived at Montague Street that morning, I still had no idea of the new manager's identity, though I was sure he would come from the Dodger organization. One morning newspaper predicted that it would be an old Brooklyn hero, Cookie Lavagetto. Dick Young, having called every possible candidate, had received denials from all except Alston, who apparently was not at home.

"Who is it?" I asked Bavasi.

"Do you know Walt Alston?" he asked in return.

I shrugged. I had seen Alston several times at the team's spring-training camp in Vero Beach, Florida. He had been unobtrusive even among the minor-league managers there because several others—Clay Bryant, Tommy Holmes, Ed Head, Max Macon —had been better-known big leaguers. Alston had appeared in only one game in the majors, having come to bat as a pinch hitter for the St. Louis Cardinals in their Rickey days and struck out.

"Well, Walt's in town," Bavasi said with a little smile. "He's at the Lexington in Manhattan. Go over and pick him up and bring him back to the press conference."

There was my answer. When I reached the hotel, I called Alston's room (he had registered under his own name, secure in his anonymity), and a moment later he came down in the elevator. In his business suit he looked bigger than I had remembered him to be at Vero Beach.

"Congratulations, Walt," I said.

He grinned his thanks, and we entered a cab almost furtively, like a couple of anarchists on their way to bomb a bridge. Neither of us mentioned Alston's new job on the way to Brooklyn, as if somehow we would be violating a confidence. We talked about Vero Beach, and his successful season at Montreal, since his team had just beaten the Yankees' Kansas City team to win the Little World Series. But Walt, as the writers were to discover, sometimes to their dismay, was not a talker.

A short while later, Walter Alston was unveiled to the world at Montague Street. Most of the writers looked a little stunned, as if O'Malley had offered them a drink and then handed them soda pop. Equally baffled were a group of office workers in a building across the street. Aware of the press conference, they held up a sign in their window: IS IT COOKIE? The newspapermen signaled no but were stumped when they tried to identify the new manager by semaphore. The press conference ended with Alston posing for pictures, O'Malley beaming over him and holding up one finger to symbolize the one-year contract Alston had accepted.

O'Malley referred to him as "our enduring manager." Indeed he was, for Alston would sign nearly two dozen additional one-year contracts in Brooklyn and Los Angeles before stepping down.

If, from that time on, "good copy" was not forthcoming from the manager's office, there was a mother lode of it in the office next to mine. Irving Rudd came to the Dodgers by way of Jacobs Beach, where my father and I used to encounter him once in a while as he was going about publicizing fights at one or another of the small clubs around the city. When television diversified into other sports and entertainments, there was no longer a need for the boxing clubs, and Rudd, struggling to support his wife and two young daughters, came to the Dodgers to handle special promotions. Cherubic in figure, with a stubby clown's nose and a smile that was less a facial expression than a display of large front teeth, Rudd was, and is, one of the most imaginative promotion men of his time.

"Unswerving Irving," as baseball writer Tommy Holmes, of the *Eagle*, called him, was a master at looking ahead to a dull Tuesday night with a second-division team in town and turning it into a festival. He and O'Malley worked well together, bouncing ideas off each other and carrying them through to a successful promotion. One of the oddest was "Sym-phony Night."

O'Malley had become entangled in a dispute with New York Local 802 of the Musicians' Union. It concerned the Dodger Sym-phony (the second syllable pronounced as in *ersatz*), a group of six or seven fans who brought instruments to Ebbets Field and, between innings, played music of a sort from their seats behind first base. The union contended that these fans could not play music in public unless they were paid. O'Malley replied that they played only for their own amusement (a statement with which no one who sat near the Sym-phony would have quibbled), and since they had been playing at the park for years, he saw no reason why they suddenly should have to stop.

When the union threatened to picket Ebbets Field, O'Malley huddled with Rudd. They set aside a night game (one with a lagging advance sale, of course) to which every fan who brought along a musical instrument would be admitted free. Rudd set about interesting Brooklyn's citizenry in their Sym-phony's right to freedom of expression, and over twenty-five hundred music-loving fans appeared at the ball park, fully armed, on the appointed evening. They carried flutes, drums, and ocarinas, and ancient, rusted trombones they had disinterred from the attic. According to Rudd, a youngster was stopped at the gate and asked to open his violin case. It proved to have only a salami sandwich inside, but he was passed through anyway.

"Just before the game started, two big guys arrived at the gate hauling an upright piano," Rudd recalled. "We figured that was good for two admissions and passed them both in."

The assembled "musicians" were seated together in the left-field stands. They began to play two hours before game time and continued until the final out. While the howling dissonance nearly drove the ball players out of their minds, they manfully played the game to a finish. In this case the end justified the means: the union relented and permitted the Sym-phony to go on blaring for its own peculiar amusement.

I discovered Rudd to be a fount of enlightenment, a purveyor of information of the kind that is indispensable to anyone who deals with people. He had grown up in the tough Brownsville section of Brooklyn at a time when Murder, Inc., was flourishing, and his neighbors included such fistic worthies as "Schoolboy" Bernie Friedkin and Al "Bummy" Davis. (He once explained to me that Davis' real name was Albert Abraham Davidoff, Abraham being Ahvroom in Yiddish, and successively corrupted into Boomy and Bummy; thus the raffish Davis was marked almost from birth.) As a boy, Rudd loitered outside the players' entrance at Ebbets Field, hoping to get a glimpse of his heroes, foremost among them an obscure pitcher named Clise Dudley, who sometimes subdued the hated Giants.

"I would watch them go in and out of the clubhouse," Rudd said of the Dodgers. "It was only thirty feet from where I stood, but it took me twenty-one years to get inside."

Rudd's most sentimental and successful promotion was "Pee Wee Reese Night" in 1955, which coincided with the shortstop's

thirty-sixth birthday. Irving badgered Brooklyn fans and merchants for more than ten thousand dollars' worth of gifts for the
celebration. The most elaborate was a car he secured by working
out a stunt with seven dealers in the borough. Each contributed a
new model that was driven to home plate during the pregame
ceremony. Barbara Reese, Pee Wee's little daughter, pulled a key
out of a Dodger cap and he was presented with the car that
matched the key. The seven dealers divided the cost of the car
among themselves.

The other Dodger players afterward referred to the car as
"Rudd's Folly," since the key Barbara Reese selected proved to fit
the smallest model and they believed that Irving should have
fixed the drawing so that Pee Wee won a Cadillac. Irving insisted,
however, that the show remain on the level. The ceremony came
to a tear-jerking conclusion when, at the end of the fifth inning, all
the lights at Ebbets Field were turned out and the crowd, holding
lighted matches aloft, sang "Happy Birthday to Pee Wee."

A third arm of our press-relations corps was Allan Roth, a statis-
tician with a dry sense of humor to go with his ability to search
out the significant figure. Roth, a Canadian by birth, had compiled hockey statistics before coming to Brooklyn and convincing
Branch Rickey of the good use to which finely analyzed records of
all the players could be put; in his hands, these records could be as
revealing about a player's strengths and weaknesses as the game
films to which football coaches are addicted. At a moment's notice, Roth could glance down a set of figures and tell how Furillo
fared against left-handed pitchers in Cincinnati over the last three
seasons, or how often Erskine was successful in keeping opposing
pitchers from hitting the ball out of the infield when they came to
bat.

A story of Roth's indicates how closely meshed are the minds of
managers and players, both being content to depend on the
records compiled by their inner computers. He happened to
watch an evening sports program on which the host interviewed
Don Newcombe. When the host asked the big pitcher who was
the toughest hitter in the league for him to get out, Newk replied

that, surprisingly, it was an obscure and notoriously weak-hitting infielder with the Phillies.

"Just for the fun of it, I looked up the records," Roth said. "Just as I thought, this fellow was no threat to Newk at all. I think he had managed two singles in eighteen at bats against him. But I guess Newk psyched himself. The fellow's hitting never improved against anybody else, but from then on, he was death to Newcombe. *Boom-boom-boom.* Two doubles and a home run every time he faced him!"

At best, of course, we in the press department simply pumped the confectioners' guns, daubing our frosty little curlicues across the birthday cake. With or without the icing, the Dodgers of those years were an enthralling team, and at the heart of the team was Robinson. He remains my one burning memory of Ebbets Field. He played with an imagination and abandon that transcended baseball. After watching him harass an enemy team to the point of despair and disintegration, all of us came away from the ball park with a sense of excitement that was more than animal stimulation; we knew now that life held possibilities, if only we rushed to meet it, as Jackie drove himself to take charge of a ball game. He had the artist's gift of providing us with a high that did not let us down with the blahs on the dreary morning after. The sense of purpose remained, though we suspected we were still .220 hitters.

If Robinson the man, like other superstars, could not live up to the soaring intensity of the performer, he came closer to it than most. He was the pioneer; he had not only lived through the humiliation of oppression but had braved the agony of confrontation as well. That anger, which is hoisted like a flag by the black athletes who followed him, is too often political or self-indulgent, but Robinson's was the marrow of the man, rooted in humanity.

He could act pettishly. One of the newspapermen came to me before a game and said he had heard that Robinson was complaining about something he had written earlier in the week.

"Did you see Bill Corum's column today?" the writer asked.

271

"Well, I wrote it. Corum was sick last night and they asked me to
do the column for him. It's all about Jackie, and how much he
means to the ball club. Let him know I wrote it, will you?"

When I saw Robinson in the clubhouse, I handed him the
paper.

"Our friend wants you to know he wrote Corum's column," I
said.

Jackie glanced at the paper and dropped it on the floor. "Fuck
'im," he said and walked away.

I marveled at how this thin-skinned man had steeled himself to
endure the vilest jeers when he first played in organized baseball.
The pain must have been searing, the self-control almost inhu-
man.

Although Robinson fiercely resented any slight to himself or to
his race, he was not a slave to his convictions. O'Malley had assigned Irving Rudd to serve as an advance man for the Dodgers'
spring exhibition games in Miami, where the team traveled after
its preliminary training at Vero Beach. Irving went on early-
morning disc-jockey programs to talk about the team, hired an old
circus runner to roam the city putting up posters, and set up displays of Dodger photographs and equipment in department store
windows. During his first spring there, he also arranged a parade
for the players down Collins Avenue in Miami Beach. The city
agreed to provide the open cars. When Robinson arrived, he discovered that the city fathers, following Southern traditions, had
reserved the cars at the rear of the parade for the blacks. He refused to take part, and the other players backed him unanimously.
For a moment, the parade was off.

Rudd, aware that his plans for a city-wide reception were tum-
bling about his ears, went to Jackie with a personal plea, taking
the blame for the blunder on himself.

"Okay, Irv," Jackie said. "I'll go ahead with this thing only because of you. If anybody else was running it, I'd walk out."

There was one matter on which Robinson stood firm. That was
his dislike for Walter O'Malley. He took Rickey's part in their
dispute, but I believe it went deeper than that. He felt that
O'Malley patronized him and treated him unfairly, and Jackie

could not abide the sight of him. To some extent he carried this feeling over to the other members of the Dodgers' post-Rickey hierarchy, and sometimes during the off season he called me to find out what was going on at Montague Street.

"What are they saying about me?" he asked, with a funny little laugh. "What are they up to?"

A year after I left the Dodgers, he was sold to the Giants. (Eventually he decided to retire before he ever played a game for his new team.) I dropped him a note the day after the deal, and had a handwritten reply from him.

"You and I know it was bound to happen," Jackie wrote. "For the sake of all the players I hope my absence doesn't have an effect. The Dodgers are a great bunch and I will always wish them well.

"I was very pleased to hear how you feel about it but I want you to know I don't feel too badly about the deal. At first I did and thought back to some of the reasons but then I felt it wouldn't do any good to say anything about them."

Restraint, as well as conversion to Rockefeller Republicanism, came upon Robinson in his approaching middle age. Meanwhile, Brooklyn had seen the unsettling and then glorious opening years of Walter Alston's long tenure as manager. The first season, 1954, had been the dreariest for the Dodgers in a long while. The worst blow was an injury to a nerve in Campanella's right hand, which failed to heal when a surgeon operated on it. ("He operated on my pocketbook, too," O'Malley announced to the press when he got the surgeon's bill, and then settled the resultant defamation suit out of court.) Everything went wrong for Alston, and the Dodgers trudged home a distant second to the Giants.

The spring of 1955 must have been even worse for the Dodgers' manager, who was under fire from all quarters. The squad was a blend of aging immortals and scrappy youngsters, and Alston shifted, experimented, substituted, all through the exhibition schedule. The veterans were furious, accusing the manager of misusing them. When Robinson complained of not getting enough action, the papers all printed "Robinson Blasts Alston" stories.

"I can't talk to him man to man," Robinson said to me. "I don't know why, but I can't."

The writers found Alston uncommunicative and seemed to enjoy his discomfiture; some equated his taciturnity with mindlessness. The high point of the spring trip for the writers was when the Dodgers played the Washington Senators, whose new manager was Charlie Dressen. Dick Young and the others rushed to Dressen for a story, and he played along with them, composing what they could not extract from Alston—the Dodgers' opening-day lineup. The next day's papers were awash with mirth, but Alston was not amused.

Then the season began, and the Dodgers simply ran off from the rest of the field. They won their first ten games, justifying Alston's endless tinkering during the exhibitions. Campy slugged home runs; Robinson played dashing baseball; Reese appeared rejuvenated. Yet the Dodgers were playing in comparative privacy. The fans simply were not showing up at Ebbets Field. During a sparsely attended game early in the season, O'Malley abruptly asked us to alert the crowd that there would be an important announcement in the late innings. Having had a couple of innings to figure out what he was going to do, O'Malley then released the news that souvenirs, commemorating the Dodgers' record-breaking winning streak at the start of the season, would be sent to all the fans who turned in their rainchecks that day. After the game, the players were discussing the low attendance.

"When they said there was going to be an important announcement, I thought they were going to say that the franchise had been moved to Los Angeles," said Snider in prophetic jest.

With Alston in firm command, the Dodgers kept on winning, making a shambles of the pennant race. No longer unsure of himself or cramped by a weak bench, Alston managed with the flair of a Durocher or a Stengel. He inserted pinch hitters and called on his bullpen with daring and skill. Newcombe, a terror on the mound, also became a menacing pinch hitter, while Clem Labine and Karl Spooner headed an effective staff of relievers. But the fans remained at their television sets, and O'Malley revealed at midseason that the Dodgers would play seven of their seventy-

Before anyone realized what was happening, hundreds of wildly excited fans knocked over the barricades, pushed aside the restraining wall of police, and came charging down on us. I pulled Podres back through the front door as the crowd stampeded past, but Hodges and a couple of cops were well mauled before Gil could fight his way, like a swimmer in heavy seas, through the surging, clutching mob into the safety of the lobby. As the police struggled to shepherd the fans back behind the barricades, a distraught sergeant glared at me through the front door.

"Try that again, buddy," he growled, "and I'll have you locked up."

Beyond him the ecstatic roar incredibly sustained itself.

The Dodgers are gone from Brooklyn now, and so are Ebbets Field and the old office building on Montague Street. But the voices hurled into that long-ago night by the crowd in front of the Bossert must still be around there somewhere. They had been held in for a long time, and there was a feeling that one had better let it all out while there was still a chance. A great many of us were beginning to say a long farewell to our heroes.

seven home games in 1956 at Roosevelt Stadium in Jersey City. (When he put Irving Rudd in charge of an office there to drum up advance interest among Jerseyites, Red Smith wrote that Irving had reached the ultimate stage of the two-platoon system by becoming one-eleventh of a business manager.)

This hop-and-skip that was to precede the big jump to Los Angeles was largely overlooked by the press as the Dodgers slumped during a siege of injuries in July. Robinson, Campanella, and Snider were hobbled, and sore arms afflicted the pitching staff. But young players from the farm system kept their fingers in the dike, and the team survived. Robinson returned to the lineup in August and for about a week put on one of the friskiest displays of his career—taking the extra base on hits, stealing bases, rattling enemy pitchers by dancing down off third.

"My leg still bothers me," Jackie said of his injury, "but the club has been dead for the last week or so, and I thought I could put a little life into it."

Mission accomplished, Jackie returned to the bench and concentrated on getting his legs in shape for the World Series while the younger players took over. One of the rookies who was put on very limited display that season was Sanford Koufax, a "bonus baby" signed by the Dodgers the previous winter out of the University of Cincinnati. The stupendous fastball was already there, of course, but the pitching finesse and social savoir faire were not. Sandy's moodiness, plus the growing pains that occasionally afflicted his young body and caused him to beg off from a workout, gave some of the older players the impression that he was a spoiled and pampered kid. I was in the clubhouse on an evening when Koufax groused about some order he had received from the pitching coach. Sitting on a stool near me was another southpaw pitcher, a stumpy, peppery little guy of only marginal ability who failed to win a single game in his two trials with the Dodgers. His name was Tommy Lasorda. He looked at the sullen Koufax across the room and then shook his head wistfully.

"I'd give anything to have his ability," Lasorda said. "Do you think he's ever going to do anything with it?"

It was October, and the Dodgers were in the World Series, trying once more to beat the Yankees. Robinson electrified the crowd in the opening game at the Stadium, sliding under Yogi Berra's tag to steal home in the eighth inning, but the Yankees beat Don Newcombe. They won again the next day, and as the Series shifted to Ebbets Field, the traditional Brooklyn cry of "Wait till next year!" could already be heard.

Alston chose his young left-hander, Johnny Podres, to pitch against the Yankees' Bob Turley in the third game. The score was tied, 2–2, in the second inning when Robinson took over. He singled with one out, and the Dodgers quickly filled the bases. Jackie went into his classic act, moving up and down the third-base line, feinting a dash toward home, pulling up, suddenly feinting again. Unnerved by the show of bravado, Turley walked Jim Gilliam on four pitches, forcing in Robinson. Another run scored before the Yankees retired the side.

In the seventh inning, Robinson (who had been playing well at third base, too) humiliated the Yankees once more. He doubled to left, took a wide turn around second, and feinted a dash to third. Elston Howard, who had retrieved the ball in left field, hesitated, then threw to second base in an attempt to trap him. Instead, Robinson wheeled and raced to third, sliding in ahead of Billy Martin's high relay. He scored a moment later when Sandy Amoros dribbled a hit through the drawn-in infield. Podres, using his change of pace beautifully, held on to win, 8–3, and the Dodgers were still alive.

Now the Dodgers began to play as they had during the pennant race. Campanella, Snider, and Hodges provided the long ball while Clem Labine stifled the Yankees in relief, and the Dodgers won the next two games. Everybody went back to the Stadium, and the Yankees tied the Series at three games apiece. It was Podres again, as the Dodgers attempted what they had never been able to do since the ancient trolley dodgers began playing ball in what was then the City of Brooklyn more than seventy years before. Hodges drove in a run with a single in the second inning and another with a sacrifice fly in the sixth, sending the Dodgers to a 2–0 lead.

It was then that Alston made the move that saved the game. As

the Dodgers took the field in the seventh inning, he sent S Amoros, a little left-handed Cuban, into the game to pla field. The Yankees put two runners on base, and Berra, a clutch hitter, came to bat. Podres threw, and Berra lifted drive toward the low barrier in the left-field corner. A playing Yogi in left center, had to run more than a hundred catch up with it. Just before crashing into the railing, he str out his glove and caught the ball. Bouncing off the rail, he and fired to Reese, who relayed the ball to Hodges to dou McDougald off first base.

The tension mounted into the ninth inning, which w torture for all of us from Montague Street. We rocked in o and groaned with every pitch. Bill Skowron, the Yankees' ful first baseman, grounded out, and Bob Cerv flied out. change-up was a thing of beauty, but none of us was a tician at that moment. Might was right. He threw to Howard, who bounced the ball to Reese, and the Dodg the champions of the world.

That night, more than two thousand screaming, sta Brooklyn fans, held in check by police lines, jammed walks in front of and across from Brooklyn's Hotel Bosse the Dodgers' "family" was celebrating the victory. Th roared with the arrival at the hotel of each Brooklyn he riotous lounge, where players, club officials, and newsp and their families swarmed in an endless round of toasts slapping, somebody pulled me aside and shouted into "That crowd out on the street is yelling for Podres an Why don't you give the fans a break and let them see a the players?"

Good idea. I pulled Podres and Hodges from the c circle of admirers and asked them to come out and w crowd. We pushed our way through an advance guar managed to penetrate as far as the lobby, and walked o steps. The two stars of the Dodgers' victory lifted the response to the crowd's wild roar. Hodges, called to by standing in front of the nearest police barricade, des steps to sign his autograph album.

Chapter Twenty-three
Libel

In the spring of 1963, two prominent football men, coach Paul "Bear" Bryant, of the University of Alabama, and former coach James Wallace "Wally" Butts, of the University of Georgia, each sued the *Saturday Evening Post* for ten million dollars. They charged that the *Post* had libeled them in an article called "The Story of a College Football Fix," which appeared in the magazine under the byline Frank Graham, Jr.

"I don't know whether the stuff you wrote was true or not," the sports editor of a Midwestern newspaper said to me at the time, "but I do know it's the most amazing goddamned magazine article I ever read!"

Hyperbole discounted, the man neatly summed up the article's virtues and defects. The *Post*, which was then in its death throes (a condition, I hasten to add, that antedated my association with it), received enormous publicity as a result of the story, making it once more a household word across the country. Yet the entire enterprise was so slipshod and the article so flawed by inaccuracies that in the long run the *Post*'s position was further weakened. Here was a publication tied by tradition to high professional standards, and here was a writer prodded by every element in his background to strict journalistic integrity, entangled together in ineptitude like a couple of drunken sailors. The details of this fiasco, as I know them, compose a sad little cautionary tale.

I left the Dodgers for journalism after their triumph in 1955. Like an ambitious high-school student, I had been training for my opportunity, waiting for my big chance, in a kind of vacuum, getting up a couple of hours early every morning at our apartment in the Village and writing for my own instruction and amusement: street scenes, incidents at the ball park, reflections on life and letters. I played with words in those gray dawns, I clinked them like coins on the counter of my typewriter and tested their ring. It was pretty stilted stuff at first, but gradually it smoothed out.

When Gil Hodges took Pee Wee Reese's throw for the final put-out of the World Series that year, I knew I had extracted all I wanted to from baseball, and this was the time to climb out of the rabbit hole. I sent two of my articles to *Sport.* Ed Fitzgerald, the magazine's editor, called me at the Dodgers' office to say that he couldn't use the articles, but would I join the staff there as a writer and editor? Within minutes I told Walter O'Malley that I was leaving. He was, I think, a little offended, but he did not ask me to post any of his correspondence on the way out.

Sport was fertile ground in which to cultivate an aspiring talent. Management operated on the Rickey principle, keeping the staff youthful and hungry, with lots of hustle. One learned not so much by stricture as by permissiveness, tempered by competition. John Lardner, W. C. Heinz, and Graham *père* were among the contributors, as were such upwardly mobile moppets as Roger Kahn, Ed Linn, Jimmy Breslin, Al Silverman, and Josh Greenfeld. One didn't dare pen a sloppy sentence. Besides sharing in the duties of a copy, photo, and cartoon editor, I wrote articles at lengths that varied from a column of miscellany (my byline supplanting that of a conglomerate *nom de plume,* Biff Bennett) to "triple-book-length features." I wrote pieces about Floyd Patterson, Hurricane Jackson, Sal Maglie, and Henri Richard, and ghosted others for Rocky Marciano, Bob Feller, and Vic Raschi. I suffered painful sunburn and a violent siege of the runs while covering a grand prix auto race around the *malecón* in pre-Castro Havana, and sprained my knee when I slipped on a turd while doing roadwork on a Central Park bridle path with a West Indian boxer named Ludwig Lightburn.

A classmate of mine at Columbia who had become a literary agent saw my articles and signed me to his stable of writers. From this happy circumstance emerged my first book. My agent set up an appointment for me with an editor who was interested in publishing a biography of Casey Stengel. The editor's jaw dropped in surprise when I walked into his office, and I later formed the suspicion that he had been expecting Frank Graham, never having heard of Junior. But after reading some of my articles, he gamely went through with the deal. Stengel refused to cooperate with me, preferring to hoard his experiences for an autobiography, but I did my research and went up to Yankee Stadium as often as I could to sit unobtrusively in the dugout and observe him in action.

When my book was published in 1958, Stengel vented his frustration by refusing to talk to my father, who had been his friend for almost forty years. The situation became very sticky. My father stoutly defended my right to choose a subject to write about, and confronted Stengel angrily in the dugout one day when Casey refused to answer his questions about the Yankees. Stengel finally gave him the information he wanted, but in uncharacteristic monosyllables. Amity was restored the following spring when George Weiss, the Yankees' general manager, invited my mother and father to join him for dinner with Edna and Casey Stengel at a St. Petersburg restaurant.

By that time, I was gone from the scene. With one book published and a contract for another in hand, I left *Sport* to freelance; a year later, Ada and I gave up our apartment and went to live in Europe for more than two years. The city no longer enchanted us. I was being drawn more and more toward the natural world, toward wild things and remote landscapes, which I had come to feel, paradoxically, kept me in touch with life more faithfully than ball parks and sporty saloons; and when we returned to the United States in the early 1960s, we bought a home in eastern Maine. (I told the story of my bucolic conversion in an earlier book, *Where the Place Called Morning Lies*.) Since nature and conservation were still not broadly popular subjects, we kept a small apartment for a while in New York, which I used as a base of operations while continuing to write often about sports.

In February, 1963, I received a phone call from Roger Kahn at the apartment that Ada and I had sublet in Brooklyn only a day or two before. Kahn was now the sports editor of the *Saturday Evening Post*. I had recently finished two articles for him, one a profile of the aging but still controversial Branch Rickey, who had become a consultant for the Cardinals ("It is difficult for an eighty-one-year-old man to serve in the capacity of a consultant and not be suggestive," he told me), and the other a harking back to the Flores tragedy, under Roger Donoghue's byline.

"Can you come over here to the office in the morning?" Roger asked me. "Don Schanche, the executive editor, wants to talk to you about an important assignment."

What could be so big that Roger himself was not handling the arrangements? I wondered. I was excited as well as curious when I reached the *Post*'s office in the Tishman Building, on Fifth Avenue, the next morning. For several years, I had been living in small cities or rural areas in Europe and Maine, away from the centers of action, and I approached the ranking editors of this great magazine—of this great American *institution*—with a touch of giddiness. Kahn met me and took me to Schanche's office, where we were joined by Davis Thomas, the managing editor, and the outlines of the story began to unfold.

The previous fall, Furman Bisher, of the Atlanta *Journal* (an excellent reporter who had done some work for *Sport* while I was there), wrote an article for the *Post* called "College Football Is Going Berserk." Bisher described the increase in violence and injuries that plagued the college game and attributed much of the mayhem to coaches who wanted to win at any cost. In the course of the article, Bisher identified Alabama's Bear Bryant as a prime offender. Bryant denied the charge and, when the *Post* refused to publish a retraction, sued the magazine's parent company, the Curtis Publishing Company, for $500,000.

The *Post*'s lawyers began to investigate Bryant's background and prepare a defense. (A reliable defense against libel is to prove that the plaintiff is so corrupt that no one can inflict further damage on his reputation.) Then, hosanna! The law firm of Beddow, Embry & Beddow, which was representing the *Post* in Birmingham, Alabama, uncovered a sensational report about Bryant and Wally Butts that was then circulating among university and athletic officials in the Deep South. The Birmingham lawyers passed on the report to Pepper, Hamilton & Scheetz, the prestigious firm that for many years had handled the legal affairs of the Curtis Publishing Company in Philadelphia. The Philadelphia lawyers, in turn, took the message to Clay Blair, Jr., who was the *Post*'s editor in chief, and exuberantly suggested that they had Bryant by the short hairs.

Briefly, the story was this: George Burnett, an insurance salesman in Atlanta, had tried to call a business associate one morning during the previous fall and, after a series of queer noises on his telephone, found himself plugged in by an electronic quirk to another person's long-distance call.

"Coach Bryant is out on the field, but he'll come to the phone," Burnett heard an operator say. "Do you want to hold, Coach Butts, or shall we call you back?"

"I'll hold, Operator," said a man's voice.

Like almost everyone else in Atlanta, Burnett was a football fan, and he realized that he was about to overhear a conversation between two of the colossi of Southern football. Indeed, he was slightly acquainted with Butts, having met him around town on occasion. Although the University of Georgia had eased Butts out as coach a year or two before, he still served as athletic director. Burnett ("I was curious, naturally") kept the phone to his ear. When Bryant came on the line, according to Burnett, Butts almost at once began to disclose Georgia's plans for its opening game against Alabama, which was only eight days away. Burnett reached for a pencil and scratch pad that he kept on his desk and began to make notes on the conversation.

Later, Burnett said that he was disturbed, even frightened, by the implications of what he had heard. Butts, who had made his call from a phone in the office of the firm that Burnett was trying to reach, was apparently feeding the Georgia team's secrets to the enemy. When the two teams met in another week, Alabama gave Georgia a bad beating, 35–0, which was considerably worse than the margin of fourteen points or so established by bookmakers beforehand. On the advice of a friend, Burnett then gave his notes on the call to Johnny Griffith, who had succeeded Butts as head coach. The university's officials asked Burnett to take a lie-detector test, which he did, and he passed to everybody's satisfaction. At that point, although no announcement of the action was made to the public, the officials confronted Butts with their information, and he resigned as athletic director, effective immediately. Meanwhile, a similar investigation by officials of the University of Alabama cleared Bryant of any wrongdoing.

Here was a story to match Clay Blair's image of what the "new" *Saturday Evening Post* was all about, something that would help to get people talking about the magazine as they did in days gone by. Shortly before this, Blair had sent a memo to the *Post*'s staff, assessing its situation: "The final yardstick: We have about six lawsuits pending, meaning we are hitting them where it hurts, with solid, meaningful journalism." The memo was leaked to *Newsweek*, which published it in an article about the new *Post*, and within a year Blair was to rue his words. Meanwhile, he had the makings of another hard-hitting piece, which he confided to only three members of the staff, and they had just passed the gist of it on to me.

"Several other magazines—*Newsweek, Sports Illustrated*—and we hear even CBS are interested in this story, but we've got the inside track," Schanche told me. "This fellow Burnett wants to sell his story to us. We're sending a lawyer and a private investigator from Birmingham over to Atlanta this week to talk to him and get an affidavit about what he heard. We want you to go to Atlanta and write a story based on that affidavit."

While Schanche and Thomas were momentarily occupied on another matter, I turned to Kahn and asked the obvious question: "Why me?"

"Furman Bisher would be the logical choice, but we're being

sued because of that earlier piece he wrote," Kahn said. "It would make us look vindictive if he came right back with this one. So Schanche asked me to suggest someone who was an accurate reporter, with no skeletons in his closet in case this thing ever went into court, and I suggested you. Everybody liked those other two pieces you've done, so they agreed."

When Schanche returned, I received my final instructions. I was to check into the Heart of Atlanta Motel and get in touch with George Burnett's lawyer. Then, after I had negotiated the purchase of Burnett's story for the *Post,* I was to call the lawyer in Birmingham, who would fly to Atlanta to receive Burnett's affidavit. No one else must know that I was in the city, and that included Furman Bisher.

This was cloak-and-dagger stuff, outside of anything in my previous experience, but I set off on the assignment without qualms. I was not a lone reporter, digging up a shocking story and trying to justify it to any old editor. A great magazine had handed me the material on a silver platter, and I was merely to be present during the taking of a sworn statement. A lawyer and a private detective, both of them familiar with the vagaries of Southeastern college football, were to pass on the truth or falsity of what they heard. Finally, another formidable law firm, acting in concert with the *Post*'s highest-ranking editors, would decide on whether or not they could publish the story without exposing themselves to successful legal action by Butts or Bryant. It was heady indeed to feel a part of such a power structure. Max Schmeling, setting sail for New York to fight Joe Louis for the second time, must have radiated just as much confidence in his mission's success as I did on my flight to Atlanta.

When I arrived there, I went to see Pierre Howard, a prominent lawyer and legislator in Atlanta who was representing Burnett. I offered five thousand dollars for Burnett's story, if the *Post*'s lawyer found that it rang true, and another five hundred dollars for Milton Flack, Burnett's friend who was acting as his agent and adviser.

We agreed that all parties to the arrangement would meet early that afternoon in my motel room. Half an hour before the scheduled meeting, Roderick Beddow, Jr., the *Post*'s lawyer, arrived from Birmingham with a private investigator. The detective, who was described to me as thoroughly informed on Southeastern Conference football, was there to see if Burnett's story sounded plausible and to make a secret tape of the meeting. He had a bulky tape machine, which he concealed in one of the bureau drawers in my room. The microphone was built into the lock on his briefcase, which he kept beside him at all times.

Pierre Howard arrived with Burnett and his friend, Milt Flack. Beddow, the detective, and I looked over the affidavit Howard had brought with him, which included all of the pertinent details. We asked questions to fill in certain gaps or clear up vague points, and Burnett, an earnest, soft-spoken man of forty-one years, with a round face and a receding hairline, answered them straightforwardly. He volunteered the information that a couple of years before, he had been convicted of passing two bad checks—one for twenty-five dollars and the other for twenty dollars; the judge fined him a hundred dollars and put him on probation for a year. He had a large family and a penchant for mismanaging his financial affairs, but all of us believed him to be basically truthful.

I committed my first mistake here by taking only rudimentary notes, having been told that the tapes of this interview would be made available to me when I returned to New York. While I was questioning Burnett and Flack about their backgrounds, as well as more details of the overheard conversation, Beddow and the detective discovered they had to leave to catch their plane back to Birmingham. Since Howard and the others showed no disposition to leave immediately, the tapes could not be extracted from their hiding place. But now the microphone was gone with the detective, so I began making more detailed notes.

I completed my questioning of Burnett and Flack, and they agreed to the *Post*'s offer for exclusive rights to the story. After they left, I called Roderick Beddow, who had just returned to his office after the short flight from Atlanta. Yes, he and the detective had discussed Burnett's story and found it plausible. The affidavit was in order, but they wanted to transcribe the tapes as soon as possible. Could I mail them to Birmingham? I suddenly remem-

bered that the next day was George Washington's Birthday and
the post office would be closed, so I drove to the airport and put
the tapes on the next plane to Birmingham, where Beddow had
them picked up.

I also called Don Schanche in New York and told him what I
had learned. He was faintly disturbed about the bad-check
charges, but those were matters that were to be passed on by lawyers. I asked permission to stay over until the next morning; since
I could not visit a local newspaper office without disclosing my
identity, I wanted to go to the public library to check on some of
the facts concerning the Georgia-Alabama game. Schanche
agreed to this and suggested that I get in touch with Roger Kahn
as soon as I returned to New York. At the library, I read through
back issues of the local papers, making notes on the game in question, quotes by the players and coaches, and comments by the
writers.

By the time I reached New York, enthusiasm for the story had
surged among the few *Post* editors who were aware of it. Even
Roger Kahn, who had been skeptical of the story at first because
the details of fixing a game or altering a "point spread" were so
difficult to prove in court, became a believer. "All my training
goes toward 'Get the story,' " he said afterward. The editors asked
me to produce a draft of the article as quickly as possible, and, of
course, warned me not to mention it to anyone. At this point, I
had not even told my father about it. Other magazines were
known to have collected many of the details, and Clay Blair was
uneasy because one of them, despite our "exclusive rights" to
Burnett's story, might piece together an article from other
sources.

I worked far into the night at our new apartment in Brooklyn.
We had no furniture yet, not even a bed or a table, and were
sleeping on a mattress on the floor. I perched on a camp chair, set
up a portable typewriter on a stool, and, bending deeply from the
waist, typed out the article. I worked from the affidavit, the few
notes I had taken of my talk with Burnett and Flack, and the news
stories I had come across at the public library. Georgia's attorney
general had impounded the notes Burnett had made during the

overheard conversation, but the *Post*'s lawyers seemed sure of re-
ceiving them as soon as the state's investigation was over. The
tapes of my interview at the motel would momentarily arrive
from Birmingham.

I delivered the finished draft to the *Post* the next day. Schanche,
impressed that I had composed a readable piece within twenty-
four hours, promptly offered me a contract as a regular *Post*
writer. (Like Walter Alston, I accepted a one-year term, with my
retainer of a thousand dollars a month to begin after I had received two thousand dollars as my fee for writing the Burnett
story.) Kahn, in a more sober mood, pointed out a few weak places
in my article, which I did my best to remedy, and he made some
further improvements on it himself. Then I awaited instructions,
expecting to be sent back to Atlanta, with the wraps off this time,
to check details that were now mostly hearsay.

For the most part, there were no more instructions. Kahn called
me to report that Furman Bisher had appeared in New York, having come upon Burnett's story from another source, but being unaware that the *Post* already had it in hand. The editors decided
that if further research was to be done in Georgia or Alabama, it
ought to be undertaken by a Southerner, rather than a Yankee
who was likely to provoke suspicion or antagonism. I joined Kahn
and Bisher in a Manhattan pub, where we agreed that Furman
would talk to players and officials at both universities and send me
material to supplement the original draft.

As it stood, the article charged that Wally Butts, embittered by
his treatment at the university and enmeshed in debt, had given
details of Georgia's offensive and defensive plans to Alabama's
Bear Bryant just before an important game. The article also implied, but did not spell out, that gambling on the final score was
Butts' motivation. Then, just in case readers were a little slow,
Roger Kahn wrote a "precede," or introductory box, for the article in which he compared this incident to baseball's infamous
Black Sox Scandal, in which players and gamblers had acted in
collusion to fix the outcome of the 1919 World Series.

Chapter Twenty-four
Quixote Tumbled

What the *Post* was soon to describe to its readers as "a shocking report" was ready to go on the presses, but almost nothing had been added to support the rough draft I had fashioned from George Burnett's affidavit. Bisher's attempts to gather more telling quotes in the South had largely failed. He sent me several comments, but the people he talked to had little of significance to add, or, as in Alabama, they refused to discuss the game at all. The tapes made by the private detective had not been received by the *Post*'s editors, having been delayed somewhere en route. The notes Burnett took at the phone were still impounded by Georgia's attorney general, and so were not available for examination by the editors.

In the end, what may have been the most damaging defect of all was that, given the excessive haste and secrecy with which the article was rushed into print, there had been no semblance of the fact-checking process that is routine in the office of every major magazine. Neither I nor any other writer had been sent to Atlanta again to verify some of the hearsay quotes passed on to me by Burnett and Milt Flack. No researcher in the office had checked dates or game scores, whose accuracy then depended only on the uncertain memory and untrained observation of George Burnett. It was as if another whispered question, another phone call to Atlanta, would shatter the secrecy and with it the *Post*'s investment in this exclusive story.

As in a classic disaster, the wheels, once set in motion, could not be stopped. A sense of excitement, of inebriated delight in pulling off a coup, held together those who were in the know. Clay Blair told me in a moment of good fellowship that, whatever happened, I need not worry about my byline on the article, because the *Post* would always stand behind me. If Blair was not completely reassuring, a word from one of the *Post*'s lawyers lifted whatever lurking doubts I had.

"Even if Butts sues, the case will never get to trial," this man said. "The attorney general has the evidence, and Butts will be in jail before he can get a suit off the ground."

Looking back on the incident, I am amazed at my naïveté, but it pales by comparison with that of the men who were making the final decisions at the *Post*. They had extraordinary faith in what they perceived to be their allies in Georgia. The attorney general was, in effect, going to carry the legal burden for the magazine by prosecuting Butts; the Atlanta *Journal* was going to carry the public relations burden by breaking the story in its pages on the same day that it appeared in the *Post*.

Dave Thomas, the managing editor, expressed uneasiness about coming down so hard on Bear Bryant. The introductory box, by equating this case with the Black Sox Scandal, surely made implications about Bryant that were not supported by facts in the article itself. But the lawyers had a ready answer: If he listened to Butts, then he was part of the conspiracy.

What kept the machinery moving toward publication? There was, of course, a compulsion to excel professionally, to pull off a stunning scoop. The *Post* at the time was immersed in an orgy of revelation, but besides professional motives there was a genuine moralistic fervor abroad in the office, fueled by Clay Blair. He saw himself as the leader of an assault on the citadels of iniquity. The *Post* would root out corruption in the sports world as it was rooting out segregation in the Old South. A moment's thought on the part of anyone in power would have suggested that whatever the merits of the Butts-Bryant story, it had little chance to survive a jury trial in the South, where the *Post* was widely viewed as the chief instrument of a new Yankee imperialism. Its self-advertised "sophisticated muckraking" plainly was contributing to the mongrelization of the races. The *Post*, in this view, was a magazine for nigger-lovers, and now it was trying to destroy Southern football. (In the furor, it was forgotten that this story was unearthed by lawyers in Georgia and Alabama, brought to Blair, who had lived in Georgia as a child, and put in the hands of Schanche, who had, I believe, attended the University of Georgia.)

Otto Friedrich observed the *Post*'s pathological symptoms during the years he served there as a high-ranking editor and described them in his book *Decline and Fall*. Of the exuberant naïveté that was a part of the problem, he had this to say: "When we were young, we assumed on trust that the corporations were the indestructible engines of our national life. They were run by wise men, and they would harvest profits forever and ever." The 1960s were still young, and many of us were inclined to live, or at least to act by, the light of those doomed illusions.

Here was a chance for me to get in my moralistic licks, too. For a long time, I had been disenchanted with collegiate athletics. (Of course, in view of the results, what Columbia man hadn't?) The revelations about dumping and rigging baseball games at the City College of New York, Kentucky, and other schools in the 1950s snuffed out whatever interest I had in that pastime. Even the strong basketball team that Columbia put together during my time there left a bad taste in the mouth, as two of its starting five players later ran afoul of the law, one of them for rigging games. Meanwhile, friends in various college athletic departments had told me horror stories about the recruiting violations and the exploitation of scholar-athletes that had become almost a necessity as football coaches scrambled to keep their jobs. Coaches themselves violated their contracts and jumped to more lucrative posts. The old college game, I reasoned, needed a good shaking up.

Wally Butts was an obvious target. An amiable rogue, he had already dug a disreputable hole for himself as he got involved with shady loan companies, used university money to take a girl friend along on football trips, and engaged in persistent backbiting at the expense of his successor. The university had already arranged for him to leave at the beginning of June, even if Burnett's revelations hadn't forced the school's authorities to demand his earlier departure. Butts' unsavory reputation undoubtedly contributed to the *Post*'s overconfidence that it could make its story stand up.

The Butts-Bryant article appeared in the March 23, 1963, issue of the *Saturday Evening Post*. With its sports editor, Furman Bisher, already involved in a suit brought by Bryant, the Atlanta *Journal* decided not to break the story simultaneously with the *Post*, since it might leave itself open to charges of vindictiveness. The two coaches, having somehow obtained advance copies of the issue, went on television to deny any wrongdoing. "Never in my life have I ever attempted to fix or rig a ball game, either as a player or a coach," Bryant protested angrily. "I did not bet on the outcome of the Georgia game or any other football game." Each coach sued the *Post* for ten million dollars, Bryant's figure being added to the half a million he was already asking for Bisher's article. My name was not mentioned in either of the suits.

In the face of the coaches' denials and the skepticism expressed by the newsweeklies, the *Post* defended itself aggressively. Schanche told me that a Southern writer, not Furman Bisher, would be assigned to prepare a second article on the case (though this plan was never carried out). "We believe that anyone who rigs a football game should be exposed," Roger Kahn wrote in an editorial that appeared in a subsequent issue. "We will continue to cling to this radical belief despite what our detractors say about us."

State politics now entered the picture. Alabama, as one voice, rose in a clamorous defense of Bryant. The state's House of Representatives joined the Senate in a resolution that backed Bryant, and sent me a telegram asking me to appear before one of its committees. A *Post* lawyer composed my reply: IN VIEW OF PREJU-

DICED STATEMENT OF ISSUES TO BE INVESTIGATED BY YOUR COMMIT-
TEE AS SET OUT IN JOINT RESOLUTION I SEE NO PURPOSE IN MY APPEAR-
ING BEFORE YOUR COMMITTEE. I STAND ON THE ARTICLE.

Georgia's attorney general Eugene Cook made public the results of his investigation, which generally confirmed George Burnett's story. The call had been made from Butts to Bryant, Cook
said, and Burnett had accidentally intercepted it. The notes Burnett made during the sixteen-minute conversation were shown to
six members of the Georgia coaching staff, all of whom affirmed
that they contained "vital and important information that could
have affected the outcome" of the Georgia-Alabama game. Cook
released a statement from the Southeastern Conference, whose
chairman agreed with his conclusions and commented, "I would
say the best you could say about the situation . . . it's unethical,
unsportsmanlike."

The attorney general, in his turn, agreed with the description of
the situation as "unethical," rather than criminal. Although he
found conclusive evidence that Butts had made sixteen phone
calls to a Chicago gambler during the period leading up to the
game, including one call from Alabama just before the game itself, Cook was unable to establish that Butts profited from gambling. These and other facts of Butts' background were merely
suggestive. Since no gambling was proved, Cook declined to press
for an indictment.

Late in the spring, Butts' lawyers came to New York to take
depositions from all of us who were involved in preparing the article. The *Post*'s lawyers coached me in advance. ("When they ask
you why you didn't check the allegations with Butts before you
wrote the article, your answer can be brief, and it will be accepted in court: 'I knew he would deny it.'")

But my answer to another question put by Butts' lawyers was
catastrophic. They asked me if I had actually talked to several of
the people, such as Coach Johnny Griffith, whom I quoted in the
article. No, I replied, I "reconstructed" their quotes from my interview with Burnett and Flack. This is a common practice in
journalism, sometimes abused, when a reporter is reconstructing a
scene at which he was not present. But, in any serious article,

either the reporter or one of his publication's fact-checkers will make an attempt before publication to verify the accuracy of the quotes with the original speaker. I was in no position to offer Butts' lawyers the added information that in the haste and secrecy surrounding this article's publication, no one contacted Griffith or the others quoted.

Ada and I moved back to Maine in June. Although I was uneasy about my deposition, I had been told by both sides that I would be asked to testify at the libel trial in Atlanta, and I assumed that under further questioning the good faith in which I had acted would be made clear. But the call to Atlanta never came. The *Post*'s law firm, having retained local counsel, decided to play down any hint of regionalism and keep "Yankees" off the witness stand. Butts' lawyers, on the other hand, were more than satisfied with the depositions they had obtained from Clay Blair, Roger Kahn, and me in New York.

At the trial, which began on August 6, the *Post*'s defense against libel was that the story was "substantially true." It then went about corroborating the points set forth in Burnett's affidavit, with officials from the telephone company testifying about Butts' various calls and Griffith asserting that he was convinced that secrets had been leaked to Alabama. Butts maintained that he had done no wrong (as did Bryant, who was called to testify in his behalf), and his lawyers showed that there was no mention of gambling in the notes Burnett had taken. The article itself used the words "fix" and "rig" in the sense of tampering with the outcome, but did not charge Butts with winning a bet on the game. The introductory box more than implied the charge that he had conspired for gambling purposes, a more difficult point to prove.

Toward the end of the trial, the *Post*'s lawyers called the president of the University of Georgia and five members of its athletic board. All testified that Butts was a man of "bad character" and that they would not believe him under oath. One member of the athletic board said that the alumni had become concerned about Butts' association with gamblers, his ill-concealed "night life," and his questionable business dealings. Much was made of Butts' expressions of bitterness toward the university after he had been relieved of his coaching duties. Much, too, was made of Butts' friendship and frequent calls to a man identified by federal investigators as a gambler.

On the other hand, Butts' lawyers focused on Clay Blair's well-publicized satisfaction at the string of libel actions brought against the *Post*, and several inaccuracies in the article itself. (A wrong date for Butts' call to Bryant was given in the article's lead sentence, no one having checked Burnett's memory against telephone-company records acquired by Georgia's attorney general.) My remark about "reconstructed quotes" was dwelt on at some length, as was the editors' admission that they had not acquired a film of the game to verify certain contentions.

The jurors returned a verdict in favor of Butts and awarded him $3,060,000 in punitive and actual damages. The *Post*, in promising to appeal the verdict, put up a brave front. Matthew J. Culligan, president of the Curtis Publishing Company, issued a defensive statement: "The story ... was carefully examined in advance by the Philadelphia law firm which has served the Curtis Publishing Company for many years. Based upon their opinion that evidence justified publication, the article was subsequently printed in the *Post*."

Later on, when he had been pushed out of Curtis, Culligan was not so respectful of the lawyers' competence, and he called their efforts in court "a comedy of errors." But the fact that they had approved this discredited article did not relieve my own chagrin. The news of the trial, as it filtered in over a tinny old radio in Maine, cast a chill over me that had nothing to do with the early-morning fog. That would burn away, but the hurt did not. Although I had already turned much of my attention to subjects other than sports, I was still a journalist, and I believed rightly that my integrity had suffered in this wretched affair. My father was quietly sympathetic, assuring me that I was right to go ahead with a story in which I believed, and my friends in the business pointed out that in their opinion Butts was "guilty as hell." But my failure to assert myself, whatever the lawyers said, and give the story its proper focus rankled for a long time.

I knew I had made a serious mistake. When it became apparent that the *Post* was not going to send me back to the South to complete the investigation, I should have asked that my name be removed from the article. A writer must be responsible for the work he signs, and not leave unfinished business to his colleagues—even if they are the editors and lawyers of a time-honored publication. The right words I had groped for in those gray dawns of my apprenticeship a decade earlier are worse than useless in a haphazard context. The very word "writer" implies individual effort and responsibility. I had permitted other elements to intrude—a misplaced confidence in the trappings of power, a desire to be part of a "big story," a spasm of sanctimoniousness that made me want to become an instrument of moral endeavor. Snares and delusions!

I was cushioned somewhat by distance from the area of the direct impact. Clay Blair did not shake off the blow, which loosened his hold on the magazine, and a series of later financial shocks caused him to let go entirely. Meanwhile, he behaved well in the Butts affair. When the lawyers could not secure a change of venue for the impending trial of Bear Bryant's several grievances, they recommended that the *Post* settle with him out of court. It did, for three hundred thousand tax-free dollars. I happened to be in New York in February, 1964, when the settlement was reached, and Blair courteously invited me to come to his office with Kahn and the others so that he could give us the news before it was released to the press. He said he had agreed to the settlement only grudgingly, without admitting to error, because the experience in Atlanta had convinced him that the *Post* had no chance at all with a jury in Alabama. Yet the fact remains that there had never been evidence to connect Bryant with any such conspiracy as a "Black Sox Scandal."

Blair and his colleagues did not abandon the Butts case. On appeal in an Atlanta court, they managed to get the award to him reduced to $460,000, under conditions in which Butts was required to pay a large slice of it in taxes. They unsuccessfully appealed the trial judge's order to bar evidence that would have further damaged Butts' reputation, including testimony by a woman to whom Butts had given expensive gifts and whom he had taken on various trips. And, belatedly, they sent investigators into the field to gather further evidence. At least three or four other Southern coaches confided to newspapermen that the embittered old coach had called them to give away Georgia's secrets, hoping that after taking a succession of bad beatings, the university would give him his job back. But none of the coaches was willing to testify for the *Post*.

Yet, after all, the *Post* almost pulled it out. In a case involving the New York *Times*, the United States Supreme Court ruled that public officials, even if falsely accused of misdeeds, could not recover damages under the libel laws unless they were able to prove that the defendant had acted with "reckless disregard for the truth," or deliberately printed falsehoods. Armed with this new ruling, the *Post*'s lawyers pushed on. When the Butts case reached the Supreme Court in 1967, the justices were almost equally divided, but finally came down against the *Post* by a vote of five to four. The deciding element, in the majority's view, was evidence that "cast serious doubt on the adequacy of the [*Post*'s] investigation."

One of life's little ironies that cropped up in the affair's aftermath was that many people refused to believe I had written the story. This was especially true in Alabama, where Furman Bisher was repeatedly fingered as the villain, and Bryant nourished that suspicion in magazine articles and in his autobiography. The story persisted for so long and interfered so seriously with Bisher's football assignments in Alabama that a dozen years after the event, he asked me to write a letter affirming my authorship of the article.

"They still don't believe it over there," Bisher told me not long ago. "Time after time I'll be introduced to someone in Alabama, and this person will say to me, 'Oh, yes. You're the fellow who wrote the Butts-Bryant story.' "

The ultimate irony? In 1965 my first book on conservation was being brought out in New York by a small publishing company whose titles were distributed through the larger firm of J. B. Lippincott. A vice-president of Lippincott, which had its headquarters in Philadelphia, noticed my name as author and refused to agree to distribution until his company's lawyers had looked into the manuscript for mischievous statements. After a close reading, the lawyers found nothing to carp at in the manuscript, and Lippincott sent on to my editor a bill he had not planned on in his original production estimates. The bill bore the letterhead of Lippincott's law firm—Pepper, Hamilton & Scheetz.

Epilogue

A year or two ago I searched the card catalog in a public library far from home to see if its collection included any of my books on conservation. There, behind a card on *Since Silent Spring*, stood one for my biography of Casey Stengel, but after the author's name someone had carefully typed my father's dates; 1893–1965. A smalltown librarian, perhaps an old fan herself, had been unable to imagine any other Frank Graham who could have written this book about the incomparable Casey. For there, in the same library, was *A Quiet Hero*. The daydream world my father conjured up for me has become a part of other lives, too.

The last years were not kind to him. In 1960 a terrible operation took most of his stomach, so that his small body wasted away to much less than the flyweight he had been as a boy. ("He weighed what his bones weighed," Jimmy Breslin wrote of him toward the end, "and he was standing up to cancer like it was the flu.") He was not one of those who wait for death. He went on writing his column, though only three times a week, and through it all the prose remained as fine and generous as the man.

299

[FRANK GRAHAM, JR.]

"A gentle man who seemed to walk on the tips of his toes as if he intended to pass through the world without disturbing anyone," his colleague Jimmy Cannon wrote of him. "He was, this shy and noble man, exactly as he wrote. The copy was pure, and so was he. He typed it quickly on his toy machine with a dainty tapping of polite fingers. He frisked the characters of even the rogues for their good traits and cherished them for that. He was an original, this embarrassed poet, who changed sports writing and brought to it the dignity of folk literature."

I think the worst knock I ever heard put on a man in boxing was when a manager said of some scoundrel, "Why, even Frank Graham thinks he's a bastard!" The audience stood mute, overwhelmed by such ignominy. Yet he always seemed unaware of the admiration and affection others held for him. I like to believe that the veil was lifted for him a bit one evening, a few years before he died, when the Turf Writers held their annual dinner in Saratoga. Four hundred of racing's luminaries were present—the writers, owners, trainers, jockeys, and stewards. A highlight of the evening was to be an award to the eminent Captain Harry F. Guggenheim as the breeder of thoroughbreds who had done the most for the sport during the past year. The dinner's organizers asked my father to make the presentation.

Only his unfailing good nature compelled him to assume chores of this kind. Illness and age had made him increasingly unsure of himself, and he was a bundle of nerves all through dinner as he contemplated the ordeal of standing up and saying a few words in front of the throng. His hands shook; his face reflected unalloyed misery. At last Guggenheim was called to the dais, to polite applause. Then, when it was announced that Frank Graham was to present the award, the diners rose to their feet in a spontaneous demonstration of affection.

"They gave him what I can only describe as a *booming* ovation," Pat O'Brien, a racing official, said afterward. "It kept coming, wave after wave of applause, and it lasted for more than four minutes."

My father stood there, the plaque in his hands, facing the sea of cheering people, absolutely dumbfounded. He never smiled, or bowed, or otherwise acknowledged the applause. When it subsided, he simply stepped off the platform and returned to his table, still clutching the captain's coveted plaque.

In later years, separated by distance and new interests, we did not make the rounds together as often as before. He liked horses, I liked birds, and we were respectful if not enthusiastic toward each other's preference. Acting not by conscious choice but on an increasing pull toward natural things, I carved out a career in a different field. Nor did my father regret this. He had always wanted me to be my own man. My pleasure in sports became retrospective. Like an old fossil who revels in the deeds of Arthurian knights and Bengal Lancers but has no interest in neutron bombs or nuclear subs, I found that my arena was an anachronism. It had flourished only in the relationship between father and son.

He kept his interest—that is to say, he was able to keep alive that world of heroes and stirring feats in his imagination even after it had stopped living in my own. The world of heroes exists for me now only in his books and the columns, pasted down in tall ledgers, which are on my shelves at home. I reach for them once in a while in the evening to renew a part of myself, the boy and the young man for whom events on the field had the power to brighten or darken a day.

Toward the end of my father's life, his thoughts often turned back to the heroes of his boyhood in Harlem, more than sixty years before. In one of his later columns he remembered the old Polo Grounds, where, as a boy, he had found the perfect seat in the left-field bleachers, on a line with third base and just over the visiting team's bullpen. Reading the column, I feel again that I am my father's son, sharing a moment of unique intensity and, I am sure, a throb of gratitude for what this sport added to our lives. He is the senior author, and he has the last word here.

The opening day of a season was, of course, a very special day. You received permission at home to stay out of school or, failing that, played hookey. In either case, you were at the Polo Grounds by noon. The game didn't start until three-thirty, but who minded the wait? On the way, you stopped at a delicatessen and bought five-cents' worth of ham and three cents' worth of rye bread, suffi-cient to make three sandwiches. You had a quarter that you laid on the line at the gate and two or three nickels for hot dogs or pop. You were closer to the ball game than many a rich stiff who sat in the grandstand. Only you did not think about that at the time. You were just happy to be there.

If you got there early enough, you could get a seat overlooking the bullpen and have a nodding, talking acquaintance with the enemy. Or, if you really didn't like them, you were close enough to them to spit on them. Still, there were advantages, too, in sitting farther out, where you practically were one with the left-fielder. Spike Shannon, for instance, burly, bull-throated, red-faced, the first outfielder ever to wear sun glasses. Rimless and black, they were, making Spike look like a blind man, but he could see through them all right and, once he took to wearing them, he never lost a ball in the sun.

You saw the Giants—and the Brooklyn Dodgers, or the Phillies, or the Boston Braves—work out. You saw the parade across the field and the ball game. If the Giants won, you were so happy it hurt. If they lost—that hurt, too, but worse. One year, the Giants were beating the Dodgers, 2 to 1, but in the ninth inning Brook-lyn's Tim Jordan hit a home run with a man on.

The walk home wasn't long. It only seemed that way. When you arrived, your grandmother said:

"Would you run down to the grocer's and get a pound of but-ter?"

"What's the matter?" you yelled. "Am I the only one around here who can buy butter?"

And your sister-in-law said:

"Well, I gather the Giants lost."